Contemporary Arab Women's Life Writing and the Politics of Resistance

Edinburgh Studies in Modern Arabic Literature
Series Editor: Rasheed El-Enany

Writing Beirut: Mappings of the City in the Modern Arabic Novel
Samira Aghacy

Women, Writing and the Iraqi State: Resistance and Collaboration under the Ba'th, 1968–2003
Hawraa Al-Hassan

Autobiographical Identities in Contemporary Arab Literature
Valerie Anishchenkova

The Iraqi Novel: Key Writers, Key Texts
Fabio Caiani and Catherine Cobham

Contemporary Arab Women's Life Writing and the Politics of Resistance
Hiyem Cheurfa

Sufism in the Contemporary Arabic Novel
Ziad Elmarsafy

Gender, Nation, and the Arabic Novel: Egypt 1892–2008
Hoda Elsadda

The Arabic Prose Poem: Poetic Theory and Practice
Huda Fakhreddine

The Unmaking of the Arab Intellectual: Prophecy, Exile and the Nation
Zeina G. Halabi

Egypt 1919: The Revolution in Literature and Film
Dina Heshmat

Post-War Anglophone Lebanese Fiction: Home Matters in the Diaspora
Syrine Hout

The Modern Arabic Bible: Translation, Dissemination and Literary Impact
Rana Issa

Prophetic Translation: The Making of Modern Egyptian Literature
Maya I. Kesrouany

Nasser in the Egyptian Imaginary
Omar Khalifah

Conspiracy in Modern Egyptian Literature
Benjamin Koerber

War and Occupation in Iraqi Fiction
Ikram Masmoudi

Literary Autobiography and Arab National Struggles
Tahia Abdel Nasser

Latin American and Arab Literature: Transcontinental Exchanges
Tahia Abdel Nasser

The Libyan Novel: Humans, Animals and the Poetics of Vulnerability
Charis Olszok

The Arab Nahdah*: The Making of the Intellectual and Humanist Movement*
Abdulrazzak Patel

Blogging from Egypt: Digital Literature, 2005–2016
Teresa Pepe

Religion in the Egyptian Novel
Christina Phillips

Space in Modern Egyptian Fiction
Yasmine Ramadan

Gendering Civil War: Francophone Women's Writing in Lebanon
Mireille Rebeiz

Occidentalism: Literary Representations of the Maghrebi Experience of the East–West Encounter
Zahia Smail Salhi

Arabic Exile Literature in Europe: Forced Migration and Speculative Fiction
Johanna Sellman

Sonallah Ibrahim: Rebel with a Pen
Paul Starkey

Minorities in the Contemporary Egyptian Novel
Mary Youssef

edinburghuniversitypress.com/series/smal

Contemporary Arab Women's Life Writing and the Politics of Resistance

Hiyem Cheurfa

EDINBURGH
University Press

In memory of my father, Hassen Cheurfa

Edinburgh University Press is one of the leading university presses in the UK. We publish academic books and journals in our selected subject areas across the humanities and social sciences, combining cutting-edge scholarship with high editorial and production values to produce academic works of lasting importance. For more information visit our website: edinburghuniversitypress.com

© Hiyem Cheurfa, 2023, 2024

Edinburgh University Press Ltd
13 Infirmary Street
Edinburgh EH1 1LT

First published in hardback by Edinburgh University Press 2023

Typeset in 11/15 EB Garamond by
Cheshire Typesetting Ltd, Cuddington, Cheshire

A CIP record for this book is available from the British Library

ISBN 978 1 4744 8968 3 (hardback)
ISBN 978 1 4744 8969 0 (paperback)
ISBN 978 1 4744 8971 3 (webready PDF)
ISBN 978 1 4744 8970 6 (epub)

The right of Hiyem Cheurfa to be identified as author of this work has been asserted in accordance with the Copyright, Designs and Patents Act 1988 and the Copyright and Related Rights Regulations 2003 (SI No. 2498).

Contents

Acknowledgements	vi
Note on Transliteration and Translation	vii
Series Editor's Foreword	ix
Introduction – Arab Women's Life Writing and Resistance Literature: History, Theory and Context	1
1 Genre and Twentieth-century National Struggles: Arab Women Write the Resistance	38
2 A Bricolage of Genre, a Montage of Selves: Autobiographical Subjectivity, Generic Experimentation and Representational Contestation	64
3 *Shahādāt Nisā'iyyah*: Testimonial Life Writing, Accounts of Women's Resistance	106
4 Dissident Laughter: Diaries of National Struggles and the Aesthetics of Humour	144
5 Arab Women's Digital Life Writing: Resistance 2.0	186
Conclusion – Arab(ic) Resistance Non-fiction: Critical Trajectories	225
Bibliography	236
Index	260

Acknowledgements

This book was made possible by a generous PhD scholarship offered by the Algerian Ministry of Higher Education and Scientific Research, for which I am grateful. I would like to thank Edinburgh University Press for the opportunity to publish with them. Many thanks to the series editor Professor Rasheed El-Enany, to Emma Rees and Louise Hutton for their comments and endless support throughout the stages of the completion of this book.

I am particularly grateful to the community of scholars and colleagues at Lancaster University who have encouraged me and believed in the value of my research. The completion of this book would have not been possible without the consistent guidance and enthusiasm of my wonderful PhD supervisor Lindsey Moore. She has supported me during the course of researching, writing and completing this project. This book is dedicated to her. I also owe a debt of gratitude to Lynne Pearce, Philip Dickinson, Jo Carruthers and Brian Baker for their constructive feedback on earlier versions of my project. The MENAWA reading group at the English Department also needs to be acknowledged. It had been an important and intellectually stimulating space that helped me develop many arguments and ideas throughout the course of my research.

I am thankful to many friends and colleagues for their invaluable comments on the manuscript. I would like to thank Rachel Gregory Fox, Anastasia Valassopoulos, Layla Alammar, Ghazouane Arslane, Alberto Godioli and Rania Said for sharing their expertise, for taking the time to read my work, and for their incisive commentary on different versions of my chapters. I am also indebted to Hocine Maoui for his administrative assistance and to Chabha

Ben Ali Amer and Afaf Rabehi for their help in providing access to a number of resources when I was writing from home during the COVID outbreak. My sincere thanks go to the talented Hassan Al Mohtasib for diligently designing the stunning cover of this book.

I am utterly grateful to my family for their unswerving encouragement and help. Everything I have accomplished so far, including this book, goes to my parents and siblings. My father, who passed away so early leaving behind so much love and memories, my mother Malika, my sister Soaada and brother Lamine have always believed in me and inspired me in so many ways. And to Kamel Eddine, *habibi*, who brings so much love and joy into my life, this book is dedicated to you.

Note on Transliteration and Translation

I have followed the IJMES (*International Journal of Middle Eastern Studies*) standard system of transliteration from Arabic to English. For the names of authors, political parties and places, I have used the common and preferred spellings used in publications (without transliteration).

Throughout the book, I cite the published English translation of Arabic texts when available; my own translations from Arabic are noted in the text. All translations from French are mine, unless otherwise noted in the bibliography at the end of this book. In instances when I translate from French, my English translation is followed by parenthetical citations that refer to the original. I am working with texts in the original French language due to the unavailability of translated versions. Italics and capitals used in quotes throughout this book are in the original texts.

Series Editor's Foreword

Edinburgh Studies in Modern Arabic Literature is a unique series that aims to fill a glaring gap in scholarship in the field of modern Arabic literature. Its dedication to Arabic literature in the modern period (that is, from the nineteenth century onwards) is what makes it unique among series undertaken by academic publishers in the English-speaking world. Individual books on modern Arabic literature in general or aspects of it have been and continue to be published sporadically. Series on Islamic studies and Arab/Islamic thought and civilisation are not in short supply either in the academic world, but these are far removed from the study of Arabic literature qua literature, that is, imaginative, creative literature as we understand the term when, for instance, we speak of English literature or French literature. Even series labelled 'Arabic/Middle Eastern Literature' make no period distinction, extending their purview from the sixth century to the present, and often including non-Arabic literatures of the region. This series aims to redress the situation by focusing on the Arabic literature and criticism of today, stretching its interest to the earliest beginnings of Arab modernity in the nineteenth century.

The need for such a dedicated series, and generally for the redoubling of scholarly endeavour in researching and introducing modern Arabic literature to the Western reader, has never been stronger. Among activities and events heightening public, let alone academic, interest in all things Arab, and not least Arabic literature, are the significant growth in the last decades of the translation of contemporary Arab authors from all genres, especially fiction, into English; the higher profile of Arabic literature internationally since the award of the Nobel Prize in Literature to Naguib Mahfouz in 1988; the growing number of Arab authors living in the Western diaspora and writing both in English and Arabic; the adoption of such authors and others by mainstream, high-circulation publishers, as opposed to the academic publishers of the past; and the establishment of prestigious prizes, such as the International Prize for Arabic Fiction, popularly referred to in the Arab world as the Arabic Booker, run by the Man Booker Foundation, which brings huge publicity to the shortlist and winner every year, as well as translation contracts into English and other languages. It is therefore part of the ambition of this series that it will increasingly address a wider reading public beyond its natural territory of students and researchers in Arabic and world literature. Nor indeed is the academic readership of the series expected to be confined to specialists in literature in the light of the growing trend for interdisciplinarity, which increasingly sees scholars crossing field boundaries in their research tools and coming up with findings that equally cross discipline borders in their appeal.

Life writing, not a traditional genre of Arabic literature, has seen some salient exceptions to the rule in the twentieth century written by prominent figures, whether in direct form or thinly disguised as fiction; the most famous example is Taha Hussain's classic, *Al-Ayyam* (1929), or *The Stream of Days*, as it is titled in translation. Since that time, nearly a century ago, the genre has established itself and ramified, assuming all kinds of different shapes and forms across Arab countries, including the blog, as it embraced in its lively adaptability the digital age. And just as happened with the genre of the novel, which entered Arabic letters in the late nineteenth century, coming of age only in the 1930s and 1940s at the hands of male writers before women writers joined the ranks with full force a few decades later to become prominent exponents, so it was with life writing too. This is the context in which the current monograph belongs. Arabic life writing in general is beginning to attract scholarly attention with already three volumes in this EUP series dealing with the genre whether partly or exclusively: Valerie Anishchenkova's *Autobiographical Identities in Contemporary Arab Culture,* Tahia Abdel Nasser's *Literary Autobiography and Arab National Struggles,* and Terese Pepe's *Blogging from Egypt.* The current monograph, focusing entirely on life writing by women, is a welcome addition of much needed scholarly work. While Dr Cheurfa's book, anchored in life writing, feminist and postcolonial theory, focuses on women's contemporary life writing in the last few decades taking particular interest in writing as an act of resistance, usefully it also offers a contextualising brief survey of such writing in the earlier parts of the twentieth century. On the other hand, the geographical scope of the study is broad enough to cover the Arab countries most significant for the genre, while not limiting itself to Arabophone writing but also going on to examine Francophone and Anglophone texts of relevance.

Rasheed El-Enany, Series Editor
Emeritus Professor of Modern Arabic Literature
University of Exeter

Introduction

Arab Women's Life Writing and Resistance Literature: History, Theory and Context

This book aims to provide the first detailed investigation of Arab life writing as part of a cultural corpus of resistance literature. This literature, it contends, must be contextualised and understood within specific fields of power discourse. More specifically, this book argues for a reinvigorated postcolonial understanding of contemporary Arab women's autobiographical writing as revolutionary and dissident cultural practice. In doing so, it also aims to promote a critical dialogue between the sub-fields of Arab women's writing, auto/biographical theory and resistance literature. Modern and contemporary Arab auto/biography has flourished in contexts of diverse, yet overlapping, colonial and anti-colonial struggles, and thus situates its subject at a particular political and historical juncture (Nasser 2017: 2). In the twenty-first century Arab world, a volatile region marked by (post)colonial histories and ongoing manifestations of Orientalism, colonialism, (neo)imperialism and revolutionary resistance movements (uprisings/ḥirāks), autobiographical discourses have become important cultural vehicles which highlight the relationship between political movements and artistic forms of literary expressions. They constitute an important, and ever-emerging, cultural corpus for bearing witness, testimony and dissidence as well as for political responses which foreground the relationships between writing and fighting and between the activist writer and the writer activist.

However, there remains a surprising lack of sustained academic discussions on forms of Arab life writing as politically driven practices which emerge in contexts of revolutionary and dissident moments, particularly from a gendered perspective. The leading scholarly discussions on and conceptual frameworks of resistance literature do not give much attention to life writing forms, including Ghassan Kanafani's seminal work *'Adab Al-Muqāwama fī Filasṭīn al-Muḥtalah 1948–1968* (1966) (*Resistance Literature in Occupied Palestine 1948–1966*, 2013), Barbara Harlow's classic *Resistance Literature* (1987) and, more recently, Karima Laachir's and Saeed Talajooy's edited collection of essays *Resistance in Contemporary Middle Eastern Culture* (2013). While the latter, the closest study to the context of my book in terms of conceptual framework and geopolitical scope, establishes an important and elaborate connection between cultural forms of expression and dynamics of power in some of the countries of the contemporary Arab world, its scope is broad in terms of media of artistic expression. It investigates fiction, drama, cinema and music as cultural forms of resistance but does not include a rounded discussion of life writing forms. Similarly, gender has been flagrantly deprioritised within the modestly emerging field of Arab auto/biography criticism, which mirrors a long tradition of critical marginalisation of the female Arab subject (both pre-modern and modern) within mainstream feminist and auto/biographical studies. This historical marginalisation has ignored a persistent tradition of Arab women's deployment of the genre in relation to Arab feminisms and thereby obscured a crucial critical understanding of women's first-hand narratives developed within specific conditions of resistance. It has also overlooked the political and ideological conditions within which Arab women write auto/biographically to assert their role and position within (post-)colonial contexts and national histories and records, issues that this book closely addresses.

Contemporary Arab Women's Life Writing and the Politics of Resistance joins recent interventions in focusing upon a range of generic and thematic characteristics of contemporary Arab autobiography (Nash 2007; Bugeja 2012; Anishchenkova 2014; Nasser 2017; Sheetrit 2020). Its distinctive character, however, lies in its gendered and comparative perspective that captures a convergence of feminist, literary and historico-political questions across different linguistic (Arabophone, Francophone, Anglophone) and national contexts (including Egypt, Algeria, Syria, Palestine and Tunisia), with consideration given to regional imperatives. This book considers life writing forms emerging from the contemporary, revolutionary Arab region as cultural sites for the articulation of resistance. It addresses the role and implications of life writing genres by Arab women in critically engaging with, reflecting on, and rethinking key sociopolitical and cultural contexts that shape their enunciation. Looking closely at texts set in contexts of Arab national struggles and revolutionary movements and published in the twenty-first century – with a first chapter surveying life narratives from the twentieth century – my book highlights deliberate redefinition, experimentation and rejection of the genre's formal and thematic conventions in addressing and interrogating mainstream power narratives, including discourses of narration and self-representation. It also foregrounds ways in which forms of first-hand narration enable women to write themselves into revolutionary history, to devise new venues of active involvement in the national narrative of combat and to reclaim public spaces of participation and representation of which they have been historically denied.

There is, as yet, no full-length critical study in English that focuses exclusively and comparatively on Arab women's autobiographical discourses within such recent historical parameters and across as generically, contextually and linguistically rich a corpus as this book. Recently, Valerie Anishchenkova's *Autobiographical Identities in Contemporary Arab Culture* (2014) and Tahia Abdel Nasser's *Literary Autobiography and Arab National Struggles* (2017), published in the same series of Edinburgh Studies in Modern Arabic Literature as this book, have contributed important discussions of various forms of modern/contemporary Arab auto/biographical writing. While Anishchenkova's monograph examines the expression of cultural identity, selfhood and subjectivity as manifested in Arab autobiographical narratives – in a range of forms across literary, cinematic and cyber modes of self-expression – Nasser's is more interested in the notion of solitude during colonial and anti-colonial movements and ambitiously attempts to cover autobiographical texts from the second half of the twentieth and twenty-first centuries. However, neither of these two studies has a specific gendered/feminist focus nor comprehensively investigates dynamics of power and resistance implicated in the use of the genre by Arab women authors. *Contemporary Arab Women's Life Writing and the Politics of Resistance* extends this scholarly conversation by investigating the ways in which sociopolitical resistance is represented, negotiated and sought in Arab women's life narratives in a range of autobiographical forms.

This book specifically speaks to and expands on these few discussions on the effects of national struggles on modern Arab autobiography mainly to focus on the role of genre in revolutionary moments from a gendered (female) perspective. I adopt a comparative, cross-national and cross-linguistic approach to read Arab women's texts and address more experimental and less predictable forms of life writing within recent and/or ongoing revolutionary contexts. The overarching aim is to examine the manifestation of resistance through genre strategies of autobiographical writing by contemporary Arab women. All authors under scrutiny and selected for this study are politically committed intellectuals and/or partisans of organised revolutionary movements against the ruling regimes in their national context but who also reflect regional preoccupations. They are all insiders living in and writing from their country of origin and define themselves both nationally and regionally as 'Arabs'. While I acknowledge the status of the selected authors as relatively privileged, they provide a significant model that highlights the fundamental role of the woman writer within national revolutionary moments. I argue that the female life writers selected in this book (often transnationally influential through international prizes and translation), use the genre – with an awareness of its ideological potentials – to rewrite mainstream narratives of national struggles. They enact their active involvement in the resistance and within revolutionary movements through various thematic and formal strategies of autobiographical narration. In doing so, they attempt to shift the established ways in which Arab women's presence and participation in national conflicts in the region are represented and to reflect the way their personal life is intertwined with the sociopolitical status quo in their countries.

An exhaustive coverage and conclusive analysis of the ever-expanding corpus of Arab women's life writing would be impossible. Instead, my selection of texts has been based on thematic and generic criteria, politically urgent contexts and my endeavour to widen the critical field by including less known/ critically discussed works. The selection of texts is based on their relevance to key concepts by which this book has been driven: Arab postcolonialism, resistance literature and women's auto/biographical writing. They all emerge from urgent contexts of recent and/or ongoing zones of political conflict which reflect popular and deliberate struggles for justice and dignity, and thus urge for a prompt critical consideration of cultural productions which emerge thereof. However, the texts under scrutiny are only examples which reflect the plural sensibilities and variety of forms, modes and approaches to woman's autobiographical narratives as sites of resistance within contemporary Arab culture. I have chosen to illuminate particular literary forms and models of resistance as a first stage of mapping out this area of study which still requires further exploration.

By focusing on Arab women, a historically and representationally marginalised category in social, political and cultural scores, I am by no means recycling gender-based critical tropes by excluding men from the focus. Undoubtedly, many contemporary politically committed Arab men have used life writing to manifest their dissent to political and social structures of power.[1] By focusing on women's life writing, I am not excluding the male mainstream that has been at the centre of scholarly discussions; I am, rather, highlighting the ostensible margin. Equally, resistance is much more complex in the case of women because it reflects, in addition to the nationally shared oppressive mechanisms, an imbrication of struggles based on gender, sexuality and cultural mis/under-representations. In this sense, the consideration of women's texts yields insights into the role of life writing as a possible site of womanly resistance, which is the main critical trajectory I pursue in this study.

Contemporary Arab Women's Life Writing and the Politics of Resistance is contextualised within an intersectional framework of feminist and postcolonial lens that is recent, gender-focused and politically informed; as such, closely relevant to the newly-emerging, and shifting, femino-political concerns of the contemporary Arab region. The main questions that this monograph asks are: why is resistance important when writing about the self for Arab women? and how is it articulated through experimental, formal and thematic approaches to the autobiographical genre? The remainder of the introduction explores the history, theory and context of feminist autobiographical theory, postcolonial life writing and resistance literature and foregrounds their interface as an important paradigm that I propose for critically considering contemporary Arab women's literary non-fiction.

Autobiographical Theory and the Feminist Genre(s)

Although autobiography was recognised as a distinct literary form in Western culture(s) in the last half of the eighteenth century,[2] autobiographical criticism is a fairly recent field of inquiry that began in the 1950s, flourished in subsequent decades, and remains fraught with controversies. It has failed to establish, efficiently, incontestable definitions of the genre or firm critical boundaries around fundamental notions such as subjectivity, authorship, truth-telling and the distinction between narration and creation, and fiction and non-fiction. The emergence of multiple subgenres of autobiographical expression has contributed to the malleability of both the genre and the critical field. These were further problematised with the advancement of poststructuralist and postmodernist theories, which privilege intertextuality and inter-genericity, and emphasise language as preceding and exceeding the subject.[3]

Inaugural studies of the genre have engendered numerous critical contestations due to their generic characterisation of the form and, most importantly, their exclusion of social, cultural, racial and gender heterogeneity. Founding fathers of autobiographical criticism, including first- and second-wave predominantly male critics – notably German philologist Georg Misch (1907), French critic Georges Gusdorf (1956) and English scholar Roy Pascal (1960) – limited their focus to narratives by 'great Western men' of public presence who are, as they claimed, worthy of remembrance for their high personal and professional achievements.[4] Most prominently, in his seminal article 'Conditions and Limits of Autobiography' (1956), Gusdorf problematically structures his theorisation of autobiography around a reductive, Eurocentric and masculine frame of analysis. Gusdorf claims that the genre 'is not to be found outside of our [the Western] cultural area' because it is only suitable to reflect 'a concern peculiar to Western man' (1980: 29). He stresses that any non-Western autobiography is necessarily a replication of the Western, original model. Likewise, Misch states that 'a history of autobiography . . . cannot reach back to the primitive people' (1973: 18), and Pascal declares that 'there remains no doubt that autobiography is essentially European' (1960: 22). This reductionist scope of master criticism, which reflects the politics of cultural imperialism, does more than deauthorise the autobiographical agency of the non-Western other. It also confines its literary practice to the masculine gender, assuming that the proper autobiographical subject is white and male.

Such views have been challenged in many ways. The exclusory trope of 'great men' was particularly problematic for feminist critics of the 1980s who showed dissatisfaction with what Domna C. Stanton, a founding feminist autobiography critic, describes as 'cases of maddening neglect' of the female autobiographical agent (1984: vii). The publication of *Women's Autobiography: Essays in Criticism* (1980), the first anthology of critical essays on women's autobiographies edited by Estelle C. Jelinek, signalled the beginning of a sustained, feminist tradition of critical inquiry into women's autobiographical practices. The main drive of this feminist criticism is toward 'building the archive of women's writing, claiming models of heroic identity, and revising dominant theories of autobiography' (Smith and Watson 2016: 7). Jelinek's foundational monograph offers thorough analyses of the specificities of women's autobiographical practice as opposed to the dominant male tradition. However, while her work remains influential, having contributed to the visibility of women's autobiographical writings, it was criticised for being monolithically structured around gendered identity and sexual difference as defining measures of generic classification. It neglects geopolitical specificities and hence stands as 'uninflected by class, ethnicity, genres, or life cycle' (ibid.: 14). By foregrounding the Western female autobiographical subject as a universal model, this study eventually reproduces models of coherence that were introduced by foundational male-centred critics. Excluding other forms of oppression in favour of a gendered one 'effectively erases the complex and often contradictory positioning of the [female] subject'; this ultimately suggests 'a central instance of the universalizing agenda of the Western theorization' (Smith and Watson 1992: xiv).

This exclusory critique led to the emergence of a second wave of feminist autobiographical studies, which particularly thrived during the second half of the 1980s. Critics associated with this wave moved beyond the essentialist argument that gender provides consistent meaning and unified experiences. Through 'map[ping] women's dialectical negotiations with a history of their own representation as idealized or invisible' (Smith and Watson 2016: 17), they focused on investigating the complexity of women's life writing not simply as men's 'other'. Theorists such as Domna C. Stanton (1984), Sidonie Smith (1987), Bella Brodzki and Celeste Schenck (1988) and Shari Benstock (1988) highlight the inadequacy of adopting a gendered identity as the sole criterion for classifying autobiographical practices, which would only lead to monolithic categorisation. Their studies stress the need to address generic and historical specificities in the study of women's autobiographies beyond the essentialist stereotypical dichotomy of male/female writing.

Equally, there was a persistent need for what Sidonie Smith and Julia Watson describe as 'de/colonizing the [autobiographical] subject' (1992: iii) through a rigorous theorisation of autobiographies by postcolonial women who are historically and representationally marginalised. Among the most prominent publications which brought to the fore issues of ethnicity, historical specificity and gendered experiences of colonisation and oppression in the analysis of women's autobiographies are Françoise Lionnet's *Autobiographical Voices: Race, Gender, Self-Portraiture* (1989) and her *Postcolonial Representations: Women, Literature, Identities* (1995), Smith and Watson's edited collection *De/Colonizing the Subject: The Politics of Gender in Women's Autobiography* (1992), Leigh Gilmore's *Autobiographics: a Feminist Theory of Women's Self-Representation* (1994) and Gillian Whitlock's *The Intimate Empire* (2000). These texts have been useful in offering historically contextualised readings of autobiographies by postcolonial women. They raise important questions about the relationship between self-definition, gender and power discourses and explore the ways in which female autobiographical identities are inextricably informed by discursive historical, cultural, political and social domains. This development in feminist studies of the genre also confirmed that women's life writings do not necessarily conform to generic forms and concerns established by mainstream male genre criticism. Therefore, such formal shifting has led to the emergence of new terms to describe women's autobiographical practices such as 'autogynography' (Stanton 1984) and 'autobiographics' (Gilmore 1994).[5]

It is due to this generic complexity in the history of the development of the genre, which has been exacerbated by the constantly emerging forms and media of autobiographical expression, that I classify my selected texts under the umbrella term 'life writing',[6] which I also refer to synonymously as autobiographical discourse(s)/text(s).[7] The specific category of autobiography is problematic for the context of my book for the reason that most of my selected texts cannot be classified as proper or strict autobiographies in the modern, Western sense. Traditionally, an autobiography refers to a particular way of writing; it 'recomposes and interprets a life in its totality' (Gusdorf 1980: 38) and denotes a 'self-interested . . . autonomous individual and the universalizing life-story' (Smith and Watson 2001a: 2–3). It implies a retrospective account of the life of an individual starting, traditionally, from childhood and ending at the moment of writing while following a chronological sequencing and offering a professional and intellectual exemplary model (Smith and Watson 2001a: 112–13; Kelly 2005: 31). Autobiography, thus, enfolds an implicit reference to a specific mainstream genre. It cannot help but refer to 'an uncritical Western understanding of the subject of autobiography' (Smith and Watson 1998: 29). The term autobiography, challenged by feminist, postcolonial and postmodern scholars, 'is now generally reserved for a literary canon that privileges a specific Enlightenment archetype of selfhood: the rational sovereign subject that is conceived as Western, gendered male, and . . . racially white' (Whitlock 2015: 3). The writings of non-Western, women, and postcolonial life writers are non-monolithic. They often represent the lives of migratory and shifting subjects who are affected by historical and cultural conditions, and hence tend to move beyond a normative, Western-derived 'formal arrangement of the development of the protagonist's subjectivity and identity' (Moore-Gilbert 2009: 69). The relevance of the term 'autobiography' as an encompassing life narrative category has also been contested by the emergence of new, hybrid forms as well as approaches to, and channels of, self-expression.

My texts fall into different and notably self-reflexive literary subgenres that are broadly encompassed by the generic category of life writing. The latter denotes literary 'writing of diverse kinds that takes a life as its subject' (Smith and Watson 2001a: 3); it is a term that can describe '"minor" genres that flourished in [post]colonialism's literary cultures' and is thus a category that 'is critical for de/colonizing the subject' (Whitlock 2015: 3). The term life writing is also useful to think about the processes of writing as it 'is widely used to capture the creativity involved in the construction of narratives based on "real lives"' (Summerfield 2019: 4). That is, the concept of life writing, which I opt to use in this book, specifically describes different literary modes of presenting experiences as lived, perceived and endorsed by the postcolonial writing subject based on the criteria of self-referentiality, but often incorporating reflexive insights about the process of writing the self and non-fiction. Each narrative I analyse here solicits, but also complicates, Philippe Lejeune's famous '*pacte autobiographique*' (1975) (autobiographical pact) which still holds sway as a defining criterion of non-fictional, self-referential writings. This pact implies that autobiographical texts should be read as referential since 'the author, the narrator, and the main subject of the narrative are identical' (Lejeune 1982: 193); it thus establishes a contractual agreement between the autobiographical subject and the reader that the autobiography is 'true'. My texts endorse non-fictionality but at the same time complicate, and enrich, it. They reflect a critical attitude towards representation by drawing attention to the exhaustion of the conventions of the genre and expanding generic possibilities of autobiographical writing. The selection deliberately includes memoirs, literary auto-portraits, diaries, testimonies and blogs, which do not necessarily reflect the conventional and individualistic 'bio', or the life of the subject in its 'totality'. They are often about fragments of a personal itinerary that is situated within a larger national narrative of resistance and struggle. The implicit reference to the mainstream genre that the inadequate use of the term autobiography implies is the main reason behind its substitution in this context as I am dealing with non-canonical texts by non-Western subjects who choose to move beyond thematic and formal conventions in the enunciation of their experiences of revolutionary movements and national struggles.

Postcolonial Life Writing

The lack of critical interest in the postcolonial subject within the traditions of autobiographical criticism, which I outline above, is not gender specific. Foundational feminist critics were no more open to the postcolonial subject than their mainstream counterparts. The foundational criteria for evaluating the autobiographical subject (proper) arguably reproduces the driving principles behind colonial projects by advocating cultural and racial 'purity' as the superior sources of knowledge. But conversely, inaugural postcolonial studies paid limited attention to the autobiographical genre. The critical dialogue between postcolonial theory and auto/biography studies is fairly recent despite the fact that a substantial amount of 'postcolonial life-writing has flourished since the decolonisation of European empires' (Moore-Gilbert 2009: xi). Bart Moore-Gilbert remarks that even the founding text of modern postcolonial studies, Edward Said's *Orientalism* (1978), does not discuss the role of the autobiographical genre in his exploration of cultural imperial projects and relations (2009: xiii).[8] This paucity of nuanced theorisation that intersects both areas of study might be partly attributed to the recent development of both fields of enquiry. Perhaps, also, the lack of an incontestable and uncontroversial set of generic notions and definitions of the mainstream genre complicated the potential of its earlier critical development within the postcolonial context. And, as Moore-Gilbert rightly observes, 'the task is further complicated by the heterogeneity of contexts and cultures from which postcolonial life writing has emerged' (2009: xiv).

Certainly, the pluralities of postcolonial identity do not accommodate the traditional essentialist premises of the autobiographical subject that privilege a unified model of a coherent subjectivity reflected in a specific generic style. The controversial conventions of the genre 'prioritize authenticity, autonomy, self-realization, and transcendence' (Whitlock 2015: 3). They reflect a 'Romantic notion of selfhood' and offer 'an unmediated and yet stabilizing wholeness for the self' (Anderson 2011: 4–5). This sense of the autobiographical selfhood as autonomous, self-conscious and cohesive are virtues propagated by Western modernity and are not intrinsic characteristics of postcolonial subjects, who are generally conflicted '*proximate* subjects . . . with a more hybrid genealogy' (Whitlock 2015: 3). The history of the Western autobiographical subject's sense of achievement and irrevocable knowledge of himself is contrasted with the generally conflicted, ambivalent and alienated postcolonial subject who is inextricably affected by discursive material and power relations. A 'history of postcolonial life writing is [characteristically] shaped by . . . social activism and resistance' (Whitlock 2015: 6), as I detail throughout this book. Postcolonial subjects tend to rework the genre to inscribe the effects of the colonial legacy and its enduring power. Therefore, 'postcolonial autobiography often elaborates . . . models of decentered, even disjunctive, subjectivity' which 'is generally represented as the effect of the material histories and relations of colonialism, in which new and sometimes radically conflicting identities are inscribed in palimpsestic fashion on the subaltern' (Moore-Gilbert 2011: 95–6). Having said this, it is important to note that decentred subjectivity and generic experimentations are not intrinsic characteristics of postcolonial auto/biography.[9] However, the availability of models which conform to mainstream autobiographical conventions does not negate the destabilising effects of colonialism on peripheral (autobiographical) identities nor the political implications of the postcolonial genre.

Postcolonial life writing is an emerging critical field that attempts to address this flagrant gap in prior scholarship. The most recent and influential academic interventions, notably Debra Kelly's *Autobiography and Independence: Selfhood and Creativity in North African Postcolonial Writing in French* (2005), Moore-Gilbert's *Postcolonial Life-Writing: Culture, Politics, and Self-Representation* (2009), Norbert Bugeja's *Postcolonial Memoir in the Middle East: Rethinking the Liminal in Mashriqi Writing* (2012), and Whitlock's *Postcolonial Life Narratives: Testimonial Transactions* (2015), establish a significant theoretical framework for the study of life writing by situating the complex experience of the postcolonial subject within discursive relations of power. These studies reconsider the genre as defined and advocated by Western critics and question the conceptions of autobiographical subjectivity as static or stable. They also interrogate the dominant culture of representation that reproduces social and racial stereotypes and duplicates the asymmetric relations between the (formerly) coloniser and (formerly) colonised.[10]

The feminist trope of 'de/colonizing the [autobiographical] subject' (Smith and Watson 1992: iii) from critical and cultural exclusion has served as a useful paradigm for the evaluation and theorisation of postcolonial life writing by both men and women. Both postcolonialist and feminist critics stress the need to investigate the relationship between personal and public discourses. They foreground personal sources and histories that emerge from the marginalised rather than mainstream discourses that tend to be governed by systematic 'othering'. Postcolonial and female autobiographical subjects are marginalised agents who are speaking through a genre believed to be exclusive to the dominant discourse, and through which they attempt to reclaim and reconstruct their repressed subjectivity. Their narratives often do not conform to what Gusdorf refers to as 'fine logical and rational order' (1980: 43) nor to the strict generic boundaries (Lejeune's pact), the developmental structure and the exemplary model of the autobiographical subject that are advocated by mainstream criticism of the genre.

Kelly (2005) and later Moore-Gilbert (2009), most prominently, provide particularly useful readings of postcolonial life writing. Although neither of their studies exclusively focus on postcolonial women, they both establish a pertinent critical dialogue between postcolonial theory and feminist autobiographical studies. Kelly argues that feminist autobiographical theory is 'a useful analytical tool in the reading of colonial and postcolonial texts . . . in a situation where the writer is resisting oppression and challenging the historically imposed image of the self' (2005: 48). Similarly, Moore-Gilbert writes that both women's and postcolonial life writing have challenged the rigid conceptions of autobiography 'as a properly coherent genre with its own protocols and boundaries' by contesting cultural politics of the canon in terms of form and selfhood (2009: 69). However, while postcolonial and feminist writings overlap in terms of their contestation of mainstream essentialism and conventions of self-representation, they present a 'different set of cultural politics and histories at both its source and as its goal' (Moore-Gilbert 2011: 97). They are often inflected differently and have divergent driving forces. Unlike mainstream women's auto/biography, Moore-Gilbert rightly contends, the postcolonial genre is usually conditioned by material histories of colonialism (2009: xxi). Regardless of the gender of its author and the level of its generic experimentation, postcolonial life writing is generally politically informed, reflecting engagement with the history and legacies of the colonial experience.

In this book, I am particularly interested in the political implications of genre, as it is stressed by postcolonial and feminist studies. I draw from postcolonial studies and feminist autobiographical theory in order to examine ways in which contemporary Arab women's life writings situate their subjects in relation to gendered, social, historical and political axes of power. I explore how these subjects write themselves out of the dominant discourse of genre criticism which is a source of patriarchal, racial and colonial authority. They do so, as I demonstrate, by producing 'an "I" that becomes a place of creative and, by implication, political intervention' (Smith and Watson 1992: xix). By challenging the dominant discourse of the genre, I do not mean to suggest that all of my texts necessarily deviate from formal and thematic structures promoted by mainstream critics of autobiography; some Arab women life writers selectively maintain these, as I shall explore. I wish rather to emphasise how my writers reclaim voice as gendered and marginalised subjects through a literary practice that has traditionally privileged the Western male subject. Thus, power relations must be considered when approaching life writing by subjects who have been denied literary discourses (Schmidt 2012: 65). In this sense, their autobiographical practices become, in Linda Anderson's formulation, 'both a way of testifying to oppression and empowering the subject through his/her cultural inscription and recognition' (2011: 97).

While postcolonial life writing is a recent field of inquiry which urges further critical interventions, a particular focus on life writing practices from the contemporary Arab world as a postcolonial context remains relatively insubstantial within autobiographical and postcolonial studies.[11] Both fields have not sufficiently examined the role of autobiographical discourses as cultural modes of reflecting, scrutinising and engaging with the power dynamics that govern the contemporary Arab region, despite the rich cultural tradition of autobiographical expression that has influenced the modern and contemporary expression of Arab subjectivity, as I outline in what follows.

Arab(ic) Autobiographical Traditions

Despite the common opinion that the emergence of autobiographical works in non-European cultures is directly influenced by the modern Western model of the genre, Arab(ic) literary autobiography is not a modern phenomenon.[12] Critics agree that autobiographical writing is not an unusual mode of literary expression within the Arab culture but, in fact, goes as far back as pre-Islamic Arabia (Rosenthal 1937; Rooke 1997; Enderwitz 1998; Reynolds 2001; Anishchenkova 2014; Nasser 2017). However, it is the distinction between the modern form and concerns of autobiography as theorised by Western critics and the pre-modern Arab(ic) analogue that came to be a central point of dispute among critics. The period between the mid-nineteenth and early twentieth centuries in the region mark the era of cultural modernity that came to be known as the Arab Renaissance, *al-Nahḍa* (Arabic for 'awakening'). This period witnessed unprecedented waves of experimentations and innovation in different artistic expressions, accelerated mainly through the cultural exposure to the West (Nasser 2017: 7–8; Hafez 2002). It also witnessed the development of the modern Arab(ic) autobiography which started with the publication of Egyptian author Taha Hussein's *al-Ayyām* (1929) (*The Days*, 1997), recognised as the inaugural text of the modern Arab genre. *Al-Nahḍa* brought about several subgenres of autobiographical expression that are generically similar to their Western analogue, particularly *sirāh dhātyyah* and *tarjamah dhātyyah* (*auto*biography), *tarjamah* (self-account or curriculum vitae), *mudhakirāt* (memoir) and *yawmyyāt* (diary/personal notes) (see Nasser 2017: 6).

While the modern Arabic autobiography flourished as a recognised category in the second half of the twentieth century, pre-*Nahḍa* autobiographical literary practices are almost impossible to classify into a distinguishable category. They present distinctive and heterogeneous forms which include *sirāh* (biography), *akhbār/nawādir* (oral narratives), *riḥlah/adab al-riḥlah* (travelogue), religious tracts, lyric poetry and slave narratives (Rooke 1997: 75–83; Reynolds 2001; Anishchenkova 2014: 17; Nasser 2017: 7). These variant forms of self-expression do not fully meet the modern criteria that are critically outlined to describe the autobiographical in terms of unity of structure, stylistic character, developmental subjectivity and self-representational frames.[13] Thomas Philipp (1993) makes the point that the lack of consensus over a specific Arabic terminology that refers to the genre demonstrates the way the form is unestablished as a cohesive category and thus suggests its non-Arab origin. Contrary to Gusdorf, Philipp unbinds the genre from a particular culture and links it instead to an era. He proposes looking at autobiography as 'an expression of modern man, not simply of Eastern or Western man' (1993: 576). He insists that the abundance of pre-modern Arab(ic) autobiographical practices should be considered as 'autobiographical materials' (ibid.: 574) because these do not present the social concerns, aesthetic tendencies and conceptions of selfhood which reflect the social changes and the historical moment of the modern time. In this sense, Arab autobiography proper remains, for Philipp, an irrevocably modern (post-*Nahḍa*) mode of self-expression (ibid.: 601).

This complexity in categorising modern and premodern Arab literary self-expression is evidently complicated by Western canonical conceptions and representation of autobiographical subjectivity. Autobiography as a distinguished form of life narration has emerged from an exclusive focus on the autonomous individual that reflects the Enlightenment archetype who was perceived as exclusively Western (Smith and Watson 2001a: 3). Other 'primitive' cultures, Gusdorf reductively contends, are characterised by their 'unconsciousness of personality' and hence are incapable of creating and producing a genre that values and reflects upon the uniqueness of the individual (1980: 30). This blatantly racist perception of subjectivity entails a political dimension which 'positions "Western individualism" against "Eastern connectivity" as collective and monolythic [sic] identity markers located in particular societal order' (Schmidt 2012: 50). It hence overlooks the notion of subjectivity as a complex and multidimensional construct.

However, many studies agree that the sense of Arab subjectivity is generally characterised by its collective and relational ethos (Berque 1978; Enderwitz 1998; Ostle *et al.* 1998; Moore-Gilbert 2009; Anishchenkova 2014). French scholar and sociologist Jacques Berque, for instance, in *Cultural Expression in Arab Society Today*, contends that the Arab self and identity are constituted as 'country as self, people as self, history as self' (1978: 238). More recently, Anishchenkova notes that the sense of selfhood in contemporary Arab society and culture is often constructed around a 'collective identification and valorization of the communal' (2014: 13). In this sense, basing the classification of the form on the criterion of subjectivity as linked to ideals of individualism and the sovereignty of selfhood ignores and overlooks the complexity of notions of selfhood and agency in non-Western contexts. Equally, attributing the genre exclusively to the modern Western model flagrantly denies a rich tradition of autobiographical practices in other cultures such as the Arab world. This ultimately dismisses the plethora of creative forms and subgenres that have subsequently emerged. Contrary to Gusdorf and Philipp, Dwight F. Reynolds, in *Interpreting the Self: Autobiography in the Arabic Literary Tradition* (2001), does not detach previous practices of literary self-expression in the region from the modern ones. He concludes that twentieth-century Arab(ic) autobiography reflects new 'formal characteristics' that are but a continuation of the pre-modern form (2001: 251). These characteristics, Reynolds contends, have emerged due to a number of influences, mainly 'the new socio-political context of resistance to the European colonial powers, the struggle for political independence, the rise of Arab nationalism, and the sudden emergence of a strong Arab women's autobiographical tradition, as well as new regional and national identities' (ibid.: 11); elements that are particularly pertinent to the context of my book.

In fact, the (post-)*Nahḍa* literary oeuvre does offer excellent examples of narratives that reflect the intellectual, exemplary and developmental models of the modern autobiographical subject, including, for example, Ahmad Amin's *Ḥayāti* (1950) (*My Life*, 1978), Nawal El-Saadawi's *Mudhakirāt Tabībah*

(1958) (*Memoirs of a Woman Doctor*, 1988a) and Fadwa Tuqan's *Riḥlah Jabaliyyah, Riḥlah Ṣaʿbah* (1984) (*Mountainous Journey: An Autobiography*, 1990). However, a sense of continuation of a longer historical tradition of self-expression can be still observed in these works and in other modern and contemporary literary autobiography. Most notably, the dualism of the collective/national and the individualistic continues to be a defining feature of Arab life writings. They tend to reflect a communal sense of identity and collective conception of nationhood, nurtured mainly through the anti/neocolonial struggles and the entailing growing sense of nationalism (Hafez 2002: 22). This point is further stressed by Anishchenkova who explores, in her 2014 monograph, novel conceptions and artistic articulations of contemporary Arab selfhood. She observes that Arab autobiographical expression has gone through crucial transformations in both form and method, reflecting unorthodox themes and forms of self-expression – including mixing *fuṣḥā* (classical Arabic) with dialectical Arabic, exploring elements of corporeal identity and overtly negotiating sexuality. However, Anishchenkova argues that the binary between the collective/national and the individualistic is a prominent characteristic that persists in Arab autobiographical writing; she also notes that life writers continue to place their experiences within the larger sociopolitical landscape in which personal identity is also inextricably national (2014: 14). Similarly, Nasser contends that the rise of modern Arab life writing 'dovetailed the private and the public, the individual and the national'; it 'is connected to modernity, national movements, and independence and its contemporary reworkings show these complex intertwinings in a new light' (2017: 2, 4). In this sense, the evident national and sociopolitical preoccupations and collective tendencies of Arab autobiographical discourses necessitate placing the genre critically within a postcolonial scope of analysis.

Postcolonial Arab Life Writing

It is important to define the contested terms 'Arab' and 'Arab world' that I am using in these pages in order to illuminate the way I classify my literature as postcolonial life writing. Indeed, it would be reductive to classify the region in a homogenising fashion and dismiss its inherent polycentric character; it is culturally, geographically and ethnically plural and reflects substantial linguistic variations. This plurality is further enhanced, or rather demarcated, by the geo-cultural division of the region into the Gulf, Mashriq (the Arab East, including Egypt and the Levant) and Maghreb (North Africa, west of Egypt) regions. This multicultural nature is also undeniably affected by Western influence throughout history, whether through travel and other cultural exchanges such as missions and expeditions, colonial/imperial projects and mandates or current cross-cultural movements enabled by globalisation. It is perhaps this ethnographic heterogeneity and variant geographic localities within the region that has hindered the emergence of a nuanced theorisation of Arab autobiography as a definite category that is able to encapsulate the rich traditions of the genre practice.

Throughout this book, I use the term Arab, with an awareness of its limitations, to position the authors and their texts within a specific geo-cultural context. Evidently, the term Arab is reflective of an ideological claim of a regional political affiliation. The ideological implication of its use gained popularity after the rise of Arab nationalism in the 1950s which aspired to political unity beyond the national boundaries established by imperialist policies (Pan-Arabism) (Golley 2003: 7). However, the term 'Arab' equally retains relevant cultural connotations. The Arab world does maintain a shared cultural heritage and societal structure defined mainly by a shared language (Arabic) and predominant Islamic traditions – although it is worth noting that the use of Arabic remains problematic in specific cases like the Amazigh and Berber population in North Africa, the Kurdish people in Iraq and Syria, and the Arabic dialectical varieties spoken across the region. I use the term 'Arab' as a defining paradigm of a specific cultural and geographical frame, particularly to describe authors (and their texts) who are writing from countries in which the official language is Arabic, a language that is institutionalised and spoken by the majority of the population. Algeria, Morocco, Egypt, Iraq, Jordan, Palestine, Syria and Tunisia (among other countries covered in the following chapters) are Arabic-speaking countries whose governments declare their regional affiliation through their membership in the Arab League.[14]

Most importantly, a shared history of colonial and neocolonial struggles defines the region and has had a great impact on the formation of modern Arab identity. The range of literary autobiographical expressions in the Arab world today reflects a political dimension that is inherent in the definition of contemporary Arab subjectivity and experience. The modern history of the Arab region has been shaped by anti-colonial movements, multiple political conflicts and renewed revolutionary uprisings which reflect 'continuities between historical and contemporary manifestations of colonialism, imperialism, and Orientalism' (Ball and Mattar 2019: 6).[15] These include, most notably, the founding of the state of Israel in 1948, the Algerian War of Independence of 1954–62, the Arab–Israeli War of 1967, the Lebanese Civil War of 1975–90, the US invasion of Iraq in 2003, and, most recently, the pro-democratic upheavals that have swept across the region since 2011. The fact that Arab autobiography has flourished in such contexts has influenced representations of subjectivity as predominantly political. As Moore-Gilbert argues in relation to postcolonial life writing, and this applies to the Arab context: 'an adjustment of the existing autobiographical tropes of subjectivity is deemed necessary adequately to narrativize the effects of [post]colonial history on the identity' of life writers as well as 'to express their resistance to its cultural norms, which include those ideologically dominant models of selfhood' (2011: 96). That is, modern Arab autobiography generally reflects the enduring effect of national struggles. It places the author's individual experience within larger confrontational contexts of national, colonial and anti-colonial/imperial landscapes that are equally affected by dynamics of 'pan-Arabism, pan-Islamism, and local nationalisms' (Anishchenkova 2014: 38).

Undeniably, the contemporary Arab world is characterised by intertwined national conflicts. It is torn by sectarian wars, revolutions, counter-revolutions, military interventions, *coup d'états* and armed conflicts that are motivated by extremist Islamist groups. The region has, consequently, become a central arena for international interventions and a site for conflicting political interests, geo-strategic negotiations and global score-settling. Overarching the national specificity of particular social and political contexts, the region 'suffers from lack of democracy, freedom of expression and individual as well as collective liberties'; it is also characterised by 'predominant autocratic and authoritarian regimes with their curb on democracy and civil liberties' (Laachir and Talajooy 2013: 3). This current political complexity in the Arab region reflects the enduring history of the colonial and imperial projects, which has shaped the modern sociopolitical scene and history of the region (Gregory 2004; McMillan 2016). The colonial legacy did not simply end with the declaration of independence and detachment from 'traditional' imperial hegemonies. On the contrary, traditional imperialism continues to function in the region through less visible systems (Young 2003: 3). In the Arab world, an 'intrinsically colonial modernity' is sustained through what Derek Gregory terms the 'architecture of enmity' (2004: 17). This enmity is constructed through imaginative division of geographies on the bases of ideological and cultural otherness. It establishes the Arab region as the West's 'other' whose values are incompatible with the principles of Western freedom, individualism and democracy (McMillan 2016: 224).

Moreover, the effect of the enduring colonial legacy on the failure of the modern Arab state to sustain economic stability, social welfare, democracy and peace led to the emergence of neocolonial regimes. These act as what Tamim al-Barghouti describes as 'vassal states' to the superpowers in which 'dependence becomes the precondition for independence and servitude the precondition for sovereignty' (2015: 44–5). Consequently, the growing public 'coming to consciousness' (Huggan 2013: 1) of the failure of Arab regimes motivated renewed revolutionary narratives that materialised in the prodemocratic uprisings against autocratic governments. They started in Tunisia in December 2010 and had a snowballing effect – yielding disillusioning outcomes in Egypt, Libya and Yemen, stifled in Bahrain, still ongoing as a civil war in Syria and are metamorphosing since early 2019 in Algeria, Sudan and Lebanon as ongoing *ḥirāks* (popular movements). While these new movements of revolt (known as *thawrāt*) have emerged in post-independence nations, in Western media under the problematic term 'Arab Spring',[16] they reflect what Graham Huggan refers to as 'unfinished [Arab] struggle' (2013: 1). They denote the *longue durée* of struggle for self-determination against regimes that replaced the colonial order with new local ones, and thus fall 'within a larger historical pattern of national and transnational social movements' (ibid.: 1). That is, contemporary revolutionary discourses that have emerged against a new (neocolonial) enemy mark a continuing history of oppression and resistance and represent 'as much creative engagements with the present as they are critical interrogations of the [colonial] past' (ibid.: 15). They reveal a continuing desire for collective emancipation, self-determination and freedom, and present a space for the people to envision and reclaim a nation in the process of (re)making for which and about which the literature I examine speaks.

It is in the light of these historical trajectories and renewed revolutionary discourses for freedom and emancipation from oppressive systems in the region that I look at the Arab world as a postcolonial context. While I do acknowledge the specificities of each national context throughout my textual analysis, I classify these sociopolitical conflicts under the category of national struggles. The latter, as I use it, encompasses ongoing anti-colonial struggles for self-determination, new popular movements against neocolonial oppression (the Arab uprisings and *ḥirāks*), and the enduring effect of the colonial history that is still affecting national identity formation in the region and is constantly revisited in contemporary cultural productions. Thus, the concept of national struggles in this context reflects an imbrication of sociopolitical dissidence, resistance and revolutions, terms which I use throughout the book. Resistance, as a framework that I am outlining and deploying here, is located within a specific field of social and political power, which informs the texts I discuss (as I explain further below). This field is intrinsically revolutionary and contestational in the sense that it reflects the people's desire and fight for social justice. In the contemporary Arab world, there is a newly articulated terminology of resistance which is no longer exclusive to national independence. While the contexts examined here are characterised by different waves of popular resistance against varied and multi-layered oppressive powers, they all reflect the popular desire towards individual freedom, social justice and dignity. What brings these contexts of national struggles under the trope of resistance literature is the ways in which the authors under scrutiny are partisans in popular oppositional movements and are all writing about and for the nation that is in the (re)making. They are using the genre, as I argue, as a cultural medium that engages with established social and political systems that are (or were) being contested on the streets and through which they reflect a dynamic interplay between the individual and the collective. In this sense, their writing becomes bound up with activism. Equally, these authors, as I demonstrate, are writing autobiographically to create narratives that document the conditions, the various forms and the drives of popular dissent and to echo the people's desire for (re)new(ed) nations that are in progress. It is in this sense that a postcolonial approach is necessary for forging my argument.

The postcolonial paradigm of analysis is particularly relevant to the framework of my study which looks closely at non-fictional texts that act as discourses of resistance against oppressive social, political and representational powers within contexts of conflicts and national struggles. As Robert Young explains, the postcolonial will persist as 'an interrelated set of critical and counterintuitive perspectives, a complex network of paronymous concepts and heterogeneous practices that have been developed out of traditions of resistance to a global historical trajectory of imperialism and colonialism' (2012: 20). A postcolonial lens enables us to analyse cultural manifestations of oppositional forces in Arab women's autobiographical discourses which reflect the complexity of historical processes of imperialism and colonialism and their enduring effects on identity formation and multiple neocolonial struggles. It helps, as Caroline Rooney puts it, 'to engage with questions of national self-determination through attending to the cultural forms in which a nation expresses itself, reflects on itself and critiques itself' (2011: 373). While, as I explain, Arab life writing should not be perceived monolithically, overarching political concerns and national interests continue to define Arab autobiographical practices as a cultural corpus. Both regional and specifically national concerns are intrinsic to the works that I am examining in this book. All my selected texts define their subjects as national subjects and place the author either within a post-independence context (Algeria and Egypt), ongoing national struggles (Palestine and Syria), or evoke new national concerns (the countries of the so-called Arab Spring), which they revisit and/or interrogate, as I shall elaborate. This focus also helps to extend the current critical corpus of postcolonial/autobiographical studies which continues noticeably to marginalise both pre-modern and modern Arab women's literary autobiographical practices.

In their Own Words: Arab Women Writing the Self

Until recently, Arab women's autobiographical discourses have been inexcusably overlooked in critical and theoretical discussions on the genre in English. Second-wave revisionist feminist criticism paid little, if any, attention to Arab women's autobiographical narratives,[17] and neither did inaugural postcolonial autobiographical scholarship. This critical marginalisation continued until the end of late twentieth century, which marked a modest rise of interest in Arab women's autobiographical discourses but almost exclusively within a feminist representational framework. The few existing book-length discussions in English on Arab women's literary self-expression, mainly Fadia Faqir's edited collection *In the House of Silence: Autobiographical Essays by Arab Women Writers* (1999) and Nawar Al-Hassan Golley's academic monograph *Reading Arab Women's Autobiographies: Shahrazad Tells Her Story* (2003), are preoccupied with the dichotomy of voice and silence. They focus mainly on the potential of 'the "master narrative" of neopatriarchy to be challenged and disrupted' through autobiographical enunciation, on the ability of Arab women 'to weave a "language" of their own' (Faqir 1999: 23), and on 'the ways [they] express themselves and how these texts are presented to the West' (Golley 2003: 52).

Golley's monograph *Reading Arab Women's Autobiographies: Shahrazad Tells her Story* (2003), which is the prime, and one of the few, extended critical studies in English on Arab women's autobiographies, offers interesting discussions of the genre and the way it 'provide[s] spaces within which women can talk about the complexities and pluralities of their selves' (69). It is preoccupied with questions of individualism and agency and the way autobiographical writing is used by Arab women to express themselves and how their texts are presented in the West. Like the authors in Faqir's edited collection, Golley specifically highlights the way the genre is invested in correcting the orientalist image of the Arab woman through her own 'words', which remains arguably relevant. However, such framing, I believe, needs to be re-evaluated as it implies that Arab women's use of the genre is in itself an achievement that solely demonstrates an ability for self-representation while focusing almost exclusively on issues of (mis)representation and reception. Additionally, Golley's monograph examines texts that fall into what I consider the canonical or classical category of Arab women's autobiographical writing;[18] it is also mostly Egypt-centred, and noticeably marginalises Maghrebi narratives. Golley extends her discussion through a subsequent edited collection of critical essays entitled *Women's Lives Retold: Exploring Identity through Writing* (2007),[19] which considers a range of autobiographical expression by Arab women 'from autobiographies to fiction, poetry, memoirs, and even photographs' to show 'diverse ways in which Arab women are examining and exploring contemporary issues in terms of their own lives' (xxvii). However, similar to her earlier monograph, it does not offer a sustained interrogation of the political implications of the use of the genre or propose a nuanced category of Arab women's autobiographical writing, of which it assumes to speak. While Golley's contribution – as the only critic who has produced gendered book-length scholarly discussions (in English) on the genre – is indeed significant, and her trope of 'writing back' is still relevant, her study needs to be updated and rethought. Her critical paradigm needs to be contextualised within an intersectional framework of feminist and postcolonial perspective that is politically nuanced and more recent and, as such, more relevant to contemporary femino-political concerns of the Arab region, which my book addresses.

It is the ongoing shared peripheral status of women in the sociopolitical scene in the region that begs continued critical consideration of their creative enunciation of revolutionary discourses in contexts of national struggles. National commitment is generally reserved to men through an enduring spatial division between the 'home' as feminine and the 'front' as masculine (Cooke 1993). Such a trope is reproduced by the problematic use of the name 'Shahrazad' in the title of Golley's monograph (2003), for instance, which appropriates the mythical image of the Eastern storyteller whose resistance to patriarchy is exercised within the confinement of a home. Such a spatial division has, consequently, 'compartmentalised the participation of men and women into binary distinctions between acknowledged and unacknowledged service to present a particularly male-oriented agenda of active national commitment' (Mehta 2007: 32). Women's role and participation in contexts of national struggles in the Arab world is generally obscured, as was the case in nationalist disavowal of women revolutionists in post-independence Algeria.[20] Women are denied nationalist agendas and subjectivity through a reductive conception of their role in politically fraught contexts. Even their acknowledged engagement, which is determined by the predominant nationalist discourses, is restricted to a few iconic figures who ostensibly operate as a 'décor', rather than 'as serious sites of decision making' (El Said *et al.* 2015: 237). This nationalist male-centred dogmatism unveils an underlying power structure which 'creates a hierarchy of discrimination in which men are active subjects of nation-building while women are marginalized through conceptual or fetishized imagery' (Mehta 2007: 32).

Similarly, in the literary critical field, Arab women's writings and contributions have been, until recently, perceived through an orientalist lens of criticism.[21] While the international literary sphere has developed an appreciation for Arab women writers who are being increasingly translated, published and circulated, the growing interest in Arab women's writings is still, however, relatively limited in the critical reception of their works 'as only [having] one thing to offer: an affirmation of oppression' (Valassopoulos 2007: 2, 4). This is due to the ontological stigma that the region has been associated with as a locus of patriarchy in which women are deprived of their voices and rights and treated as inferior to men in public and private sectors. This is also related to the popular perception of Islam, the region's dominant religion, as fundamentally masculine and phallocentric (Al-Ali and Pratt 2009: 1). It is the orientalist perception of the image of Arab women that led them to be subjected to representational ambivalence; they are either silenced subjects 'deprived of subjective particularity' (Mehta 2014: 14) or hyper-visible subjects in a way that 'overemphasize [their oppression and] racial and sexual attributes' (Minh-ha 1989: 6).

In this sense, postcolonial feminist insights into the study of life writing by contemporary Arab women help dissect an intersection of issues of voice, representation and participation in revolutionary moments through various approaches to literary self-expression. Many Arab women writers have transcended the phase of writing cautiously and selectively as a way out for the oppressed, confined self. Their literary subjectivity, I argue, has gone beyond the abstract meaning of autonomy, or what is condescendingly perceived, by nationalist and Western critics alike, as '"daring" to put pen to paper' (Amireh 1996); it is rather manifested in their use of self-referential forms, that fall into the category of life writing, as oppositional political acts that assert their right to speak for and about the nation through the individual lens of experience. They offer autobiographical proclamations that dissolve the line between personal writing and activism, and present themselves as active, self-defined and (self) recognised participants in the sociopolitical landscape. Hence, there is a persistent need to address the implications of the use of this genre to express political dissent, to reflect on regional conflicts and to rethink, critically, the socio-cultural predicaments of the time.

Life Writing, Sites of Resistance

In *Cultural Resistance* (2002), Stephen Duncombe points out that 'artistic creation' can constitute a 'political practice' that acts as a site of resistance to dominant political, economic and/or social structures through the way it (re)writes and/or interrogates the discourses of power that governs them (5). Cultural resistance, according to Duncombe, is possible because it is able to create ideological and material '"free space" for developing ideas and practices. Freed from the limits and constraints of the dominant culture [it offers] new ways of seeing and being' (2002: 5, 12). While, in the Foucauldian understanding, culture can constitute a propaganda device through which dominant discourses maintain and justify their semblance of power, it is equally a powerful dissident tool. Cultural production constitutes a medium of formulating new epistemologies and alternative resources that aim to destabilise asymmetries of power. It is on the basis of this alternative, artistic space for contestation that Barbara Harlow (1987), building on Ghassan Kanafani (1966), conceptualises the notion of resistance literature. Harlow argues that literature that emerges as part of organised national resistance movements is a 'politicized activity'. Literature that negotiates, (re)evaluates, questions and condemns hegemonic narratives of power – in its social, political and cultural guises – constitutes a 'part of the larger struggle for liberation'; it is 'immediately and directly involved in a struggle against ascendant or dominant forms of ideological and cultural production' (Harlow 1987: 10, 28–9).[22]

It is important to outline the way resistance functions in order to understand how literature constitutes one of its cultural forms. Resistance denotes a state of opposition to a given power that is uneven, unjust, abusive and/or dehumanising, and that is exercised through political, economic, social and/or psychological repressive apparatuses. These apparatuses can be (non)violent and (in)visible and are usually determined by the uneven possession of knowledge, material means and/or difference in gender, race, nationality or class. Resistance can be physical or symbolic, expressed through action or endurance, through breaking or embracing silence and is sociopolitically or culturally engaged. Resistance aims to bring about change or manifests against (the attempts to impose unwanted) change and can emerge from both the powerless and the powerful. It can be collective or individual, spatially limited or widespread, intentional or unintentional, conscious or unconscious, conspicuous or concealed (Hollander and Einwohner 2004; Tripp 2013). In the context of my study, when resistance is carried out on the streets and driven by the desire for human dignity and freedom (and from which my selected texts emerge and to/for which they speak), resistance is necessarily oppositional as it attempts to (re)inscribe alternative forms of power discourses. Charles Tripp, in *The Power and the People: Paths of Resistance in the Middle East* (2013), discusses the dynamics of power and political resistance in the Arab world; he asserts that any resistance movement needs to be identified and understood within specific fields of power. He rightly explains that it 'follows and contests the lines of inclusion and exclusion that are integral to all systems of power' (4); hence, resistance cannot exist outside a dichotomy of uneven power relations and certain ethical and political conditions, which give such acts (whether intentionally oppositional or not) their ideological meaning.

According to Michel Foucault, the relationship between power and resistance is mobile and multidimensional. He explains that:

> Where there is power, there is resistance, and yet, or rather consequently, this resistance is never in a position of exteriority in relation to power ... [The existence of power] depends on a multiplicity of points of resistance: these play the role of adversary, target, support, or handle in power relations. (1990: 95)

That is, power abuse may breed resistance; acts of defiance, in turn, may lead the dominant to exercise more power in an attempt to defeat this opposition. Power can also use resistance movements to legitimise and justify itself through exposing 'the dark side that will erupt unless power can keep it in check' by playing on the idea of maintaining the status quo and choosing stability over chaos (Tripp 2013: 12).

Such complex relationship between power and resistance also materialises in literary expression. Literature that takes as its subject contexts of oppression by appropriating, engaging with, interrogating and attempting to subvert power dynamics is a politicised activity. This literature, which is described by Fanon as 'the literature of combat' (1963: 193),[23] becomes a medium of 'writing human rights and righting political wrongs' (Harlow 1992: 256) in the sense that it is used as an aesthetic reflection of/on structures of hegemonic powers. It can also act as a political catalyst which works to 'ease the way into political activity' (Tripp 2013: 8). This is the case, for instance, with Palestinian writers who have contributed, since *al-Nakba* (catastrophe) of 1948, to fostering the resistance movement and highlighting the role of popular-based resistance through a myriad of oppositional and politically informed literary forms (see Kanafani 1966; Harlow 1987).[24] As I have explained, in the contemporary, politically fraught Arab world, the aesthetic and the political are intertwined in cultural productions that emerge within nations in the (re)making, and its literature cannot be divorced from the material context from which it emerges. Forms of cultural resistance 'can be a force for change, contesting hegemonic narratives on socio-political and economic issues and revealing the agency and the role of the people in pushing for reform' (Laachir and Talajooy 2013: 5). And as Syrian author Samar Yazbek, in her introduction to *Writing Revolution: Voices from Tunis to Damascus*, points out, 'writing in the time of revolution, is part of the process of change' (2013b: 7). Writing within the contexts of conflict is a form of interrogating power discourses which entails envisioning an alternative future for the writers as individuals and for their nation.

More recently, Brinda Mehta (2014) examines the relationship between creative dissidence and power, particularly through the inscription of violence in the writings of North African women, in a range of forms including fiction, testimony, poetry and drama. Similar to Laachir and Talajooy, Mehta stresses that contemporary literary expression in the Arab world constitutes 'a medium of contestation, resistance and denunciation to expose and condemn human rights violations in the region through the beauty and power of the written word' (2014: 10). While resistance literature is by no means exclusive to women writers in the region, the inscription of dissent through literature by women highlights more complex relations of power as it tends to echo, in addition to national experiences of oppression, gender-based concerns of subjugation. Gendering resistance literature thus would allow a move beyond the restricted feminist conception of women's resistance as only limited to the subversion of patriarchal norms. It stresses patriarchy as only one part of a concentric power dynamics that demarcates the status of women in the contemporary, politically fraught Arab region.

Resistance literature, like the national struggles it depicts, demands to be recognised as 'independent'; it challenges the conventions of literary theory and criticism which are developed in/by the West (Harlow 1987: xvi). This literature should not be divorced from its aestheticism, particularly its literary strategies of representation and generic tactics of experimentation. My conceptualisation of resistance literature extends its available critical framing to life writing sub-genres by contemporary Arab women. It looks particularly at literary narratives that engage with the sociopolitical and historical settings of their enunciation and which 'recount not only their [author's] personal itinerary but also the historical agenda in which they participate' (Harlow 1987: 181). I look at literary autobiographical discourses that emerge from and/or speak to national struggles as sites of resistance through which the authors intentionally interrogate existing structures of power that demarcate the agency, autonomy, freedom, dignity and basic rights of the people on a larger scope, and of women specifically. This contested structure of power, as I conceive it, is intersectional. It is represented by state oppression, colonial and neocolonial domination, social and gender-based oppression, and cultural (mis)representational dynamics. These form a concentric space where the very act of producing culture of self-representation becomes an act of resistance that 'demonstrat[es] a capacity for independent action' (Tripp 2013: 5). I argue that the authors under examination enact the importance of resistance to forms of self-expression through using (re)new(ed) styles, themes, languages and media of life writing in order to make political commentaries and interventions, to destabilise unwanted and despised powers and to potentially push for social, political and cultural reform.

An analytical study of life writing in its different forms and aspects is an important way of understanding the aesthetic models of self-expression that Arab women writers choose for enunciating resistance. However, the efficacy of life writing as political and politicised sites for the expression of resistance by Arab women, I argue, is not dependent on whether an actual change may take place. The genre, rather, gives visibility to women's presence during revolutionary moments and thus demonstrates that 'the significance of women's agency is in *being within* [and critically engaging with] *contexts of resistance* not [exclusively] in *doing as an instrument* to achieve a particular goal' (El Said *et al.* 2015: 12). Because the idea of representation is at the heart of the politics of women's resistance, their non-fictional literature helps us to understand the way they rewrite narratives of national struggles from a personal perspective in an attempt to revise representational historical discourses that are notorious for obscuring their role and presence within histories of wars and conflicts. They become actors instead of observers, operators of power instead of sites for exercising powers, subjects of their stories rather than objects of representation and they constitute what Harlow refers to as 'the active reconstruct(ors) of interrupted histories' (1987: 200). They reclaim the task of inscribing their personal history within contexts of national struggles while at the same time preserving a collective memory as they experience it.

Book Outline

This book examines Arab women's life writing emerging as part of, or in response to, national struggles and revolutionary movements as a cultural corpus of resistance literature that speaks to, interrogates and/or challenges an imbrication of power discourses. It starts by briefly contextualising women's autobiographical discourses within a twentieth-century scope of Arab national struggles and resistance writing, with a focus on works published in the last two decades of the century. The first chapter traces the major characteristics and tendencies of women's use of the autobiographical genre to engage with (post)colonialism, national movements and independence struggles, which have shaped the history and national landscapes of the region. The aim of this non-exhaustive survey chapter is to expand the critical discussion foregrounded by this Introduction on Arab woman's autobiographical writing and frame it within a twentieth-century tradition of resistance writing.

The following chapters then turn to investigate emerging literary autobiographical strategies (formal, thematic and representational) that are used to express and mediate resistance to intersectional structures of power in a range of life writing subgenres that have appeared in print, or digitally, since the onset of the twenty-first century. I start by examining models that revise and challenge mainstream self-representational modes (Chapter 2). I then move to examine models that re-appropriate and re-work life writing conventions (Chapter 3), narratives that experiment with innovative registers and oppositional writing styles (Chapter 4) and those that use new media as autobiographical sites for protest (Chapter 5).

Chapter 2 sets out the conceptual groundwork for an intersectional paradigm for the study of Arab women's life writing which I foreground in the Introduction and Chapter 1 and propose throughout this book. Chapter 2 offers ways of thinking about the relationship between literary models of autobiographical subjectivity in contexts of national struggles and strategies of resistance to dominant representational discourse. It does so by looking at the implication of revisionist approaches to the representation of fragmented subjectivity in texts by Radwa Ashour (Egypt) and Maïssa Bey (Algeria), which revisit colonial experiences and its effects. The chapter signals the way the book moves from narrative engagement with – and contestation of – both traditional and rigid strategies and critical paradigms of approaching the genre towards more ground-breaking modes and media of autobiographical expression (mainly digital life writing). It also marks a reorientation, evident in all the material I engage with in this book, from earlier postcolonial struggles (national liberation movements of the twentieth century in Chapter 1, *al-Nakba* of 1948 in Ashour's text, and the Algerian War of Independence of 1954 and the civil war of the 1990s in Bey's), to more recent national concerns in the region, particularly the Arab uprisings.

Chapter 3 considers narrative models in which Arab women life writers reappropriate conventional forms of non-fictional storytelling, particularly narratives of bearing witness, for the negotiation of context-specific political and cultural dissent. It examines the relationship between testimonial modes of writing and sociopolitical resistance by looking specifically at texts by Samar Yazbek (Syria) and Suad Amiry (Palestine). The chapter argues that the expository and contestatory nature of testimonial writing allows politically engaged life writers to dissolve the lines between writing and sociopolitical activism. It hence creates a space for challenging the normative, gender-based division of roles and spaces within contexts of national struggles. This writing strategy, the chapter argues, gives way to new archival practices to emerge which provide alternative histories on women's participation in revolutionary moments.

Chapter 4 moves to a relatively new literary strategy of inscribing postcolonial Arab women's experiences of war and revolutions. It dissects the potential strategic functions of humour in diaries that recount national struggles by contemporary Arab women, looking specifically at texts by Suad

Amiry (Palestine) and Mona Prince (Egypt). It argues that humour that stems from a sociopolitically gendered position of marginality and oppression is an intentional dissent strategy. By laughing in contexts where they are expected to weep, these women authors, the chapter contends, problematise the non-fictional literary conventions of representing political conflicts and resist the stereotypical image of the grieving woman in settings of wars and revolutions.

The shift to social media platforms, as one of the most recently emerging sites for the autobiographical expression of dissent, is examined in Chapter 5. The chapter looks closely at the ways in which digital dissidence enables the mediation between the virtual/personal spaces of autobiographical expression and the physical/public spheres of participation and activism, with reference to issues related to audience, privacy and censorship. It does so by looking at selected examples by Arab women from across the region and offering a close reading of late Tunisian blogger and social activist Lina Ben Mhenni's trilingual blog and her subsequent monograph. Mediation between the virtual/personal and the physical/public, the chapter argues, not only problematises the literary conventions of autobiographical expressions. It also reworks ways in which women in politically fraught contexts are able to channel and participate in the public domain through digitising life writing forms.

While the overarching critical paradigm is postcolonial and feminist autobiographical criticism, this book is interdisciplinary. Each chapter extends its theoretical framework according to the sub-genre it explores, including concepts of *testimonio*, humour theories and digital media studies. I examine Anglophone, Francophone and Arabic life writings from different national contexts within the region. A cross-linguistic focus, such as the one pursued here, will help avoid an essentialist perception of a singular Arab culture and a monolithic literary self-representation by Arab women. By not conforming to a language that reflects the 'authentic' Arabic culture, I consider that the selected authors 'engage in the revolutionary poetics of literary worldliness' which 'highlights the struggle to crave safe spaces of mutual understanding, compassion, justice and tolerance when engaging in the boldly expressive ethos of creative dissidence' (Mehta 2014: 18). Such a scope helps to widen the critical focus on postcolonial life writing by highlighting the nuances in approach and the aesthetic/linguistic range of Arab autobiographical discourses. The impact of language choice upon the genre, censorship politics, registers and tactics of resistance, and its relationship to the target audience (which is diverse in each case) will be addressed in each chapter.[25]

Recent and ongoing developments in Arab women's life writing are not limited to the examples I discuss in this monograph. Throughout this book, however, I propose future research trajectories for the study of Arab (auto) biographical writing and draw attention to an array of available, yet under-examined, forms of life writing by Arab women that need to be brought to the fore of critical attention, including graphic auto/biography, journalistic memoirs, autobiographical essays, creative non-fiction and autobiographical literature from the Gulf. Other forms and contexts of Arab(ic) resistance non-fiction are yet to be explored. My aim is to offer a critical approach for the study of some modalities of contemporary Arab women's life writing and its limits and capacities as a form of resistance literature that operates within a larger and diverse cultural corpus of self-representation and narration.

Notes

1. These include, for example, Moroccan author Mohamed Choukri (1935–2003); Syrian novelist Hanna Minah (1924–2018); Palestinian life writers Mourid Barghouti (1944–2021), Raja Shehadeh (b. 1951) and Atef Abu Saif (b. 1973); and Egyptian writer Sonallah Ibrahim (b. 1937), to name a few.
2. I use the terms West and Western, with an awareness of their limitations, to refer to Euro-American countries and culture(s). These terms have been advanced by colonial discourses, which have fostered the problematic division of the world into culturally homogenous categories. West and Western are terms deployed in this study mainly with the intention to draw some distinctions between the traditions and conventions of the autobiographical across cultures – specifically Euro-American on the one hand and postcolonial (and Arab) on the other. However, I do not consider these contexts, as I discuss in this introduction, as homogenous entities but tend to problematise such divisions through reference to the rich and shifting autobiographical expressions in both contexts.
3. See Anderson's chapters on poststructuralist and postmodernist autobiography criticism in her *Autobiography* (2011).
4. Issues of transparent self-representation and absolute truthfulness propagated by first-wave autobiographical criticism were questioned by a second wave of critics, who insisted that autobiographical writing is creation rather than mere transcription. Yet, like their predecessors, second-wave critics have maintained the notion

of 'high culture' in relation to the genre and ignored gendered and other marginal and minority lives (Smith and Watson 2001a: 123–8).

5. 'Autogynography' is a term coined by Domna C. Stanton to describe women's autobiographical writings which 'gave the female "I" substance through the inscription of an interior and an anterior' (1984: 14). According to Stanton, 'autogynography' has 'a global and essential therapeutic purpose: to constitute the female subject' (ibid.: 14). Gilmore's 'autobiographics' is detailed in Chapter 2, see pp. 68–9.

6. While the category of life narratives includes other forms of self-expression like performance, life writing is predominantly literary (Smith and Watson 2001a: 4–5).

7. Within feminist autobiographical criticism, there has been a shift from using the term 'women's autobiography' towards more encompassing terms such as 'women's autobiographical practices' and 'women's lifewriting' (Smith and Watson 2016: 50).

8. It is worth noting that in *Orientalism* Said, however, highlights the involvement of his own autobiographical experience in producing his seminal work. In discussing the personal dimension that motivates his course of research and writing, Said asserts that his study of Orientalism is 'an attempt to inventory the traces upon me, the Oriental subject' (2003b: 25).

9. Edward Said's memoir *Out of Place* (1999), most notably, has been critically argued to be predominantly self-centred, following the formal and thematic developmental structures that characterise traditional models of auto/biography. See, for instance, Moore-Gilbert (2009: 115–17).

10. Other recent studies that establish a dialogue between postcolonial theory and life writing include Cynthia G. Franklin's *Academic Lives: Memoir, Cultural Theory, and the University Today* (2009), Stef Craps' *Postcolonial Witnessing* (2012), Anna Bernard's *The Rhetorics of Belonging* (2013), the special issue of *Biography*, 'Baleful Postcoloniality', edited by Salah D. Hassan and David Alvarez (2013), and Lindsey Moore's *Narrating Postcolonial Arab Nations: Egypt, Algeria, Lebanon, Palestine* (2018).

11. I expand further on the idea of the contemporary Arab world as a postcolonial context in the following section. Also, see Anna Ball and Karim Mattar's 'Introduction' to *The Edinburgh Companion to the Postcolonial Middle East* (2019) for further details on the critical frameworks of the growing subfield of the postcolonial greater Middle East.

12. There have been some scholarly studies that investigate the tradition of Arabic

autobiographical writing which predate the publication of Gusdorf's controversial seminal essay. Particularly, Frantz Rosenthal's 1937 article 'Die Arabische Autobiographie' (The Arabic Autobiography) discusses the practice of literary life writing within the Arab culture by surveying a substantial number of texts produced between the Islamic period until the sixteenth century. Another equally substantial, yet more recent, study that argues against 'The Fallacy of Western Origins' is Dwight F. Reynolds' *Interpreting the Self: Autobiography in the Arabic Literary Tradition* (2001: 17); a book in which he discusses almost 100 literary autobiographical texts written between the ninth and nineteenth centuries. Both Rosenthal and Reynold demonstrate that there exists a long history of Arab(ic) literary autobiographical texts that predate the Western recognition and theorisation of the genre.

13 The major functions of pre-*Nahḍa* forms of life writing, as outlined by Dwight Reynolds (2001), are thanking God for his bounty, recording one's academic and professional achievements, leaving a landmark in history, and providing intellectual and academic example to be followed by the coming generations. These are, interestingly, very similar to the preoccupations of modern Western autobiography, but the main distinction is their predominant collective ethos and political implications.

14 The Arab League, also known as The League of Arab States, founded in 1945, is a regional pan-Arab organisation established on the basis of geographical proximity, culture and common language. It aims to create economic, structural, legal and political interrelations and coordination between its twenty-two member states.

15 On the concept of 'post/colonial modernity' as a critical framework for approaching the Arab region, see Ball and Mattar's 'Introduction' to *The Edinburgh Companion to the Postcolonial Middle East* (2019).

16 The term Arab Spring, used at the early stages of the Arab uprisings to designate a hopeful 'one-time political mutation' when democracy 'blossoms' in the region, has become a sarcastic phrase after the disillusioning outcomes of the uprisings did not rise to the aspirations of the people (Achcar 2016: 1).

17 An exception is Donna Robinson Divine's examination of the Palestinian Fadwa Tuqan's autobiography (first published in Arabic in 1984) in Domna C. Stanton's edited collection *The Female Autograph* (1984).

18 Mainly texts by Egyptian authors Huda Shaarawi (1879–1947) and Nawal El-Saadawi (1931–2021) and Palestinian poet Fadwa Tuqan (1917–2003).

19 Other scholars have also included Arab women's autobiographical writings as the

subsequent focus of different studies on the genre, mainly Debra Kelly (2005), Moore-Gilbert (2009, 2013), Norbert Bugeja (2012), Geoffrey Nash (2007), Silke Schmidt (2012), Anishchenkova (2014) and Nasser (2017).

20 See Brinda Mehta's discussion of the post-independence nationalist marginalisation of Arab women revolutionaries (2014: 15).

21 This perception rendered the use of the term 'feminism' problematic in the context of the Arab world. Nawar Golley attacks mainstream Western feminism as insufficient and racist as it maintains 'colonial assumptions about Arab women' (2003: 6). In their introduction to *Opening the Gates* (1990), Margot Badran and Miriam Cooke acknowledge the existence of feminism within the Arab/Muslim world although there is no single Arabic term to refer to the notion. The closest equivalent would be *nisā'i* which also means feminine or womanly. More recently 'the term *al-niswiyya* has entered into common usage as an equivalent of the term "feminism"' (Ball 2012: 9). Feminism is a term grounded in the commitments to gender equality in sociopolitical and representational spheres, it 'can retain a level of fluidity and multiplicity which enables it to translate across cultural perspectives and experiences' (ibid.: 10). Badran and Cooke (1990) refer to feminisms (plural) to indicate the intersection and universality of the notion as well as the commonalities of differently located feminists' experiences and agendas while at the same time acknowledging their diverse roles and approaches.

22 An equally important work which examines theories and strategies of resistance literature is Harlow's *After Lives: Legacies of Revolutionary Writing* (1996). It investigates the politics of assassination of political writers and intellectuals (including Kanafani) 'who have been instrumental in organizing resistance to systems and discourses of domination, and whose life work had been committed to redefining the very "politics of shed blood"' (Harlow 1996: 26).

23 According to Fanon, literature of combat, like the concept of resistance literature, 'calls for the whole people to fight for their existence as a nation. It is a literature of combat, because it moulds the national consciousness, giving it form and contours and flinging open before it new and boundless horizons; it is a literature of combat because it assumes responsibility, and because it is the will to liberty expressed in terms of time and space' (Fanon 1963: 193).

24 Resistance in Arabic translates as *mu'āradah*, *muqāwamah* (as elaborated by Kanafani) or *ṣumūd*. *Mu'āradah* indicates a clear-cut opposition to a system or a body of power; the term is also used to refer to the collective oppositional parties in a given political system. It can as well be used to mean a literary form known as *al-mu'āradah al-shi'ryyah* (literally translates as poetry competition

of imitation/mimicry). *Muqāwamah* is generally 'used in Arabic to suggest popular, organised resistance to colonial occupation or imperialist oppression and gives a literary-critical implication to the idea of resistance' (Harlow 1987: 24). The term *al-muqāwamah al-shaʿbyyah* (popular resistance), for instance, was used to describe the first waves of organised movements of colonial resistance in Algeria (1830–1919) which were characterised by the participation of *al-shaʿb* (as an inclusive term for 'the people'). *Ṣumūd* is specifically, yet not exclusively, used in relation to the Palestinian context. *Ṣumūd* literally means endurance, steadfastness and stamina. It 'indicates a person's ability to remain in place in the face of indignities, injustices and humiliation at the hands of the colonial power, . . . In other words, steadfastness is not about *doing* but, rather, doing by not doing' (El Said *et al.* 2015: 13).

25   The issues of language choice and target audience are discussed in more detail in the following chapter, see Chapter 1, pp. 56–8.

1

Genre and Twentieth-century National Struggles: Arab Women Write the Resistance

In *Interpreting the Self: Autobiography in the Arabic Literary Tradition* (2001), Dwight F. Reynolds surveys Arabic autobiographical literary productions between the ninth and the nineteenth centuries. He rightly demonstrates that the motivations for writing autobiographical accounts were often multifarious, ranging from creating 'biographical dictionaries', 'works in history', 'family history', 'edifying entertainment', to creating 'narratives of conversion to the true faith' (2001: 9). However, Reynolds explains that since the turn of the twentieth century, 'sociopolitical context of resistance to European colonial powers, the struggle for political independence, the rise of Arab nationalism' and 'the emergence of a strong Arab women's autobiographical tradition, as well as new regional and national identities' have all contributed to a shift in the use of Arab(ic) literary autobiography as mainly a 'means of sociopolitical expression' (ibid.: 11). Indeed, national struggles against colonial powers and the emerging movements for independence that characterised the region have deeply influenced contexts of literary production, particularly during the second half of the twentieth century, and have brought to the fore the relationship between autobiographical practices, national identity and political activism. As Tahia Abdel Nasser discusses at length in her *Literary Autobiography and Arab National Struggles* (2017), 'Arab writers produced forms of autobiography that challenged imperial cultural formations by chronicling the writers' self-formation and public involvement in independence struggles' (11). This is particularly important in relation to women's autobiographical accounts which explicitly engage with an intersection of issues of feminism, nationalism and (neo)colonialism, and hence reveal highly complex processes of identity formation, self-revelation and 'sociopolitical expression'. While Reynolds notes that 'only three [Arab] women autobiographers can be identified with certainty' between the ninth and nineteenth centuries (2001: 8), such an insignificant number has drastically changed. The second half of the twentieth century witnessed a boom in the production and publication of Arab women's autobiographical writings, most of which are rooted in historical and political events and often situate their postcolonial female subject within a broader national history of social movements and anti-colonial struggles.

This chapter offers a brief introduction that situates Arab women's autobiographical practices within a modern history of social and anti-colonial movements. It provides a short survey of Arab women's life writings that emerged in, and speak to, the context of twentieth-century national struggles, with a focus on the major works published in the last two decades of the century.[1] It traces the main characteristics of, and motivations behind, Arab women's use of the autobiographical genre to engage with (post)colonialism, national movements and independence struggles, which have shaped the history and national landscapes of the region. The aim of this chapter, which should not be read as exhaustive or conclusive, is to contextualise contemporary Arab women's life writing – the main subject of this book – within an earlier tradition of autobiographical literature in order to examine and highlight the historical role of the genre as resistance literature.

Since the publication of Taha Hussein's *al-Ayyām* (The Days) (1929), often seen as the foundational text of modern Arabic autobiography, the genre has become a major form of expression in Arab culture, which flourished particularly in the last two decades of the century and has extended beyond a single literary form and language (Arabic) to include a rich tradition of, mainly, Anglophone and Francophone autobiographical writings (Nasser 2017: 2). Since the publication of *al-Ayyām* in 1929 and up until 1988, approximately sixty Arab autobiographies were published (Rooke 1997: 1–20).[2] The publication rate has rapidly increased in the following decade to mark the boom of Arabic memoirs and auto/biographies of the 1990s. In a period of seven years, particularly between 1992 and 1999, 'more than thirty full-length autobiographies were published in different Arab countries' (Faqir 1999: 6). These writings include forms as diverse as autobiographies, testimonial narratives, memoirs, autobiographical fiction and prison accounts. This substantial rise of modern Arab autobiography is closely connected first to cultural and political relationships with the West; the socio-cultural and literacy transformations during *al-Nahḍa* (the Arab Renaissance) of the nineteenth century; and histories of revolutionary struggles and national resistance movements in the late nineteenth and first half of the twentieth century (Reynolds 2001: 251). These factors have resulted in the rise of new forms of subjectivities and sensibilities and influenced and transformed premodern traditions of Arabic autobiographical writing.[3] This increase is also recently related to the changing geopolitical landscape in the world since the 1990s.[4] The ideological and politically fraught terrain of the Arab region has caused fundamental changes in identity discourses and subjectivity formation which is materialised in modern and contemporary life writing. The genre has become a vehicle for engaging with the complex relationship between the individual, the nation, the (former) coloniser and the Western other (Anishchenkova 2014: 10). New and renewed national identities and modes of autobiographical expression have emerged in the wake of anti-colonial struggles and are, as I argue throughout this book, continuously redefined and renegotiated in the light of recent national movements and ongoing processes of nation-building.

Particularly, the turn of the twentieth century witnessed a surge in the production of Arab women's life writing which led prominent critics and observers, such as Margot Badran and Miriam Cooke, to assert that the 'writing and publication by Arab women of their own memoirs and journals is mainly a twentieth-century phenomenon' (2004: xliii). Arab women's autobiographical literature emerged in contexts in which writing has become an imperative cultural and political intervention and a 'privileged site for thinking about issues of writing at the intersection of feminist, postcolonial, and postmodern critical theories, where the processes of subject formation and agency occupy a prime position' (Smith and Watson 2016: 9–10). The genre has largely acted as means to empower women's feminist and national voices and to highlight the way women have been doubly oppressed by colonial powers and local patriarchal authorities. Women's need to write life stories emerged from their 'need to define their position in history and locate themselves *vis-à-vis* the male master narrative, and to explore and formulate a separate individual identity . . . due to their suffering "the double jeopardy" of being women and political dissidents in the Arab World' (Faqir 1999: 8–9). This rise, therefore, urges for a comprehensive critical attention to Arab women's autobiographical literature beyond a simplistic recognition of their life writing as mere representation of personal struggles against their social environment; rather, this body of work, as I argue, functions as a political intervention and as a form of cultural resistance.

Arab women's autobiographical writing produced within, and in the aftermath of, colonial contexts often intertwine personal history and feminist voices with concerns of national sociopolitical movements. Between the 1920s and the 1960s, there was a conspicuous rise in public feminist movements (mainly among upper- and middle-class educated women) that simultaneously called for women's advancement and for national independence, including in Egypt (between 1920s and mid-1950s); Lebanon, Syria and Iraq (in the 1930s and 1940s); and Sudan (in the 1950s) (Badran and Cooke 2004: xxix). The best-known early autobiographical text of the mid-twentieth century, and arguably the founding text of modern Arab women's autobiography, reflects the juncture of commitment to feminist and national causes. In the 1940s, Egyptian feminist Huda Shaarawi (1879–1947) dictated her memoir *Mudhakkirāti* (My Memoirs),[5] which was published posthumously as *Mudhakkirāt Hudā Sha'rāwī: Rāi'dat al-Mar'ah al-'Arabiyyah al-Ḥadīthah* (1981) (The Memoirs of Huda Shaarawi: The Modern Arab Woman Pioneer). It was then translated from Arabic, edited by Margot Badran, and appeared in print as *Harem Years: The Memoirs of an Egyptian Feminist* (1986). *Harem Years* records Shaarawi's private life during her years of harem seclusion, her participation in the Egyptian revolution against the British in 1919 and her daring act of public unveiling in 1923. Shaarawi, a Muslim upper-class Egyptian woman, presents her public image as both a feminist and nationalist activist. While her memoir – conventional in form, written retrospectively and organised chronologically – focuses on the narrating subject's private harem life and personal itinerary, it also records her fight on behalf of gender and the nation. The memoir situates Shaarawi's feminist agenda within a nationalist context of anti-colonial movements and records her struggle against the cultural and institutional containment of Egyptian women's rights and emancipation as parallel to her growing political and collective consciousness. Shaarawi established the first Egyptian Feminist Union

(EFU) in 1923 and was involved in the Egyptian nationalist movement; she was also the president of the political Wafdist Women's Central Committee which led the fight, along with men Wafdists, for national independence.

Like Shaarawi, whose dictated memoir aims to challenge the notorious historical marginalisation of women's engagement in the public sphere, her compatriot Nabawiyya Musa (1886–1951), feminist activist and nationalist, and one of the founding feminists of the twentieth century in Egypt, published one of the few autobiographical works by modern Egyptian women. Musa's account, *Tārīkhī bi Qalamī* (My History in my Word: An Autobiography) (1938–42),[6] is a collection of autobiographical essays which highlights the role of feminists in the national history of anti-colonial struggles through the female personal experience. These pioneering texts offer pertinent examples on the interaction of class, gender and politics and the increasingly visible role and engagement of Egyptian women during the early twentieth-century nationalist movement and the preceding reforms of the late nineteenth century. The rise of Islamic feminist writing, which became evident in the late twentieth century, and some of which is autobiographical, has further highlighted the diverse discourses on women's rights and Arab feminism(s) but similarly tied women's liberation with that of the nation and maintained women's commitment to contribute to national independence movements.[7] One of the first Islamic feminist women to engage autobiographically with this discourse is Egyptian Zaynab al-Ghazali (1917–2005), the founder of the Muslim Women's Association in 1936, and arguably the first Arab woman to publish a prison memoir *Ayyām min Ḥayātī* (Days from My Life) first published in 1972, to which I will return later.

The autobiographical works of Arab women produced in the twentieth century often highlight the historical role of women in Arab liberation movements since the late nineteenth century, during which women's feminist consciousness became conspicuously visible along their growing national political awareness and regional preoccupations. However, it should be noted that women's feminist awareness in the Arab world preceded the emergence of nationalist consciousness (Badran and Cooke 2004: xxxv). In her introduction to Shaarawi's memoir, Badran explains that through twentieth century life narratives, 'we see that [Arab] women's participation in the national movement[s] did not produce feminism (as frequently assumed) but was the turning point for moving from changes in consciousness and the using of close and expanding connections between women to public activism' (1986: 20). Arab feminists considered the recognition of women's rights and their role in the national struggle as crucial to effective political and social change, despite states' co-optation, and later elimination, of women's voices to advance nationalist agendas.[8] This is illustrated in Shaarawi's letter to Saad Zaghloul (on 12 December 1920), the leader of Egypt's nationalist Wafd party and later Prime Minister, in which she dismisses the misconception that women's renaissance is 'a mere ploy to dupe civilized nations into believing in the advancement of Egypt and its ability to govern itself' (Shaarawi 1986: 122). Rather, Shaarawi describes Egyptian women as 'half the nation' and asserts the significance of acknowledging the role of women in the liberation struggle (ibid.: 122). This reminds us that '[f]or many Third World women, feminism means women's liberation and women's liberation is seen as part of a popular struggle against the forces of oppression'; this struggle 'must have its roots in the material conditions of the people themselves but must also contain the possibilities for a larger collective vision' (Harlow 1986: 521).

Prior to the publication of Shaarawi's memoir (though not to its recording), Lebanese feminist and political activist Anbara Salam Khalidi (1897–1986) published her personal account *Jawlah fi al-Dhikrayāt Bayna Lubnān wa Filasṭīn* (A Tour of Memories Between Lebanon and Palestine) in 1978, later translated into English by the author's son, Tarif Khalidi, and published in 2013 as *Memoirs of an Early Arab Feminist: The Life and Activism of Anbara Salam Khalidi*. Like Shaarawi's personal narrative, Khalidi's memoir is an example of women's growing engagement with political movements and the intersection of feminist activism and national struggles in twentieth-century Arab history as reflected in autobiographical writings. Khalidi's memoir, straightforward and formally conventional, situates its subject within a familial tradition and outlines the social life in Beirut between late nineteenth and early twentieth centuries; it also describes the author's social emancipation journey, including her public lifting of the veil in Beirut in 1928. However, personal history in this memoir is intertwined with social and political events. The author describes her account as 'a history of a generation' (2013: 2), offering a nuanced personal testimony to key historical events of the twentieth century in the region through reflecting on early Arab nationalism and her active participation in the early feminist movements, such as establishing The Society for the Awakening of the Young Arab Woman in 1914. In the prologue to her memoir, Khalidi asserts that 'I do not intend to write a journal or a history of my family or private life as is common nowadays with autobiography', referring to dominant conventions of focusing on the individual self in autobiographical narration, but 'recollections of my own generation, and some of its major events' that characterised 'the political history of the Arab countries' (2013: 2). Such an approach to the genre impacts the conventions of autobiography as it shifts the focus from the subject's individual experiences to the larger historical context surrounding her life.

In fact, Arab autobiographies of the twentieth century are often characterised by their 'autohistory style'; they 'were structured as *historical* narratives where the construction of the autobiographical self was often over-shadowed by reports on various important historical and political events that took place during the course of their lives' (Anishchenkova 2014: 20). Both Shaarawi and Khalidi produced sociohistorical testimonies in which the individual lens of experience is closely affected by political events and autobiographical accounts in which history writing competes with personal storytelling. For instance, Shaarawi situates her personal story within a relational scope of national Egyptian collective. Nawar al-Hassan Golley describes Shaarawi's memoirs as having a 'nonreflective narrative and gentle style' (2003: 48) in reference to the accessible narrative structure and the historical documentary style of her memoir. Similarly, Khalidi explicitly invites her readers to observe, through the pages of her memoirs, 'some tableaux of life from the era during which I lived, and to share the feelings of disappointment that our generation experienced in the shadows of imperialism and foreign occupation' (2013: 1). This reflects earlier, and arguably continuous, politico-ideological orientations of women's life narratives which range from local nationalist movement, feminist issues to Pan-Arab and/or regional orientations, as my following chapters will discuss in detail.

Women's involvement in twentieth-century national struggles as reflected in life narratives can also be observed in biography form,[9] and in life sketches published in biographical dictionaries or periodicals. Biography and biographical dictionaries have a rich tradition in Arabic literature, which goes back to the oral traditions of pre-Islamic times (Reynolds 2001: 36). In the modern era, Arab(ic) biographical writing continued to be a common literary practice that was increasingly used to record women's lives and public/cultural achievements. From 1892 to 1939, for instance, 'Egypt alone saw the publication of 571 biographies of women (written by both men and women) in eighteen periodicals' (Ashour et al. 2008: 4).[10] Among the earliest and most prominent modern women biographers was Syrian author May Ziadeh (1886–1941), who inscribed biographies of three Arab women, namely Aisha Taymur, Arda al-Yaziji and Malak Hinfi Nasif (see Booth 2001: xvi). In her extensive study of the writing of women's biographies in modern Egypt, Marilyn Booth argues that modern life narrative discourses by Arab women were 'anything but separate from emerging apparatuses of identity definition and social regulation inherent to the practices of nationalism' (2001: xiv), an aspect that is not exclusive to full-length autobiographies and memoirs. Particularly, 'biography was one means by which women might assert subject positions within the nationalist collectivity, writing themselves into life narratives' (ibid.: xiv). However, unlike other forms of autobiographical writing, book-length biographies by modern and contemporary Arab women are not abundant. This can be attributed to the spread of education and the significant decrease in illiteracy among women in the region, women's growing access to channels of publication and the way they are increasingly documenting their experiences in their own voices and avoiding literary mediation – which reflects their growing awareness of the revolutionary potentials of writing in their own language as a means to power and knowledge.[11] One of the few, and most prominent, Arab women's biographies of the mid-twentieth century that explicitly engages with national resistance movements is Leila Khaled's *My People Shall Live* (1973). The biography, ghost-written in English by Lebanese academic George Hajjar, records the life story of Leila Khaled (b. 1944), a Palestinian infamous militant whose name is notoriously associated with the hijacking of a passenger jet in 1969, which she diverted, together with Palestinian Salim Issawi, from its scheduled route from Rome to Cairo to fly over occupied Palestine and land in Damascus.[12] This account, told in the first-person pronoun, merges political statements with personal history to create a powerful, yet highly controversial, account of a Palestinian woman's involvement in the armed resistance against Israeli occupation.[13]

Early-twentieth-century feminism(s), nationalism and colonialism have had a great impact on the formation of modern Arab identity, and – as I argue throughout this book – on the development of a tradition of women's life writing that constitutes, in different forms, an important part of Arab resistance literature. A common practice among Arab women life writers of the last two decades of the twentieth century was deploying the genre to portray and reflect on their fight against patriarchal and colonial structures that contained their liberties and personal, social and institutional rights. Between the 1980s and the 2000s, there was a surge in autobiographical productions by Arab women that offer important and personalised accounts of the harem and secluded life, Arab social traditions, and women's sociopolitical position during, and in the aftermath of, colonial oppression. Many of the accounts published in this period are characterised by their developmental and progressive 'journeys' towards self-knowledge and emancipation, a motif which is evident in texts by pioneering figures such as Palestinian poet Fadwa Tuqan's *Riḥlah Jabaliyyah, Riḥlah Ṣaʻbah: Sīrah Dhātiyyah* (1984) (*Mountainous Journey: An Autobiography*, 1990) and its sequel *Al-Riḥlah al-Aṣʻab: Sīrah Dhātiyyah* (1993) (The Most Difficult Journey: an Autobiography), Jordanian writer Najmiya Hikmat's *65 ʻAman min Ḥayāt ʼImraʼah Urduniyyah: Riḥlatī maʻal-zaman* (1986) (Sixty-five Years in the Life of a Jordanian Woman: My Journey with Time)[14] and Lebanese author Fay Afaf Kanafani's *Nadia: Captive of Hope: The Memoirs of an Arab Woman* (1999). This motif can also be observed in educational and border crossing journeys of women who wrote about their encounter with the West such as Egyptian Radwa Ashour's *Al-Riḥlah: Ayyām Ṭālibah Miṣriyyah fī Amrīkā* (1983), translated as *The Journey: Memoirs of an Egyptian Woman Student in America* (2018), and Leila Ahmed's *A Border Passage: From Cairo to America, A Woman's Journey* (1999). Despite their personal and individual itineraries, which should not be perceived uniformly, the subjects of these narratives share an experience of the passage/journey (*riḥlah* in Arabic) from the enclosed home, or national boundaries in some instances, to the public sphere, which is evident in the dynamic verbs and adjectives used in the books' titles to denote movement and mobility and/or the lack thereof. These accounts not only offer a sociohistorical testimony on Arab women's life and the predominant patriarchal traditions, but also ways in which they have been overcome and challenged.

However, many Arab women's autobiographical accounts treat the progressive dimension of their textually mediated predicament with a sense of irony, often querying the extent to which this sense of progression is absolute. They often gesture towards the idea that emancipation remains a persisting concern to them and to other women in the region. This idea is most notably reflected in Moroccan Fatima Mernissi's fictionalised memoir *Dreams of Trespass: Tales of a Harem Girlhood* (1994a) (discussed further below), in which she depicts her crossing journey of the 'thresholds' of harem life in 1940s Fez but concludes that the social indoctrination of gender separation persists and that 'the harem [remains] within'.[15]

Memoirs recording Arab women's emancipation and border crossing journeys, which often present developmental models of the modern autobiographical subject, were produced within a culture that is predominantly male-dominated and in which social and political institutions were undergoing radical changes. The private events in the lives of these women are insistently juxtaposed with historically significant moments in their nation's history. The autobiographical self in most of these accounts is situated within a national, and very often regional, scene with which the narrating subject engages in varying degrees. For example, in *Mountainous Journey* (1990), Tuqan's self-revelation of her early years in 1920s' Nablus, her portrayal of the traditional city, issues of class and social alienation and professional growth as an intellectual and a national poet is set against the backdrop of Palestinian political history. She most notably revisits her life in British Mandate Palestine, *al-Nakba* of 1948 and the June War of 1967; and recounts her gradual involvement in the resistance movement through political poetry with an insistence on her personal voice. Similarly, Ashour's story of the two years she spent as a student of African American literature at the English Department of the University of Massachusetts, Amherst – she was the first PhD student to graduate from the newly founded W. E. B. Du Bois Department of Afro-American Studies – makes frequent and detailed depiction of Arab national movements that preceded and occurred between the years of 1973 and 1975, ending her account with the Civil War in Lebanon of 1975. Ashour also makes a few references to Algerian revolutionary icon Jamila Bouhired and engages critically with the African American rights movements in the USA. These few examples demonstrate Arab women authors' growing political preoccupations through the way they situate their narratives within national, and in many instances regional/international, contexts.

The sociohistorical context of the twentieth century has shaped women's experience and influenced their creative and literary expression, therefore 'gradually le[a]d[ing] them away from cautious, direct, and sentimental writing – and occasionally simplistic moralizing – to more complex texts that convey a desire to capture women's experience' within the social and political spheres, and to write about themselves as women and as citizens (Ashour *et al.* 2008: 9). It is worth mentioning that in the 1990s many Arab women authors made explicit political commentaries in collective narratives that overshadowed the individual experience of the narrating female 'I'. Autobiographical works such as Leila Abouzeid's *Amrīkā al-Wajh al-Ākhar* (1991) (America: The Other Face) and Egyptian communist Arwa Salih's *The Stillborn: Notebooks of a Woman from the Student-Movement Generation in Egypt* (2017) (originally written in Arabic in 1991 and published in 1996) engage predominantly with ideological issues and make informed political statements from the individual experiential sphere of their militant and/or politically engaged authors, a form that has been associated with prominent authors like Nawal El-Saadawi (1931–2021).[16] These real-life-informed, sociopolitical commentaries tend to include media reports and academic references, testimonies, historical documentaries, official speeches and statistics which dominate the narrative over personal stories and experiences. Such works aim to challenge the notorious marginalisation of women from national politics and history through dissecting, analysing and re-writing them from women's perspective.

Here, it is important to emphasise that Arab women life writers have been aware of both the artistic exigence and the ideological function of the genre as one which, in Leigh Gilmore's words, 'offers voice to historically silenced and marginalized persons who penetrate the labyrinths of history and language to possess, often by stealth . . . the engendering matrix of textual selfhood: the autobiographical I' (1994: 63). In the period between the late 1980s through the 1990s, the expression of 'the autobiographical I' in Arab women's life writing emerged along divergent formal paths. The autobiographical output of Arab women in this period reflects the idiosyncrasies of autobiographical writing but nonetheless maintains the sociopolitical preoccupation of the genre; 'Arab women's writing dealt with a diversity of themes addressed in various styles, although historical concerns and an awareness of a double burden remains a basic theme in their writing' (Ashour *et al.* 2008: 8). Women recorded their experiences in memoirs, autobiographical novels, literary portraits, prison accounts, interviews and journalistic essays, to name a few. These various autobiographical forms represent important tools in the articulation of women's voices and the emergence of feminist discourses that assert women's presence in the public space and resist a persisting culture of silencing.

In the Maghreb, between the late 1980s and 1999, women authors published several fictionalised auto/biographies and autobiographical novels, mostly in Arabic and French, which explore the complexity of female subjectivity during, and in the aftermath of, colonial oppression and the various roles of women during the national struggle, as militants, activists, artists, writers and/or housewives and order keepers.[17] This body of literary work most prominently includes Moroccans Leila Abouzeid's *Year of Elephant: A Moroccan Woman's Journey Towards Independence and Other Stories* (1989) (first published in Arabic as *'Ām al-Fīl*, 1979) and *Return to Childhood* (1998) (*al-Rujūʿ ila-l-Ṭufūlah*, 1993), Fatima Mernissi's *Dreams of Trespass: Tales of a Harem Girlhood* (first published in English in 1994) and Malika Mustazraf's *Jirāḥ al-Ruḥ wa-l-Jasad* (*Wounds of the Spirit and Body*, 1999); and Algerian francophone author Assia Djebar's semi-autobiographical quartet, which comprises *L'amour, la fantasia* (1985) (*Fantasia: an Algerian Cavalcade*, 1993a), *Ombre sultane* (1987) (*A Sister to Scheherazade*, 1993b), *Vaste est la prison* (1995b) (*So Vast the Prison*, 2001), and *Le Blanc de l'Algérie* (1995a) (*Algerian White*, 2003).[18] The original editions of these works tend to lack an explicit editorial claim of non-fictionality (the term 'autobiography/memoir' on the covers) but nonetheless have been recognised and/or extra-textually acknowledged by their authors as autobiographical.[19] While it is important to acknowledge that not all autobiographical writings were/are intended for publication, including the body of work I analyse in this book, politically engaged and dissident Arab women have often written autobiographically on and for the nation as part of an intentional resistance culture that is prevailing at a particular historical moment: to explore and articulate their voices against a patriarchal culture that tends to silence women; to address and/or voice nationalist readers (the people/the revolutionaries); to contest the prevailing national record perpetuated by the state; to achieve international visibility and circulation; and to create personal archives through the autobiographical genre.

On the one hand, for many Arab woman writers/national dissidents, writing an explicit autobiographical account – although culturally considered a daring act of self-exposure, akin to unveiling – constitutes a political proclamation and a cultural form of resistance to processes of forced concealment that Arab women have historically endured. Arab women life writers demonstrate that 'writing an autobiography constitutes a political act because it asserts a right to speak rather than be spoken for' as women, nationalists and feminist activists (Sheetrit 2020: 39), at times in which women's voices were considered *'awrah* (shameful and private like the intimate parts of the body). 'By affixing their signature to their words' in an autobiographical contact, as Badran and Cooke put it, Arab women 'eradicate namelessness ... in societies where women's voices were not supposed to be heard nor their names pronounced' (2004: xxix–xxx). Additionally, many women choose to write explicit autobiographical accounts to contrast the genre subtly and emphatically with fiction. By writing both explicit non-fiction and fiction, Arab women seek to assert their creative and artistic endeavours and evade the prevailing assumption that all Arab women's writing is autobiographical because their imagination and creative abilities are limited to a single real-life story contained within the walls of the home in which they have been traditionally confined.

On the other hand, writing autobiographical accounts cloaked within fiction has been in many cases imperative in the light of the prevalent culture of censorship at the level of the social, political and institutional (publishing) structures which encouraged some Arab women life writers to abandon/avoid Lejeune's authorial pact. Arab women have been aware of the politics of representation and their potential multiple readers, including the national patriarchal male.[20] As Lindsey Moore explains, they 'produce texts with a fictional aura in order to "veil" their own experience, ironically rendering visible a heightened anxiety of authorship' (2008: 14). Moroccan author Leila Abouzeid (b. 1950) refers to this 'anxiety of [autobiographical] authorship' in the preface to her memoir *Return to Childhood* (1998), which revisits her childhood memories as set against the background of Morocco's independence struggle. She asserts that an Arab/Muslim's 'private life is considered an *'awrah* (an intimate part of the body) – a prevalent and cross-cultural concept across the Arab region – and *sitr* (concealing it) is imperative' (1998: iii), an issue that is not gender specific but of more relevance to women who are expected to remain silent and veiled with modesty and privacy. For Arab women, the bearers of their families' honour, personal and family matters are deemed private and revealing them is a shameful act that brings social embarrassment. Non-fictional sexual and political topics were equally off limits (and are arguably still monitored and largely censored).[21] This is why the autobiographical mode in Arab women's literary discourses has been sometimes deployed 'as one register in a polyphonous whole, in conscious acts of generic destabilization that expose the constructed nature of *any* discourse' (Moore 2008: 14). The importance of late twentieth-century autobiographical fiction by Arab women resides in the historical moment of their production and publication, as well as the public context in which they appear. These texts, although not straightforwardly autobiographical, are political interventions which denote the ways in which Arab women life writers have been aware of the male-dominated context of national writing and the political frameworks of literary representation.

Social constraints on women's self-revelation in writing have also encouraged self-censorship, with many twentieth-century Arab women choosing to publish under pen names. This is the case of, for example, Egyptian Gulpérie Efflatoun (b. 1921), Kuwaiti poet Ghanima Zayd Abd Allah al-Harb (b. 1949), Syrian poet Mahat Farah al-Khuri (b. 1930), Palestinian author Samira Azzam (1927–67) (see Ashour *et al*. 2008: 319, 402, 429, 363), and Algerian novelist Maïssa Bey (b. 1950) (see Chapter 2). Among the most prominent women authors who wrote autobiographically under a pseudonym is Fatima-Zohra Imalayen (1936–2015) who chose to write as Assia Djebar in order, as she explains, to remain 'veiled' ('écrire tout en restant "voilée"') (Djebar 1999: 100). Djebar is most known for her acclaimed semi-autobiographical account *L'Amour, la fantasia* (1985) (published in English as *Fantasia: an Algerian Cavalcade,* 1993a), the first of her Algerian quartet which revises the history and cultural memory of the French colonialisation of Algeria since the invasion of Algiers in 1830. Djebar's narrative is a historiography which interrogates the French historical narrative of the colonial period in Algeria. It creates a literary orchestration of personal testimonies by Algerian women of different (post)colonial epochs merged with recollections from the author's own childhood memories; the narrative dialogically intertwines the voice of the autobiographical subject (Djebar) with those of her fictional(ised) female characters in an attempt to conjure up a revisionary communal memory of the Algerian struggle for independence from women's perspective.[22]

While Djebar makes an explicit reference to the autobiography of Ibn Khaldun in an epigraph in *Fantasia*, gesturing perhaps towards the influence of Arab indigenous traditions of autobiographical writing on her narrative, her *Fantasia* is formally experimental and constitutes a form of cultural and political resistance to dominant autobiographical discourses. In her study of Djebar's oeuvre, Jane Hiddleston comments that '[i]n *L'Amour, la Fantasia*, conflicts between the specific, the singular-plural are demonstrated by the text's complex relationship with the genre of autobiography' (2006: 69). Djebar describes her work as an 'attempt at autobiography' (1999: 218). The narrative skilfully intertwines testimonial fragments by the author's female compatriots, fictional(ised) stories, French historical documents, cultural archives on the conquest of Algeria, transcriptions of Algerian women's oral stories that Djebar collects together with her own autobiographical voice and memories from her past. The narrative's multiplicity of women's voices, in their singularity, attempts to combat their historical alienation and document the effect of colonisation and independence on both female identity and the nation through creating a collective autobiography of Algerian women under colonialism, during the Algerian war and after independence.

In *Ces Voix qui m'assiègent* (1999), Djebar contemplates the process of writing *L'Amour, la fantasia* (1985). She explains the fragmentation and generic liminality of her narrative: 'it was neither a straightforward autobiographical narrative nor a proper novel!' ('ce n'était pas une simple continuité autobiographique, et ce n'était pas un vrai roman!') (1999: 108), but rather a mélange of both fiction and non-fiction. Djebar acknowledges that *L'Amour*'s construction progressed through 'the pressing search for an obscure form, a structure that I gradually needed to invent' ('la recherche exigeante d'une forme obscure, d'une structure qu'il me fallait, peu à peu, inventer') (ibid.: 107). Clearly, Djebar acknowledges that new literary spaces for self-representation, and, to some extent, fictionalisation, emerge through experimentation with autobiographical structures. Generic manipulation complicates the traditional autobiographical discourse, allows the author to potentially evade censorship and permits subjective multiplicity to surface. This multiplicity is generally reflective of the ways in which the postcolonial subject's interrogation of the personal is inevitably implicated in a complex intersectional discourse of history, class and gender. Such a concentric discourse informs formal aspects of autobiographical writing which, 'through the lens of the interrogation of the personal, becomes a polyphony of personalised and dispersed individual voices that share a common origin or source' (Weber-Fève 2010: xxv). As such, postcolonial autobiographical narratives tend to reflect a subject that is dynamic and in process through 'frequent [formal] digression that gives readers the impression of a fragmentary, shifting narrative voices, or a plurality of voices in dialogue' (ibid.: xxix). This literary strategy of autobiographical construction will be discussed in detail in the following chapter.

Since the mid-twentieth century then, Arab women authors have produced different forms of autobiographical texts which often rewrite mainstream narratives of national struggles and enact Arab women's active involvement in the public sphere and during revolutionary moments. Among the autobiographical forms that emerged out of social and political oppression, and which collapsed the harem-centred, romantic and/or apolitical expectations of Arab women's writing, was the emergence of a strong tradition of prison memoirs. The tradition has arguably started with the publication of Egyptian Zaynab al-Ghazali's *Ayyām min Ḥayātī* in 1972 (*Days from My Life*, 1989) which records her prison experience under President Gamal Abdel Nasser and the torture she endured between 1965 and 1971 for allegations of collaboration with the Muslim Brotherhood. Other Arab women who continued the tradition of writing their memoirs as political prisoners include, most prominently, Egyptian journalist Farida al-Naqqash (*al-Sijn . . . al-Waṭan*, 1980 [Prison . . . The Homeland]),[23] Egyptian author and activist Nawal El-Saadawi (*Memoirs from the Women's Prison*, 1986), her friend and compatriot Latifa al-Zayyat (*The Search: Personal Papers*, 1996), Palestinian journalist and political activist Raymonda Hawa Tawil (*My Home, My Prison*, 1983), Saudi author Alia Makey (*Yawmiyyāt 'Imra'ah fil-*

Sujūn al-Suʿūdiyyah [Diaries of a Woman from the Saudi Prisons], 1989) and Iraqi writer and artist Haifa Zangana (*Fī Arwiqat al-Dhākirah*, 1995; first appeared in English translation as *Through the Vast Halls of Memory*, 1990). These accounts, driven by the urgency to record and document,[24] testify to the trauma of imprisonment, sexual violence, torture and isolation endured by women dissidents who stand against the violations of their national regimes. Prison memoirs by women political detainees constitute part of a national narrative of resistance,[25] and a literary site in which 'gendered values, the cultural traditions of patriarchy and women's passivity, her honor as national symbol belonging to her male guardians, hierarchical structures of domination' including race and class 'all are submitted to the systemic brutality of torture and interrogation – and transformed' (Harlow 1992: 46). For these Arab women political prisoners, memoir writing becomes a means for gaining access to history and a form of bearing witness both to the active role of women in liberation struggles and national resistance movements and to the state-sponsored violence and oppression perpetrated against them as citizens, activists and women (authors). Their stories, which document the effects of political detention on the lives of these women inside and outside the prison cells, intervene in public spheres seeking recognition of the politicisation of the female body as liable to state violence and of the different forms of trauma that the woman militants had to endure.[26]

Arab women political prisoners have had to invent new forms that testify against political injustice and oppression. The form of their prison accounts tends to blur the established generic borders between memoir, diary, notebook sketches and testimony. This is due to the challenging circumstances of the writing process which often occurs in a disguised fashion aiming to eschew the regulations of prison institutions, especially for those held on account of their political writing (El-Saadawi and al-Zayyat), and/or in a retrospective manner in which trauma affects the process of memory recollection and literary transmission (Zangana). For instance, Iraqi revolutionary activist Haifa Zangana (b. 1950), imprisoned for her involvement with the Iraqi Communist Party under the Baʿath regime in Iraq in 1972, uses multiple narrative techniques in her documentary prison memoir *Dreaming of Baghdad* (2009), first serialised in Arabic between 1986 and 1989, then published in full in 1995 as *Fī Arwiqat al-Dhākirah*, with an earlier English co-translation by Zangana and Paul Hammond in 1990 under the title *Through the Vast Halls of Memory*. Zangana's *Dreaming of Baghdad*, which introduces a new genre of women's torture memoir that is not previously found in Iraqi literature, is characterised by its fragmentation, non-linearity, lapses and shift in time and space (between her childhood in the mid-1950s Iraq, political activism and imprisonment during the 1970s, to her exile in London in the 1980s), and occasional use of the third person pronoun. It also blurs the boundaries of genre by merging epistolary prose with prison diary and a series of dreams transcription. It took Zangana eight years to write this memoir in which, as she writes, 'I tried my best to document a decade of revolutionary struggle . . . to tell my experience with torture. To break the silence' (2009: 4). In recounting her experience of incarceration, Zangana also documents the arrest of other political detainees and exposes the Ba'athist prison system and the ethical and social implications of being a woman and a political detainee. In her study of Iraqi literature during the Ba'athist state, Hawraa al-Hassan argues that the form of Zangana's memoir 'is not just a post-modern device but is used as a means of challenging grand narratives on identity, history and the family perpetuated by the state; structures which are deemed to stifle the liberties of groups as well as individuals' (2020: 190).

Indeed, Arab women's prison non-fiction, including Zangana's narrative, merges the personal with the political to produce a broader historical narrative of resistance that is ideological in essence. As Harlow maintains in 'From the Women's Prison: Third World Women's Narratives of Prison' (1986), '[t]heir personal itineraries, which have taken them through struggle, interrogation, incarceration, and in many cases, physical torture, are attested in their own narratives as part of a historical agenda, a collective enterprise' (506). Prison memoirs by Arab women attest to their personal experiences as political detainees but they are not private affairs; these experiences are depicted as part of the collective experience of women as political dissidents and the broader resistance struggle. This aspect can be also observed in Zangana's more recent autobiographical account *City of Windows: An Iraqi Woman's Account of War and Resistance* (2007). This documentary memoir makes visible women's contribution and participation in armed conflicts throughout Iraq's history, with a focus on the American occupation of Iraq of 2003. While Zangana describes her account as a form of 'cultural resistance', a description that aligns with the argument of my study, it is also part of her 'personal history' of years of activism, imprisonment and exile (2007: 138, 9). She asserts that 'in this story of Iraq, I also present myself' (ibid.:14), which highlights Arab women's awareness, and notable use, of the autobiographical genre as a form of civic and political engagement which interfaces women's individual concerns with national and collective preoccupations.

As this chapter demonstrates, the impetus behind Arab women's autobiographical writing in the last two decades of the twentieth century was multifarious, but sociopolitical independence and emancipation have been common and persisting issues which manifest in more recent works. It should be stressed, however, that Arab women's autobiographical writings are not, and should not be perceived as, a homogenous category. The form and language of Arab women's writing have been 'informed by a particular environment surrounding the production of this autobiographical work and by its geographical locality with its distinct cultural and political history' (Anishchenkova 2014: 3). For instance, the language used to write and publish life stories is of paramount importance in suggesting the author's educational background, class, geo-historical location, political stances, accessibility to publication channels and/or readership and intended audience. The issue of language in Arab literature is a contested one. Many Arab authors prefer to use standard Arabic (Arabic *fuṣḥā*) because it is the prevailing writing convention that facilitates publication and accessibility to local and regional Arabic speaking readers, a process that has been particularly challenging for women. Additionally, a renewed interest and prestige for Modern Standard Arabic (*fuṣḥā*) have particularly emerged since the Arab cultural renaissance (*al-Nahḍa* of the nineteenth century) during which socio-cultural and political projects were articulated through the ideology of Arabism.[27] *Fuṣḥā* has become the national, and arguably nationalist, language; the use of standard Arabic has been considered as a political statement and an important part of Arab nationalism and Pan Arabism, and so 'many Arab intellectuals chose *fuṣḥā* for their writing for ideological reasons' (Anishchenkova 2014: 45).[28]

However, politically informed Arab women's autobiographical works written in *fuṣḥā*, in the twentieth century and more recently, are generally only accessible to an educated audience. Modern and contemporary Arab women life writers use Arabic to 'articulate their daily experiences in a language which is neither classical nor colloquial and in some cases close to the oral or folk culture'; their 'subjectivity and daily experiences are not articulated by the classical Arabic of the establishment' (Faqir 1999: 22). Nevertheless, the political and socio-cultural subject matter of these accounts, as well as the often-experimental style of their narratives, remain accessible to an intellectual audience. This audience needs to be aware of and interested in both the working of the genre, and the historical conditions of the moment of, and about which the author is, writing and publishing. This is also the case of all the selected texts that I analyse in this book because, as Harlow rightly explains, resistance literature 'requires both historical referencing and a politicized interpretation and reading' (1987: 81).

We also need to remember that the use of Arabic, or any other language of expression, can be attributed to the authors' (sometimes exclusive) mastery of the (mother) language and inability to write otherwise. This is also true, most prominently, in the case of Maghrebi writing in French. Maghrebi writers writing in French tend to express how they are estranged from Arabic, which is often not their first language, and the ways in which the French language of autobiographical expression highlights the persisting colonial legacy in the region (such as the case of Algerian authors Djebar and Maïssa Bey, see Chapter 2). Similarly, while writing originally in English can signify an Arab authors' intention to appeal to an international audience and advocate for visibility beyond local contexts, receiving Western education can also determine the language choice of the author, who may be more comfortable writing in English. In this book, I treat the issue of language carefully by referring to the specific sociohistorical conditions of writing and production of each text I analyse in individual chapters. Women's autobiographical accounts strive to assert their subjects' voices and to achieve visibility to multiple audiences. By standing against an imbrication of sociopolitical and representational power discourses, Arab women life writers often write for an (inter)national readership, for and about other women and their fellow citizens and revolutionaries, for themselves (some authors do not intend to publish their narratives) and/or for the nation that is in the (re)making. I consider writing autobiographically, in the challenging and often life-threatening political contexts and national locations such as those selected in this book, to be about the ability to speak and articulate the women author's experience in whichever language she chooses, and that, as Kay Schaffer and Sidonie Smith assert, 'as stories circulate beyond local contexts through extended national and transnational communication flows, they enable claimants to "speak [their] truth to power"' (2004: 4).

Arab women's life narratives circulate according to different conditions that enable or constrain their movement across time and locations. Their international/global circulation and the ways in which they are received and interpreted by multiple audiences are affected by various elements, which most importantly include the politics of marketing narrated lives from conflicted zones (comprising translation, interviews, lectures and seminars, media adaptation, talk shows and podcasts and the endorsement of other public figures [mainly through reviews], to mention a few). Looking at life writing subgenres by women from conflict zones can be problematic and challenging at many levels. First, the rise of production in literary self-expression in the Arab region coincides with the increase of international interest, and in effect consumption, of the lives of others as mediated in various cultural media. The question of truth-telling has always been intrinsic to the critique of autobiographical discourses in the sense that this literary genre involves some level of artistic creation that is based on selective recollections of, often, unreliable memory (Siegel 2001: 26). Thus, the distinction between fiction and non-fiction might be perceived, as Paul de Man puts it, as 'undecidable' (1979: 921). This question of authenticity further persists when taking into account the idea of the global marketability of life stories.

Indeed, life writing has become one of the most 'talked-about literary genres' which appeal to a wide range of audiences and, hence, to publishers as a profit-generating 'boom commercial product' (Douglass 2011: 483). Gillian Whitlock warns of the danger of this rapid movement of the autobiographical through what she refers to as the 'marketability of lived experience' (2007: 16), which involves elements like translation, circulation and paratext, an issue that is specifically relevant to women writing from contexts of conflicts.[29] In *Soft Weapons: Autobiography in Transit* (2007), Whitlock argues that life writing from postcolonial contexts, and contexts of conflict zones, risks being used as 'soft weapons because it is easily co-opted into propaganda . . . a careful manipulation of opinion and emotion in the public sphere and a management of information in the engineering of consent' (3). The context of reception of these works is often governed by power relations between the centre and the periphery especially in the case of postcolonial women. It relies primarily on enduring stereotypical perception and representation of these subjects who become fetishised as 'authentic insiders' and whose experiences (generally as oppressed victims) are becoming an emblem of cultural difference (Amireh and Majaj 2000: 9). Life writing is, thus, liable to be economically politicised on the basis of a presumed 'cultural [and national] authenticity' (Huggan 2001: 157). Certainly, marketing 'exoticism' of the postcolonial experience, as Graham Huggan terms it, is a dialectical process. It may underline the implication of the writer as selling out postcolonial otherness to a metropolitan market. It can equally reflect the involvement of 'market readers' who are voracious consumers, with touristic craving, of exotic literature that provides them with an imagined access to the culture of the other (Brouillette 2007: 7). This also entails other elements such as the filtering processes of the publishing industry.[30] A prominent example is the Jordanian Norma Khouri's hoax autobiographical account *Forbidden Love* (2003), a proclaimed memoir on honour-killing, that was exposed as a fictional account after it had gained unprecedented popularity in the US and was even celebrated by Oprah Winfrey who selected the text for her show's book club in September 2005. The fabricated account was endorsed by its author as autobiographical due to her awareness of the demands of the Western market on real-life stories from 'the exotic other', and its potential commercial success.

Nevertheless, while the aforementioned issues need to be acknowledged (and will be touched upon throughout the book), full response to them is beyond the scope of this study. This book takes an ethical position that trusts the endorsement of the writers to their experiences as (re)told in their literary self-narratives. I look at the narratives as experiential constructs, as 'subjective "truth(s)" rather than "fact(s)"' (Smith and Watson 2001a: 10). This is important to the trajectory of this book. The agency of subjects who are already marginalised by virtue of their gender and sociopolitical position in national conflicted contexts, and whose autobiographical discourses are scholarly under-examined, calls for consideration. What I hope to do in this book is to evoke the 'ethics of recognition' by acknowledging 'the truthfulness of the story and to accept an ethical responsibility to both story and teller' (Schaffer and Smith 2004: 12, 6).[31] Over-investment in authenticity debates would obscure pressing issues that are important to this study, including how life writing forms sustain a tradition of resistance literature that reflect 'the powerful transformations taking place in nations around the world and the realignment of national interests across the regions of the globe' (Smith and Watson 2001a: 130). The focus here is on the position and role of Arab women authors in revolutionary moments as active cultural and political actors and the ways in which such positions are represented and negotiated through different forms of life writing.

Notes

1. This chapter introduces selected autobiographical works by politically committed, intellectual Arab women that appeared publicly and in print in the last two decades of the twentieth century. Privately kept journals, autobiographical fragments and other unpublished life writing forms are not the focus of this study.
2. In his introduction to *In My Childhood: A Study of Arabic Autobiography* (1997), Tetz Rooke explains that there have been around sixty Arab autobiographies published between 1929 and 1988. From this vast collection, he selects twenty texts as his main research corpus.
3. See the 'Introduction', pp. 14–17.
4. Since the 1990s, the world has witnessed significant geopolitical changes that have arguably affected literary and cultural productions in the region. These include the end of the Cold War, the spread of Islamism, capitalism, the first Gulf War, the second intifada, the events of 11 September 2001 and the subsequent US invasion of Afghanistan and later Iraq. See the Introduction of this book, pp. 18–19.
5. The memoirs were dictated in Arabic by Shaarawi to her secretary Abd al-Hamid Fahmi Mursi (see Golley 2003: 37).
6. The autobiography of Nabawiyya Musa was published as a series of essays (later in a book form) from 1938 to 1942 in her periodical *Majallat al-Fatah* (The young woman's magazine) in a column entitled *Dhikrayyāti* (My memoirs). Cited in Christina Civantos's 'Reading and Writing the Turn-of-the-Century Egyptian Woman Intellectual: Nabawiyya Musa's *Ta'rikhi Bi-Qalami*' (2013).
7. A rounded discussion on the rise of secular and Islamic feminisms in the Arab region is too substantial and beyond the scope of this survey chapter. For more details on the subject, see Margot Badran's *Feminists, Islam, and Nation: Gender*

and the Making of Modern Egypt (1996) and 'Between Secular and Islamic Feminism/s: Reflections on the Middle East and Beyond' (2005).

8   For more details on Arab women's feminist writing and activism, see the introduction to *Opening the Gates: A Century of Arab Feminist Writing* (2004) edited by Margot Badran and Miriam Cooke.

9   Biography is a nonfictional personal account mediated through an author, who is necessarily someone other than the narrating/main subject.

10 There are very few studies that look at literary auto/biographical fragments by (or on) Arab authors including Reynold's *Interpreting the Self: Autobiography in the Arabic Literary Tradition* (2001) and Marilyn Booth's *May Her Likes Be Multiplied: Biography and Gender Politics in Egypt* (2001).

11 Although not abundant, there are some important literary mediations of life experiences of illiterate women, women who cannot write for themselves and/or women who do not have access to channels of publication; these include works based on interviews such as *Doing Daily Battle: Interviews with Moroccan Women* (1988) edited by Fatima Mernissi; *Khul-Khaal: Five Egyptian Women Tell Their Stories* (1982) edited by Nayra Atiya; *Iraqi Women: Untold Stories from 1948 to the Present* (2007) by Nadje Al-Ali; and more recently *Tis'a 'Asharāt 'Imra'ah: Sūriyyāt Yarwiyna* (2019) (19 Women: Tales of Resilience from Syria) by Samar Yazbek.

12 For more on Leila Khaled's life and activism, see Sarah Irving's *Leila Khaled: Icon of Palestinian Liberation* (2012).

13 See Irving 2012: 70–1.

14 Cited in Ashour *et al*. 2008: 225.

15 A different edition of Mernissi's memoir was published in the UK by Bantam and the USA by Transworld Publishers in 1994 as *The Harem Within: Tales of a Moroccan Girlhood*.

16 Such as El-Saadawi's controversial feminist works *The Hidden Face of Eve: Women in the Arab World* (1980) and *The Fall of the Imam* (1988b).

17 I have compiled a list of twelve autobiographical narratives by Algerian women (published between 1968 and 2014) for *ArabLit* literary e-zine (see Cheurfa 2019c).

18 Djebar's autobiography proper *Nulle part dans la maison de mon père* (Nowhere in my father's house) appeared later in 2007.

19 For instance, in *Ces Voix qui m'assiègent*, Assia Djebara describes her *Fantasia: An Algerian Cavalcade* as an 'attempt at autobiography' (1999: 218), and in the introduction to the Arabic edition of *Return to Childhood* (al-Rujū'

ila-l-Ṭufūlah, 1993), Abouzeid stresses that the story is autobiographical (4–6). Equally, the back cover of the Perseus Books edition of Mernissi's *Dreams of Trespass* says 'memoir', although in very small characters. It is also worth mentioning that the categorisation of genre is sometimes an editorial choice that is determined through the politics of translation and marketing of such works to an international audience.

20 The idea of the multiple audience of postcolonial women's literature as affected by gender and race is explored by Mae Gwendolyn Henderson in her article 'Speaking in Tongues: Dialogics, Dialectics and the Black Woman Writer's Literary Tradition' (1993, first published in 1989). She argues that women's awareness of the multiplicity of audience to which, or against which, they write may determine the way they present their identities and voice(s) in literary discourses. She most famously argues that 'black women writers enter into testimonial discourse with black men as blacks, with white women as women, and with black women as black women. At the same time, they enter into a competitive discourse with black men as women, with white women as blacks, and with white men as black women' (1993: 261). Similarly, Sidonie Smith, in *A Poetics of Women's Autobiography* (1987), discusses this complex and contested relationship between the female life writer, her literary account and her audience. She writes that '[s]ince autobiography is a public expression, she [the female life writer] speaks before and to "man". Attuned to the ways women have been dressed up for public exposure, attuned also to the price women pay for public self-disclosure, the autobiographer reveals in the speaking posture and narrative structure her understanding of the possible readings she will receive from a public . . . They [female autobiographers] understand that a statement or a story will receive a different ideological interpretation . . . attributed to a man or to a woman' (Smith 1987: 49).

21 The many examples of literary and artistic censorship cannot be noted in this brief chapter, see, for instance, *Barriers to the Broader Dissemination of Creative Works in the Arab World* (2009) by Lowell H. Schwartz *et al.*

22 Most prominently in the third section of Djebar's *L'Amour, la fantasia*, entitled 'Voix' (Voice). This overlap of genres is similar to the collage approach adopted by Ashour in *Specters* (see Chapter 2 of this book).

23 See Marilyn Booth's 'Farida al-Naqqash, Barred from Writing in Egypt: The Experience of a Journalist who was Critical of the Government', in *Index on Censorship* 12: 3 (1983).

24 See Chapter 3 of this book.

25 For more details on prison memoirs and resistance movements, see 'Prison Memoirs of Political Detainees' in Barbara Harlow's *Resistance Literature* (1987).
26 More recently published works that recount experiences of Arab women's imprisonment (particularly in French colonial prisons) include Algerian Zohra Drif's memoir *Inside the Battle of Algiers: Memoir of a Woman Freedom Fighter* (2017) translated from the French *Mémoires d'une combattante de l'ALN: Zone Autonome d'Alger* (Algiers: Chihab Éditions, 2013).
27 For more details, see, for instance, Stephen Sheehi's *Formations of Modern Arab Identity* (2004).
28 For example, Shaarawi was French educated but preferred to dictate her account in Arabic primarily for the national Egyptian (and perhaps Arab) audience.
29 See, for instance, *Reading Iraqi Women's Novels in English Translation: Iraqi Women's Stories* (2021), in which Ruth Abou Rached explores how translation affects the literary context, meaning-making and reception of Iraqi women's fiction. Also see Graham Huggan's *The Postcolonial Exotic* (2001) and Sarah Brouillette's *Postcolonial Writers in the Global Literary Marketplace* (2007).
30 The focality of the marketing process to autobiographical narratives challenges the idea of the death of the author because the life writer, in this case, is a marketing tool whose name on the title page contributes to the sales of his/her book, see Whitlock (2007) and Brouillette (2007).
31 Kay Schaffer and Sidonie Smith remind us that 'all [life] stories invite an ethical response from listeners and readers. All have strong affective dimensions for both the teller and their audiences, affects that can be channeled in negative and positive ways, through personal, political, legal, and aesthetic circuits that assist, but can also impede, the advance of human rights' (2004: 4).

2

A Bricolage of Genre, a Montage of Selves: Autobiographical Subjectivity, Generic Experimentation and Representational Contestation

In her autobiography *Athqal min Radwā: Maqāṭiʿ min Sīrah Dhātiyyah* (2013) (Heavier than Radwa: Fragments of an Autobiography), late Egyptian scholar and author Radwa Ashour (1946–2014) draws the attention of the reader to the psychological and cognitive processes of life writing as she herself experiences it. In a chapter entitled 'A Short Essay on Writing', Ashour metatextually reflects an awareness of the theoretical protocols of autobiographical narration which presume that:

> [All] I need to do to write a strictly autobiographical text is to look around me, behind me, inside of me in order to see or to remember. As if I am only mediating previously written events, times, places, conversations, incidents, feelings and thoughts . . . the role and function of imagination is no longer needed as the mind's only mission here is to retell what I have experienced, seen, heard or felt. (2013: 252, my translation)

While Ashour does not completely dismiss these conventional assumptions on autobiographical writing, she considers them to be 'only partly relevant' (ibid.: 252). She queries the importance of linearity in the process of life writing, the pre-existence of a plot and characters waiting to be mediated, the writer's presumed prior knowledge and a clear sense of understanding of his/her life and relationships and the accuracy of memory and its relationship with fiction in the autobiographical act. Ashour closes her chapter with the following reflection:

> The act of writing an openly autobiographical narrative such as the one I am embarking on here [Heavier than Radwa], is bound up, like other narratives such as the novel, with individuality in dealing with words, and with all that I have compiled, as the author, in terms of knowledge, experiences, convictions, emotions, taste, perception and attention. All of these elements compile to form a perception, my own perception of the world and of myself. (2013: 253, my translation)

Ashour dismisses the prescribed conventions of life writing which monolithically attempt to frame the practice within a single format and process, and in doing so tend to discard the idiosyncrasies of the life of the writing subject. Instead, she privileges the experiential, or what Linda Anderson describes as the 'local uses of the self' (2011: 85). Rather than referring back to rigid conditions that used to define the genre, Ashour emphasises the ways her narrative is shaped by the individuality of experiences, the singularity of perspectives and the distinctiveness of approaches to autobiographical practices.

This chapter looks at the representation of autobiographical subjectivity in life narratives by Arab women which reflect a critical awareness, and representational contestation, of mainstream formal and thematic conceptions of the genre. Particularly, the chapter looks at autobiographical texts of the post-independence period by Egyptian Radwa Ashour and Algerian Maïssa Bey which eschew conformity to predominant patterns of non-fictional writing. I argue that Ashour and Bey engage with a double form of cultural resistance. Setting their texts within contexts of political conflicts, they reflect upon the role of Arab women as resistant to intersectional (post)colonial forms of subjugation by evoking binaries of colonial/neocolonial powers, state/society, men/women, voice/silence and agency/discourse. Equally, their texts perform an act of resistance to dominant approaches to autobiographical writing. They question, and ultimately move beyond, predefined aesthetic and critical approaches to, and homogenised definitions of, both female postcolonial subjectivity and practices of life writing. Both authors produce inexhaustible literary projects that question the validity of gender-specific production and consumption of life writing; they authorise autobiographical selves which provide alternative models to the predominant patterns of negotiating gendered, postcolonial dispersed identities.

It is worth, first, briefly reminding my readers of the critical grounds at stake, as outlined in greater detail in my Introduction. Ashour's above contemplation on the formal and thematic conditions of autobiographical narration reflects a central concern among formational, feminist and postcolonial critics of the genre. It particularly engages with the controversial premise of a unified, transparent literary representation of life and subjectivity which is critically advanced in relation to masculine autobiographies of the founding fathers of the genre. In their introduction to *Life/Lines: Theorizing Women's Autobiography* (1988), feminist critics Bella Brodzki and Celeste Schenck question such foundational assumptions on the mirror-like representative capacity of the genre which allows the channelling of an undistorted image of the writing self:

> To the uncritical eye, autobiography presents as untroubled a reflection of identity as the surface of a mirror can provide. The corresponding assumption has been that autobiography is transparency through which we perceived the life, unmediated and undistorted. (1)

The assumptions of a unity of self and identity as reflected in classical autobiographies, such as Saint Augustine's and Jean-Jacques Rousseau's, is due to the way the genre had been traditionally promoted as presenting a moralistic narrative which reflects a coherent story of a developmental life, one that is exemplary and authoritative and hence certain and undistorted. Foundational criticism in the field advocates such a monolithic view of autobiographical subjectivity. Georg Misch stresses the homogeneity of the autobiographical subject's identity 'as a whole, with unity and direction and significance of its own' while claiming that the genre presupposes 'a manifestation of man's knowledge of himself' (1973: 7, 8). Similarly, Georges Gusdorf describes autobiography as a 'comprehensive sketch' which reflects the subject's 'unity and identity across time' (1980: 35), presuming not only the coherence of autobiographical subjectivity but also the chronological order in which it needs to be presented. He compares autobiography to 'the mirror image of a life, its double more clearly drawn – in a sense the diagram of a destiny' (ibid.: 40).

Feminist critics of the genre view such essentialist perception of selfhood, which dominated the critical field for almost three decades,[1] as problematic and particularly inadequate to the study of women's autobiographical subjectivity. They attack the mirror metaphor in canonical autobiographical criticism which presumes transparency, linearity of narrative and coherence of selfhood. Shari Benstock describes this 'mirror' as reflecting a 'false symmetry' that gives an illusion of unity (1988: 11, 12), a view that is particularly problematic for postmodernist theorists. Instead, feminist theorists, such as Estelle Jelinek, stress the fragmentation of women's autobiographical subjectivity as being 'analogous to the fragmentary, interrupted, and formless nature of their lives' and socially conditioned, marginalised status (1980: 19). Similarly, Brodzki and Schenek argue for a 'provisional, undecidable, and dispersive' women's autobiographical subjectivity which they compare to the postmodernist decentred model of selfhood (1988: 6).[2]

However, mainstream feminist counterdefinitions of the genre reproduce a similarly coherent model to that which male-centred critics have introduced. The generic instability of the genre has been perceived as gender-determined, which also assumes that women's experiences can be transparently captured by the form and the language of the genre. Some feminist theories of autobiography succumb to the same mirror metaphor of autobiography which they claim to dismiss. A coherent gender distinction is used as a fixed paradigm for the evaluation of autobiographical subjectivity: a gendered experience produces a given self-representational form, voice and language. This means that 'men' and 'women' are homogenised as subject-distinctive categories and autobiographical practices are reduced to gender-determined coherent models.

Recent postcolonial as well as revisionist feminist critiques of autobiography warn against the danger of such generalised conceptions of self-representational strategies. Revisionist autobiographical criticism of the 1980s, in what was termed third-wave autobiography criticism,[3] focused on displacing the rigid formational conceptions of generic and structural coherence, authoritative narrators, authenticity and meaning making. Instead, critics emphasised flexible and inclusive approaches to the reading of autobiographical narratives by foregrounding dialogic subjectivities, provisional and relational subjects, unstable selfhood and multiplicity in form and voices. Similar arguments have been extended to the study of autobiographies by postcolonial subjects. The colonial encounter and the historical and material specificities of the postcolonial experience are argued to be crucial in conditioning subjectivities that are relational, multiple and dispersed. Bart Moore-Gilbert, notably, argues that 'the postcolonial sub-genre marks its difference from canonical western norms . . . by endorsing thematics of subjectivity identified by feminist critics in women's life-writing', one of which is 'decentered models of personhood' (2009: xx).[4] Drawing primarily from aspects of postmodern and postcolonial theories, such revisionist approaches to the study of life narratives fall into three main critical modalities – which I interlink to form the paradigm on which my analytical approach to Ashour's and Bey's narratives is based.

First, the performative view conceptualises autobiographical narratives 'as dynamic sites for the performance of identities constitutive of subjectivity' (Smith and Watson 2001a: 143). It dismisses the idea that autobiographical identity is an authentic, fixed and stable character of its writing subject. Instead, it looks at discourses of identity as interrogated through the complex intersection of language, memory, society, history, body and voice (Weber-Fève 2010: xxx). This view challenges earlier monolithic models and conceptions of autobiographical narratives as referential records of pre-existing identities. It rather puts emphasis on identities as produced by the act of writing and as informed by the contexts within which they are enacted.

With a similar intersectional focus, the second modality purports positionality: the way 'subjects are situated at particular axes through the relations of power' (Smith and Watson 2001a: 145). This view is particularly popular among feminist and postcolonial critics who stress the inadequacy of earlier mainstream models of analysis to the study of texts by gendered and/or sociopolitically marginalised subjects. This critical position argues that autobiographical narratives are inextricably situated within the social, historical and political milieux in which the subjects negotiate their identity construction.

In her reading of women's life narratives, Leigh Gilmore, most notably, emphasises the importance of attending to the subject's position in their autobiographical negotiation of identity. She proposes the term 'autobiographics' to acknowledge multiple strategies of self-representation and foreground the experiential in approaching the autobiographical 'I', a critical category which echoes Ashour's understanding of autobiographical narration outlined at the onset of this chapter. Gilmore uses 'autobiographics' to describe the changing discourse of identity and selfhood in women's autobiographical narratives and to dismisses gender as being a determinant of 'thematic continuity' that produces 'a more or less shared story of female turning points, crises, and conventions' (1994: xii). Instead, '"autobiographics" as a description of self-representation and as a reading practice, is concerned with interruptions and eruptions, with resistance and contradiction as strategies of self-representation' (1994: 42); it emphasises the need for the recognition of multiple, discursive circumstances surrounding the process of self-representation, including intersectional gendered, social and historical discourses. This approach aims to attend to 'the level of each text's engagement with the available discourses of truth and identity and the ways in which self-representation is constitutively shaped through proximity to those discourses' definition of authority' (Gilmore 1998: 183), a paradigm that is particularly important in analysing postcolonial women's life writing.

Of equal relevance to the gendered postcolonial context, the third critical modality attends to the multiplicity of voices in autobiographical narratives by women and postcolonial subjects by exploring the interface of orality and writing. Scholars of heteroglossic dialogism, including Mae Henderson and Françoise Lionnet, 'contest the notion that self-narration is a monologic utterance of a solitary, introspective subject' (Weber-Fève 2010: xxxi). Instead, they stress the dialogical character of postcolonial/women's life writing. Lionnet, for example, emphasises its intercultural territory. She emphatically argues that postcolonial women, a historically silenced category, use autobiographical writing 'as an enabling force in the creation of a plural self, one that thrives on ambiguity and multiplicity, on affirmation of differences' in order to create a space to speak dialogically of their multiple cultural locations (1989: 16). Heteroglossic style, this view purports, allows the autobiographical subject to engage with multiple sociohistorical and political discourses and cultural contexts by negotiating differences and identifications with the 'other', a point I will address further through my textual analysis.

Building on the intersection of these three modalities of autobiographical criticism, I examine gender concerns along with relevant historical and contextual factors informing the production of each narrative. My aim is to explore the ways in which the texts under scrutiny are performative discourses that present a subject in process. I am interested in the ways in which the authors' formal and stylistic choices expose the multiplicity of selfhood that is conditioned by their position as gendered (post)colonial subjects. Accordingly, I argue that multivoicedness and fragmented form in autobiographical storytelling signify the presence of multiple selves that the authors mediate and negotiate through their texts. I argue that the autobiographical narrators, whom I read as representatives of their authors, are subjects whose narratives – highly conscious and self-reflexive – highlight the relationship between experiences of national struggles, gendered, dispersed subjectivities and experimental strategies of self-expression.

In the remainder of the chapter, I examine intentional (formal and thematic) revisionist approaches to the representation of dispersed autobiographical subjectivity in Radwa Ashour's *Specters* (2011), and Maïssa Bey's *L'une et l'autre* (2009) (The One and the Other) with further reference to Bey's autobiographical article 'Faut-il aller cherecher des rêves ailleurs que dans la nuit?' (Should We Go Looking for Dreams Somewhere Other than the Night) (2003). By bringing these texts together, I look at the way Arab women's life writing deliberately deploys experimental strategies to explore, mediate and express a discontinuous sense of autobiographical subjectivity that reflects, and attempts to challenge, the effects of gendered context and an enduring colonial heritage. Ashour and Bey, both academics and intellectuals, adopt revisionist approaches to the writing of the autobiographical 'I' – through multiplicity of voices, collage of genres, metatextual techniques and sociohistorical referentiality – in order to reveal the subject's multiplicity of self as conditioned by gendered (post)colonial experience within which they write. Equally, they both self-consciously resort to metatextual strategies to reveal their knowledge of the conceptual apparatuses governing autobiographical writing. They emphasise the experiential and draw attention to the diversity in which fragmented subjectivities can be autobiographically mediated. In doing so, they highlight the exhaustion of the traditional conditions of autobiographical genre and problematise dominant representational discourses which perceive the genre as monolithically gender-determined.

However, Ashour and Bey, I argue, approach the representation of multiple subjectivities differently. While they each affirm the dynamic state of the autobiographical subject in a postcolonial, gendered context, this affirmation is diversely conveyed across their narratives, as I shall discuss. Despite their nuances in approach, I bring together these life narratives on the basis of their contextual and textual affinities. Although differently located in Egypt and Algeria respectively, Ashour's and Bey's narratives are written in the post-independence period, revisit and reflect on national political history and have predominantly postcolonial feminist preoccupations. Both authors belong to a transitional generation that lived through historically significant political struggles and witnessed their critical aftermath. Although the shared regional and gendered context is key in my approach to the texts – both authors define themselves explicitly as Arab women – my analysis also takes into account the national specificities of Egypt and Algeria, including colonial and historical conditions, language differences and the target audience.

Discursive Selves, Intersecting Genres in Radwa Ashour's *Specters*

In the above-quoted *Athqal min Radwā* (2013), an illness narrative that reflects on the Egyptian revolution of 2011, Ashour's emphasis on the impracticality of a universal, unified and linear literary form for the representation of life is indicated by the subtitle of her narrative *Maqāṭiʿ min Sīrah Dhātiyyah* (Fragments of an Autobiography). The author chooses to present discontinuous, fragmented, non-linear and scattered sketches of her life in an autobiographical format. The same subtitle is borne by the autobiography's sequel *Al-Ṣarkhah: Maqāṭiʿ min Sīrah Dhātiyyah* (2015) (The Scream: Fragments of an Autobiography) which was published posthumously in its fragmented and unfinished state. Both narratives constitute a part of an autobiographical project which Ashour started in the 1980s with her recently translated *The Journey: Memoirs of an Egyptian Woman Student in America* (2018) – originally published in Arabic in 1983 as *Al-Riḥlah: Ayyām Ṭālibah Miṣriyyah fī Amrīkā*. The author subsequently embarked on an autobiographical series that spans almost half a century (1970s–2014) and is composed of four narratives, three of which are aforementioned.

This section focuses on the second published text of Ashour's autobiographical corpus, a winner of the Cairo International Book Fair Prize, and the most generically experimental and stylistically crafted of the series. *Aṭyāf* (1999), published in English as *Specters* (2011), is perhaps the most compelling text of this autobiographical project due to the unconventional literary strategies through which the subject's experiences and life are mediated. While *The Journey* is a straightforward account of the two years which Ashour spent in the United States as a doctoral student of African-American literature, *Heavier* and *The Scream* are fragmented texts which offer sketches of the author's last years of struggle with cancer, her episodes of medical treatment in Europe and America, her distant witnessing of the events of the Egyptian Revolution of 2011 and her subsequent participation in the demonstrations in Tahrir Square. Both *Heavier* and *The Scream* are self-conscious autobiographical accounts which tend to reflect on the process of the construction of the text by directly addressing readers, for example, apologising for redundancy and repetition and inviting them to skip certain sections. Both texts revolve around the theme of Arab women's role and activism during revolutionary moment and unfold different literary techniques of life writing such as the inclusion of daily entries, testimonies, illness accounts, poetry and reflective notes. In *Specters*, however, the author's distinctive strategy of life writing operates on a more intentionally experimental level. Ashour deliberately and explicitly collapses the conventional structures and approaches to autobiographical writing by combining different literary genres into a single narrative fabric.

Specters is openly an experimental autobiographical narrative which proceeds from multiple writing strategies. Ashour deploys a variety of stylistic and formal devices in order to mediate her experiences as a university professor and an activist, and her ideological stances as a pan-Arab nationalist and a pro-Palestinian leftist. She namely experiments with what I describe as a collage of genres by weaving a patchwork narrative that includes fiction, memoir, testimonies, poetry, inter-textual references and historical documentaries. Such a generic multiplicity, as I will elaborate, is predominantly informed by the imbrication of national history and personal memory. It indicates the dynamic nature of subjectivity that tends to reflect the 'effects of the histories of colonialism which often enforced fragmentation and multiplicity' (Moore-Gilbert 2009: 14). More importantly, it gestures towards the inadequacy of one form to capture a 'life' in its unattainable 'totality', to recall the Gusdorfian claim, and is indicative of the author's deliberate reworking of rigid, traditional frameworks of autobiographical practices. Later in this section, I explore ways in which such a narrative structure allows the author to engage with discourses of resistance and to respond autobiographically to contexts of violence and sociopolitical instability.

Specters spans crucial historical and political moments in the 1970s–80s Egyptian landscape with reference to 1948 Palestine by combining two main genres: fiction and memoir. In this text, Ashour intertwines her autobiographical experience as Radwa – writer, academic at Ain Shams University in Cairo, activist, wife and mother – with that of a fictitious character, a history professor she names Shagar Abdel Ghafar. Due to the book's generic liminality, the genre of the narrative is not specified on either the cover page of the original Arabic nor on that of its (American) English translation. The chapters alternate, and sometimes intertwine, the stories of Radwa (the autobiographical subject whom I read as the author Ashour) and Shagar. The two women share the same age, profession, activities, historical interests and political ideologies. The most stylistically subtle characteristic of the narrative is perhaps the ways in which it swiftly moves across genres. Although this movement seems at first abrupt and tends to conflate between the voices of Radwa and Shagar, as at times we are not sure who is speaking, the author's metatextual comments on the process of writing bring together both narratives and progressively facilitates the distinction between what is autobiographical and what is fictitious. It furthermore draws attention to the text/form as a subject of scrutiny which has an equal value to the external reality with which autobiographical narratives are, supposedly, solely preoccupied.

Specters is a patchwork of narrative fragments that stitches together the personal and professional experiences of Shagar and Radwa whose fates are connected, as Ashour describes, 'by a process of association' (2011: 68). Their stories are crafted within the narrative in a symmetrical and discursive style, yet not necessarily synthetically, as I discuss further below. The relationship between both figures is explained by Radwa through recourse to the notion of *ka* from ancient Egyptian mythology, which, in turn, contributes to the multiplicity of (re)sources from which the narrative draws. The narrator describes *ka* as 'a person's life force, his strength of spirit and his creative power' (2011: 194), the equivalent of which in Arabic translates as *qarīn*: 'your companion, who is as one with you . . . your equal in courage and in battle' (ibid.: 195). Born on the same day of 26 May 1946, having the same interests, educational formation and ideological affiliations and suffering from similar injustice and corruption within the institutions of higher education: everything suggests that Radwa and Shagar are two personas of the same subject, the author

Ashour. In a subsequent article in which Ashour muses on her literary oeuvre, she acknowledges that Shagar is 'a kind of [my] double' (2000: 91).

Both the recourse to a fictional double in an autobiographical text and the notion of 'spectrality' evoked by the title of the narrative, *Aṭyāf*, induce an important gothic atmosphere that reflects the trope of haunting ghosts. In Arabic, *aṭyāf*, plural for *ṭayf*, translates as 'the shadow of something that has possessed you' and 'an apparition that comes in sleep' (Ashour 2011: 196–7). The word 'specters' is used in this narrative to convey the meaning of *aṭyāf* as shadows of the dead.[5] At the opening of the text, Shagar is haunted by the unexpected spectres of her demised relatives whom she talks to, listens to and questions. This trope of return is skilfully evoked by Ashour through what David Punter, in his analysis of the postcolonial gothic, describes as 'the logic of haunting'; it acts as a reminder of the persistence of the past which 'can only be inscribed and interpreted through the doubtful and phantomatic interweavings of the present' (2003: 206). This idea is also enforced by Shagar's doctoral thesis which she entitles '*Al-Aṭyaaf: the Story of Deir Yassin*' (Ashour 2011: 198). In this piece of research, Shagar revisits Deir Yassin massacres of 1948 in Mandate Palestine, which took place in Deir Yassin village west of Jerusalem, now part of the newly formed Israel.[6] She compiles the testimonies of the survivors in an attempt to 'present and disprove' the 'Zionist narrative' that justified the atrocity, and 'examine and elucidate' the Arab interpretation which condemned Jewish soldiers of murdering unarmed civilians (ibid.: 64). The use of the gothic-inspired noun 'specters' (*al-aṭyāf*) to describe the subject of historical research suggests the persistent need of a comprehensive interrogation of the past which ceaselessly haunts the predicament of the Palestinian present, a context which preoccupied Ashour throughout her life.

Many *aṭyāf* visit Ashour's narrative to convey the haunting history of violent political conflicts the legacy of which persists into the present. While Shagar is haunted by ghosts from her past, she herself constitutes a spectral figure. As a fictional character, Shagar's 'ghost' hovers around Ashour while she attempts to write her own story: 'should I keep her and interweave our stories, or drop her and content myself with telling about Radwa? But then, why did Shagar come to me when I started out writing about myself? Who is Shagar?' (Ashour 2011: 17). The element of the supernatural which intervenes into Ashour's inscription of a personal record particularly reveals the interconnectedness between approaches to writing the self and uncertainty about an unsettling past/present. Ashour orchestrates two models of a single self: the 'I' and the 'she', with the former being the autobiographical avatar and the latter her *qarīn*, her double, a fictitious alter ego. The two narrative segments of Radwa and Shagra are dialogically interwoven into a single text; this interface explicitly suggests the disjuncture of the coherent self.[7] This fragmented sense of the subject, and in effect that of the form, intensifies the gothic-inspired sense of disorder and uncertainty. It becomes emblematic of the violence historically imposed on the identity of the colonised subject. The figure of the double therefore acts as a means to 'illustrate the anxieties of . . . struggling for a postcolonial identity' (Giles 2011: 1). Equally, the use of the doubling-self trope aims to explore possibilities of the autobiographical that exceed assumptions of a single, real, autonomous subjectivity that externally (pre)exists the text. In fact, as Lionnet argues, 'it should not be surprising for an autobiographical narrative to [interface with or] proclaim itself as fiction' (1988: 261). This is because 'the narrator's process of reflection, narration, and self-integration within language is bound to unveil patterns of self-definition (and self-dissimulation) which may seem new and strange and with which we are not always consciously familiar' (ibid.: 261).

Specters, therefore, foregrounds the discursive relationship between fiction and non-fiction in the construction of life narratives. Ashour's text stresses the possible intervention of creation in the production of life writing by suggesting the possibility, and even perhaps the inevitability, of the autobiographical subject's self-fictionalisation. This strategy recalls earlier controversial conceptions of Paul de Man who emphasises the role of imagination in the autobiographical practice and describes the distinction between fiction and autobiography as 'undecidable' (1979: 921). Similarly, but more recently, Golley describes the interface of fiction and non-fiction in autobiographical writing as 'deconstructing Auto/Bio/Graphy' (2003: 59). She argues that 'in each autobiographical text the "bio" (truth) and the "graphy" (fiction) both contribute, to different degrees, to the act of constructing the "auto" or self' (ibid.: 60). Indeed, Ashour's dismissal of autobiography as a strict, reality-defined genre reflects a postmodern approach to the representation of subjectivity. The narrative collapses the conventions of genre in its process of self-representation by mediating a discontinuous sense of a subject that is split across reality and self-fictionalisation. However, the narrative also openly rejects the postmodern approach of non-referentiality which denies any political relevance and meaning outside the text. *Specters* is equally a historical account of national struggles which suggests a strong relationship between its fragmentation in form and subjectivity and the postcolonial political context it explores, as I discuss later.

Ashour's use of a metatextual framework in *Specters* makes explicit her intention to generically experiment with her autobiographical narrative. *Specters* establishes a dialogue between shifting narrative voices and between fiction and non-fiction very elegantly through the author's metatextual interventions and commentaries on the labour of writing. This strategy enables Ashour simultaneously to record the process of the construction of the text, make the readers conscious of the distinctions between the novel and the memoir parts and create a narrative bridge that holds the seemingly dispersed subjects and generic fragments together. In *Specters,* similarly to her later approach in *Heavier*, Ashour openly questions the validity of the assumptions that an autobiographical text portrays a self-knowing subject and reflects his/her life entirely and straightforwardly: 'what writer has ever been able to put her entire life into one text?'; instead, she presents 'only these fragments of my life' (2011: 135).

In her examination of metafiction, Patricia Waugh maintains the relationship between history and self-reflexivity in literary texts. She states that metatextual approaches to literature are more likely to emerge during 'crisis periods' that are 'uncertain, insecure, self-questioning and pluralistic'; such periods give rise to writing which self-consciously reflects 'dissatisfaction with, and breakdown of, traditional values' in terms of formal and thematic conditions (1984: 6). Ashour uses metatext to evaluate conventions of life writing, and in doing so questions and rejects orderly forms and authoritative approaches to self-representation as inadequate to capture contexts of national struggles in which time, space and subjectivities are liable to violence and fragmentation. She writes herself out of the dominant paradigms of self-representation in an attempt to reach an alternative way of being as a postcolonial autobiographical subject. However, Ashour is conscious of the difficulties her approach poses: 'I wonder: this narrative, suspended between two lives – where is it taking me?' (2011: 269). She lays out the stakes implied in her experimental techniques and wonders: 'would anyone put up with such writing?' (ibid.: 17). These contemplations beget an important question: who is the target audience of Ashour's narrative? Clearly, Ashour is aware of the contractual relationship between the autobiographical author and his/her audience. She is equally attuned to the potential dissatisfaction of her readers as she implicitly acknowledges their expectations of the genre to be truthful, confessional and entirely non-fictional. However, through her metatextual and critical comments, it seems that Ashour is primarily addressing readers who have a solid knowledge of genre conventions but who are also aware of the way the autobiographical can operate within a binary of truth and imagination. The author, therefore, writes for an audience who would, like her, concede that autobiographical writing is a literary mode 'that constantly reinvents itself and whose basic premise is that of self-questioning, not only of the subjectivity under investigation but of the very forms in which that investigation may take place' (Kelly 2005: 32).[8]

Clearly, *Specters* is a product of the author's creative and experimental engagement with critical debates on genre criticism. As a scholar, Ashour reflects an awareness of, and an engagement with, the critical literary field being, besides a novelist, an academic and the author of a number of critical monographs including her co-edited *Arab Women Writers: a Critical Reference Guide 1873–1999* (2008).[9] Her metatextual reflection on the writing process denotes her awareness of dominant critical approaches to life writing; it draws her readers' attention to text as artifice and, hence, interrogates intrinsic epistemologies associated with conventional autobiographical forms, including the mirror-like trope, authenticity and truth-telling. Ashour's use of metatext is integral in understanding her autobiographical experience and the form in which it is mediated; it, furthermore, foregrounds the role of the life writer in reconfiguring and reconceptualising rigorous rules of reading and critically approaching the autobiographical. In this sense, the writing form and process in *Specters* become the locus of investigation which compete with the narrative's autobiographical 'I'. Thus, *Specters* is not only a (semi)memoir, but equally a memoir on writing.

Important to the examination of Ashour's highly self-conscious writing strategy is the notion of *ijtihād*. The Arabic concept of *ijtihād* denotes an independent reasoning which entails 'a component of personal commitment and extraordinary effort' (Said 2003a: 68).[10] The word is often used to describe an ardent quest for knowledge on a matter that is controversial, ambiguous or unknown. In its Islamic connotation, *ijtihād* refers to an interpretative judgement on a religious and/or legal matter that lacks an established, robust rule. More generally, it denotes a significant intellectual and/or physical effort invested in a particular labour. Reflecting on her autobiographical writings, Algerian author Assia Djebar defines *ijtihād* as 'an inner effort . . . a '(re)search', an ardent (re)search on oneself, an inner, intellectual and moral quest' ('l'effort intérieur . . . la "rechereche", la recherche ardente sur soi, la quête intérieur et intellectuelle, et morale') (1999: 115). The concept of *ijtihād* specifically relates to the effort of research which I perceive as an integral part in the construction of Ashour's *Specters*. Ashour's *ijtihād* is manifested in the ways in which her narrative constitutes a 'writing "workshop"' for academic and historical knowledge and for self-definition (Ashour 1993: 172). The value of research to Ashour not only designates the distinctive structure she crafts. It equally grounds the narrative within a thoroughly investigated historical context which constitutes a crucial part of her text.

Specters is in part a historical documentary which reflects its author's labour of research. In the narrative, the personal stories of Shagar and Radwa are combined with a collective, (trans)national history through which Ashour takes the reader on a journey into the major political events that have shaped the twentieth-century Arab region. The narrative is dense with references to national struggles including the 1948 Palestinian *Nakba*, the Algerian War of Independence of 1954–62, the 1956 Tripartite Aggression, The Arab–Israeli War of 1967 and the Israeli invasion of Lebanon of 1982. This subtle preoccupation with historical and political issues in the region reflects Ashour's fierce sociopolitical commitment to concerns occurring across both the Egyptian nation state and the Arab national community. She engages narratively and critically with the region as a geopolitical setting and assumes the role of 'eyewitness, scribe and storyteller' (Ashour 2000: 85). Her historically grounded writing style gestures towards the ways in which modern Arabic literature, including autobiographical expression, 'is unthinkable outside the context of the struggle for national liberation and its pertinent questions of national history and identity' (ibid.: 89).

Ashour asserts that writing history as a part of personal and collective memory, mainly through autobiographical narratives, is an act of resistance to intersectional structures of power. For Ashour, to combine personal and collective histories autobiographically is 'to challenge the dominant discourse (a challenge, in my case, mounted from the triple periphery of nation, class and gender)'; it is also 'to attempt to give history visibility and coherence, to conjure up unaccounted for, marginalised and silenced areas of the past and the present' (2000: 89). A similar stance is endorsed by Djebar who states that in order to write autobiographically as an Arab Muslim woman living within a politically tense historical context, it becomes necessary to 'fight, and therefore one must first fight against oneself' ('combattre et qu'il faut donc d'abord combattre contre soi-même') (1999: 114). That is, autobiographical writing becomes a site of resistance against the indoctrinations of dominant discourses which attempt to frame women's subjectivity within the norms of the state/society and within restricted scopes of literary representation. Ashour evokes Barbara Harlow's notion of literature as 'an arena for struggle' (1987: 2) through her reference to autobiographical writing as a form of 'cultural resistance' (Ashour 2000: 89), a conception that is shared by many women life writers including Iraqi Haifa Zangana.[11] Ashour explains that as 'I write, the space becomes my own, and I am no longer an object acted upon but a subject acting in history' (ibid.: 89).

Palestinian history, in particular, is a major interest to Ashour who presents herself as a fierce proponent of the cause, reinforced perhaps by her status as the wife of prominent Palestinian poet Mourid Barghouti (1944–2021), and mother of poet Tamim al-Barghouti (b. 1977). Many of her fictional works are preoccupied with the Palestinian loss of the land, such as *The Woman from Tantoura: A Novel of Palestine* (2014), and some of her academic research is on Palestinian culture such as her *Al-Ṭarīq Ilā al-Khaymā al-Ukhrā* (The Road to the Other Tent) (1981) which discusses the works of Palestinian author, and pioneer of the concept of resistance literature, Ghassan Kanafani (1961–72). Ashour's autobiographical corpus also engages, to varying degrees, with the Palestinian resistance. In *Specters*, Radwa recounts the constant state of displacement of her family because of the status of her refugee husband. Mourid was exiled from Palestine for thirty years, and later denied entry to Egypt for eight years, mainly for his oppositional views on

President Anwar el-Sadat's accommodating relationship with Israel. Ashour also refers to Palestinian icons of cultural resistance, including cartoonist and friend of the family Naji-al-Ali, and recounts, in a historically detailed style, the way she lived through some of the most violent events in the modern history of Palestine, including the massacres of Sabra and Shatila (1982) (2011: 183–8).[12]

Similar to Radwa, Shagar is a dedicated proponent of the Palestinian resistance who opts, like her creator, for the role 'of scribe, a copier of valuable manuscripts' (Ashour 2000: 91). Due to her interest in, and support of, the rights of Palestinians to their homeland, Shagar embarks on academic research which investigates the massacres of Deir Yassin of 1948. Published later as a history book, Shagar's thesis combines testimonies of Palestinians who witnessed the massacre, quotations from historians and references from extensive archival resources; these elements reflect the importance of political history and the labour of research undertaken by Ashour to construct *Specters*. The notion of *ijtihād* becomes more evident when Ashour metatextually comments on the historical merits of her narrative: 'I was researching Deir Yassin in order to write about Shagar and her book, *The Specters*' (2011: 226).[13] The author studies and annotates maps, reads and collects testimonies of real people and refers to a wide selection of historical accounts. The accompanying 'Author's Notes' section at the end of *Specters* – which cites the names of the witnesses and dates of their accounts and provides historical and academic references and explanatory notes – further denotes Ashour's *ijtihād*; it legitimises the use of the term 'scholarly research' to describe her autobiographical quest. The labour of research is also evident in 'Chapter Eight' of the narrative: 'a chapter long pseudo-document' which describes the economic and political life in early 1900s Egypt in a historically grounded way (Ashour 2000: 92). This chapter, an intertextual extract from a memoir which Shagar inherits from her grandfather Abdel Ghafar, further enhances the distinctive generic bricolage of the narrative.

Specters, then, elegantly unfolds a miscellany of literary genres across its chapters: fiction, non-fiction, a memoir on writing, a memoir within a memoir, testimonies, mythology, poetry – recited by Radwa's husband Mourid and her son Tamim – academic research, historical and intertextual references. This collage of genres endows the narrative with its generic complexity and structural and stylistic distinctiveness. Ashour explains that in *Specters*, 'the European narrative tradition [of autobiography] is grafted into the narrative tradition of medieval Arab history books and literary anthologies, their use of free associations, episodic structure and extensive quotations from poems, prose writing, oral and written history' (2000: 90). This strategy of integrating different genres into one narrative fabric aligns with Lionnet's notion of *métissage* which she develops in relation to postcolonial women's autobiographical writings. According to Lionnet, '*métissage* is a form of bricolage' (1989: 3) which involves 'the weaving of different strands of raw material and threads of various colors into one piece of fabric' (1988: 277). *Specters*, similarly, creates a patchwork narrative which reflects the interest of *métissage* as a writing strategy that aims to 'emancipate the writer from any internal or external coercion to use any one literary style or form, freeing her to enlarge, redefine, or explode the canons of our discursive practices' (ibid.: 277). At the same time, it acts as an 'enabling force in the creation of a plural self, one that thrives on ambiguity and multiplicity, on affirmation of differences' (Lionnet 1989: 16).

Ashour's skilful bricolage of genres reflects her fragmented sense of experience as a social and political subject who is grounded within contexts of Arab national struggles. Musing on the multiplicity of genres in her *Specters*, Ashour states that 'possibly these [fragmented] elements, all constitutive of my life, had to be brought in to encompass my experience' (2000: 92). This remark reminds us that, as de Man points out, 'life produces the autobiography as an act produces its consequences' (1979: 920). This denotes that it is the nature of life and experience that contributes to shaping the form and aspects of life writings, not a pre-decided set of rules of autobiographical practices. Although its different patches of forms and subjects come together into a single fabric that is the narrative, *Specters* does not assume unity because, as Ashour acknowledges, the endeavour for coherence 'often evades me and remains incomplete' (2000: 88). The narrative does not pursue or reach a synthesis neither of its scattered subject(s) – Radwa and Shagar – nor of its dispersed form but rather celebrates its structural and thematic fragmentation. It signals and maintains a crisis in an orderly approach to autobiographical writing and subjectivity representation. This proves that a key interest of autobiography is 'that it demonstrates in a striking way the impossibility of closure and of totalization' (de Man 1979: 921).

Specters' resistance to generic limitations denotes a rejection of the recognisable traditions of autobiography which pursue structural coherence and stresses developmental, unified subjectivity. Not only does *Specters* deviate from mainstream feminist models of life writing; it equally reinvigorates earlier generic models of Arab women's autobiographical writings which are often characterised by their developmental and progressive 'journeys' towards self-knowledge and emancipation, a motif which is evident in texts like Palestinian Fadwa Tuqan's *Riḥlah Jabaliyyah, Riḥlah Ṣaʿbah: Sīrah Dhātiyyah* (1984) (*Mountainous Journey: An Autobiography*, 1990).[14] While the narrative structure of Ashour's *The Journey* does reflect inaugural styles of writing established by Arab male autobiographers who recount their journeys to study in the West, including Taha Hussein and Rifaʿa al-Tahtawi (Ashour 1993: 173), and also some Arab women's accounts of border crossing like Leila Ahmed's *A Border Passage from Cairo to America: A Woman's Journey* (1999), *Specters* deliberately attempts to rework the genre through its self-conscious deviation from any established structural patterns of modern Arab(ic) life writing.

However, while Ashour's *Specters* is formally and structurally distinctive, it echoes some shared thematic concerns with predecessor texts. Chiefly, Ashour alludes to the autobiographical writings of her friend and Egyptian author Latifa al-Zayyat. In her exploration of the notion of solitude in Ashour's work, Nasser briefly touches upon the influence of al-Zayyat on Ashour, stating that '*Specters* recalls features of al-Zayyat's memoir: campus activism, government repression, security forces, and political imprisonment' (2017: 135). Indeed, in *Specters,* Ashour interleaves passages from al-Zayaat's *The Open Door* (2000) and *The Search* (1996) to highlight thematic parallels in their works, mainly regarding the history of Egyptian women's activism and participation in revolutionary moments (2011: 50). Ashour makes specific references to al-Zayaat's participation in the 1946 students' demonstrations in Cairo and revives the events through Radwa's participation in the 1972 students sit-ins. She also evokes al-Zayyat's imprisonment, which she recounts in *The Search,* through Shagar's own experience of subjugation and detention as a consequence of her political activism. In this sense, Ashour's intertext is suggestive of an enduring tradition of Arab women's life writing that is centred around national conflicts and (post)colonial struggle; an overarching thematic concern which persists despite individual authors' generic and formal choices and experimentations with the genre; an idea which I will explore further in the following chapters.

At the end of *Specters*, Ashour ponders the difficulty of attaining a straightforward, linear and comprehensive narrative of her life while simultaneously gesturing towards the impossibility of a complete (re-)telling of (personal and collective) history. The narrative ends by evoking the image of the woman-cow goddess from ancient Egyptian mythology who appears to Shagar in a dream-like incident forming 'a roof over the horizon' (2011: 275). Perhaps suggestive of revolutionary moments, this woman-cow figure nurtures, renews and creates possibilities, but at the same time 'demands blood' and indistinctively destroys; it 'swallows her young' and leaves behind shadows, spectres striving to tell their stories (ibid.: 276). The author leaves the readers with a series of contemplations which suggest that transcribing personal/collective history about the turmoil of national conflicts, similar to Ashour and Shagar's self-chosen mission, persists as both a burden and a painful task, the completion of which should remain suspended: 'did you write everything down? What did you record . . . did you scrutinize the reckoning and divide it all up in your notebook? Have you preserved all your volumes in the catacomb?' (ibid.: 277).

'To Meet all the Others I Carry in Me': Autobiographical Writing, Alterity and Reconciliation in Texts by Maïssa Bey

Similarly to Ashour, Algerian academic and novelist Maïssa Bey (b. 1950), born Samia Benameur, acknowledges her dispersed sense of autobiographical self as a female postcolonial subject. Both authors do not subscribe to an autobiographical model of a chronological self-development that is represented in a single text. Instead, they present the self in fragments by intentionally establishing polyphonic narratives in which the 'I' is interwoven with different voices. Ashour and Bey suggest that dominant historical, social and political conditions influence the relationship between identity construction and writing strategies of self-representation. While the multiplicity of selfhood is structurally established in Ashour's text through alternating – and sometimes intermingling – her voice with that of a doppelgänger-like, fictional character in an elegant montage of genres, Bey's assertion of a discontinuous subjectivity is less cross-generic but equally self-conscious. Bey constructs autobiographical narratives in which the voice of the subject is explicitly plural and dynamic. She engages in a dialogical self-writing process through which she openly writes about her multiplicity of identity. Simultaneously, she negotiates this sense of multiplicity within a crucial historical context of (post) colonial Algeria by establishing a relationship between an enduring colonial heritage, postcolonial identity construction and strategies of life writing. In doing so, she actively and explicitly circumvents traditional approaches to life writing by escaping the dominant rhetoric of oneness and subject-oriented structural unity. Like Ashour, Bey's reworking of the genre is equally reflected through her extreme self-consciousness about the act of writing. She deploys metatextual elements in order to negotiate the adequacy of orderly forms and authoritative approaches to life writing. However, while Ashour's *Specters* does not pursue totality and coherence but rather maintains its generic and subjectivity fragmentations, Bey offers a different autobiographical model of negotiating the dynamic sense of selfhood: a subject who progresses through multiplicity towards synthetic self-definition.

In order to explore Bey's use of the genre as reflecting the relationship between (post)colonial heritage and experience and the autobiographical articulation of the (multiple) self, I pay particular attention to issues of otherness, bilingualism, gender and the position of the female intellectual in post-independence Algeria. I examine Bey's auto-portrait *L'une et l'autre* (2009) with reference to her autobiographical essay 'Faut-il aller cherecher des rêves ailleurs que dans la nuit?' (2003). The texts under scrutiny are among the most explicitly autobiographical of Bey's literary corpus, which is for the most part composed of fiction and autobiographical fiction. The texts examined in this section are paired due to the way they complementarily offer a valuable insight into Bey's own experience as a gendered subject in postcolonial Algeria, a subject who is writing in the aftermath of two witnessed wars: the Algerian War of Independence of 1954–62 and the Algerian Civil War of the 1990s.[15] Reading *L'une et l'autre*, the most openly autobiographical of Bey's oeuvres, against her 2003 article offers an accurate understanding of the author's attitude towards practices of life writing. While her monograph is a personal, self-reflexive piece on issues related to identity and belonging, the article provides a critical discussion of the author's own approaches to, and conceptions of, the autobiographical genre. This means that reference to Bey's article informs and illuminates the reading of her book. It puts into perspective both the theoretical notions she conceives about autobiographical narration and how these are later put into creative practice. Accordingly, I situate Bey as a life writer but also as a literary critic. A parallel reading of the two texts enables an in-depth examination of the ways in which national struggles affect the subject's sense of self and ultimately shape autobiographical strategies of mediating and negotiating the experiencing 'I', which is the concern of this chapter.

In *Time Signatures: Contextualizing Contemporary Francophone Autobiographical Writing from the Maghreb* (2006), Alison Rice argues that 'contemporary writers from the Maghreb are not always concerned with creating harmony, either in theme or in form'; instead, they produce autobiographical texts that are 'marked by dissonance, by innovation that departs from established spellings, syntax, and treatment of the past, the personal, and the political' (27). Rice suggests that these innovative strategies are mainly informed by the (post)colonial historical moment of writing which is marked by linguistic, cultural and political fractures. Bey's *L'une et l'autre* reflects such thematic and formal 'dissonance'; it presents a discursive subject with clashing voices in an autobiographical text that defies generic categorisation. Clearly, the text is a non-fictional narrative in which the author endorses the events narrated 'through the "I" which is the object of this text' ('à travers le "je" qui est l'objet de ces lignes') (Bey 2009: 11). However, it cannot be described as a strict memoir, 'a strategic narratorial vehicle ... carefully timed and cannily deployed' (Bugeja 2012: 19) to constitute a narrative of a social self which 'directs attention more towards the lives and actions of others than to the narrator' (Smith and Watson 2001a: 198),[16] nor as a conventional autobiography in its sequential and chronological form. Instead, it falls, as the text itself claims, into the sub-category of literary auto-portrait which Michael Beaujour conceptualises as a 'polymorphous formation, a much more heterogeneous and complex literary type than is [conventional] autobiographical narration' (quoted in Smith and Watson 2001a: 139). This short monograph can be described as a dialogical, public self-analysis. Its sixty pages reveal a highly personal self-reflexive practice on the complexity of notions of identity and belonging in postcolonial Algeria as experienced by its narrating subject. In this auto-portrait, Bey is explicitly concerned neither with adhering to traditional homogenous models of self-narration nor with meeting the common expectations of an elitist, authoritative and singular autobiographical voice. Instead, she presents herself to the reader as 'your host/guest today. The one who is received and simultaneously welcomes. You receive me at your home, and I welcome you in my house of words, at the threshold of which I stand, doors open' ('votre hôte aujourd'hui. À la fois celle qui est reçue et celle qui accueille. Vous me recevez chez vous et je vous accueille dans ma demeure de mots, au seuil de laquelle je me tiens, portes ouvertes') (2009: 12). By being both the object and the subject of the text, Bey acknowledges the intimacy that the autobiographical act creates with her audience who may be, just like the author, at an intersection of worlds, cultures and/or languages. Bey opens herself to (self-)scrutiny, which not only engages readers in the process of self-negotiation but also, like Ashour, puts into question common expectations of the authoritative, sovereign voice of the autobiographical subject.

Similarly, Bey's autobiographical article 'Faut-il aller cherecher des rêves ailleurs que dans la nuit?' establishes the author's interrogation of traditional forms of writing the self in relation to her sociohistorical position as a postcolonial 'writer' and a 'public female figure' (Bey 2003: 49). This essay takes the form of diary entries composed in the period between August and October 2002 and published as a part of a collection entitled *Journal intime et politique: Algérie, 40 ans après* (2003), edited by Martine Picard. This collection includes five Algerian authors, nationals and immigrants, who reflect autobiographically on the way they experience the country after four decades of independence (since 1962) by contemplating the past and the effects of the lingering colonial legacy on the individual and national present. Bey's essay is a self-conscious daily entry which fuses the autobiographical and the critical. It constitutes a metatextual reflection on writing which exhibits its author's explicit awareness of the generic norms governing autobiographical practices. Bey contemplates the labour of life writing, for example, the process of editing that involves 'tracking down the repetitions, cutting the long sentences, deleting or rewriting confusing paragraphs . . . Some passages to omit, completely' ('traquer les répétitions, couper les phrases trop longues, supprimer ou réécrire certains paragraphes trop confus . . . Quelques passages à supprimer, complètement') (2003: 51). Like Ashour, Bey reflects dimensions of self-consciousness about the extra-textual workings of autobiographical writing;

she uses metatextual techniques in an attempt to draw attention to the status of the text as an artefact that is subjected to channels of publication and circulation. She hence questions absolute truthfulness and totality in the labour of life writing: 'to be precise: this journal cannot be and will not be really intimate, since it is written to be published, so is fundamentally public. In addition, it will be necessary to choose the words' ('une précision: ce journal ne peut être et ne sera pas vraiment intime, puisqu'il est écrit pour être publié, donc public. De plus, il faudra choisir les mots)' (2003: 13). Like Ashour, Bey discusses the process of selection and prioritisation involved in composing autobiographical texts that are, as both authors acknowledge, intended for publication.

The seeming structural simplicity of Bey's texts unfolds a complex negotiation, and a theoretically informed critique, of notions and conventions traditionally associated with autobiographical writing. Like Ashour's narrative, Bey's life writing blurs the distinctions between the theoretical text, on the one hand, and the personal, individual story on the other. Both authors offer distinctive approaches to life writing. They explore the theory of the genre through autobiographical narration that unfolds metatextual discourses. Metatext, as a writing strategy, 'consistently displays its conventionality, which explicitly and overtly lays bare its conditions of artifice, and which thereby explores the problematic relationship between life and [writing]' (Waugh 1984: 4). In this sense, a metatextual autobiographical narrative, such as Ashour's and Bey's, 'self-consciously and systematically draws attention to its status as an artefact in order to pose questions about the relationship between [writing] and reality' and theory and practice (Waugh 1984: 2). These texts act as a reminder that life writers do 'work through linguistic, artistic and cultural conventions' (ibid.: 134) and do not simply and linearly produce texts that recall a pre-existing past experience waiting to be put into language. This, in turn, supports the idea that notions of autobiographical subjectivity cannot be prescribed or predetermined. This complexity is particularly highlighted by Bey when she quotes the first sentence from Rousseau's foundational autobiography *The Confessions*: 'I have begun on a work which is without precedent, whose accomplishment will have no imitator' ('Je forme une entreprise qui n'eut jamais d'exemple . . .') (2003: 9). She then states that 'I assure you, I do not have the ambition to follow Rousseau's example, nor the desire to confess' ('Je n'ai pas l'ambition de suivre l'exemple de Rousseau, ni le désire de me confesser, je vous assure tout de suite') (ibid.: 9). Instead, she makes 'no promises' but 'to be as sincere as I can' ('pas de promesses! Une exigence: être sincère, autant que je le pourrai') (ibid.: 13). Bey deliberately redefines the traditional autobiographical act; she consciously examines and reworks the conventions of life writing instead of abandoning them completely, an enterprise she describes as perilous: 'entreprise périlleuse' (2009: 11).

Clearly, what makes this writing project 'perilous' is the revisionist approach to life writing adopted by Bey in which she is both the subject and the object, and through which the text is not only autobiographical but also theoretically critical. This puts the notions of autobiographical credibility and truth at risk. Conventionally, readers expect an authentic autobiographical narrative to promise absolute truthfulness (*le pacte autobiographique*); to be consistent and devoid of any contradictions and uncertainties; and to present a subject who is assertive and, as Doris Sommer puts it, 'nurtures an illusion of singularity' (1988: 112). Bey's text openly diverges from such conventional measures of autobiographical consistency. It presents a subject who is neither stable nor fixed but rather imbued with self-contradictions, and a text that makes 'no promises' either of absolute 'sincerity' or of generic unity. She composes texts which speak of her uncertainty, alterity, disparity and liminality because, as she writes, 'between the expression of the dominant discourse, that is to say, the conformity to established, classified norms of assertive self-expression, I chose. I chose to meet all the others I carry in me' ('Parce qu'entre l'expression du discours dominant, c'est-à-dire la conformité à des normes établies, codifiées et l'expression de l'affirmation de soi, j'ai choisi. J'ai choisi d'aller à la rencontre de tous les autres que je porte en moi') (2009: 57).

Bey's reworking of the ethical terrain surrounding this form of writing, which pertains to assumptions about autobiographical authority and authenticity, challenges the reader–autobiographer pact of trust established by the genre, and eventually the ways in which this form is consumed. Such a strategic approach to the genre is reminiscent of the – predominantly French – literary tradition of 'autofiction': a hybrid form that mixes fiction with non-fiction, prioritises the experimental and diverges from traditional approaches to life writing, often by challenging the authority of autobiographical authenticity. In doing so, Mounir Laouyen writes, 'autofiction takes into account the impossibility of an authentic story through a language that alters, exceeds and dissociates' ('L'autofiction prend en compte l'impossibilité d'un récit authentique dans un langage qui corrompt, excède et dissocie') (2002: 4–5). Therefore, like practices of autofiction, Bey's text puts emphasis on 'the "act-value" rather than the "truth-value" of narratives' (Jordan 2012: 78, 81); a practice which highlights the performative aspect of autobiographical narration and thus allows a space for 'une shiftérisation du sujet' (the shifting nature of the subject) (Laouyen 2002: 4).

Bey's experimental approach to the autobiographical 'I', particularly her deliberate circumvention of autobiographical unity and continuity through the trope of 'the one and the other', reflects the ways in which the effect of a long colonial history on identity construction is inextricably linked to the assertion of 'plurality and multiplicity ... in polyphonic autobiographical works' (Rice 2006: 21). More broadly, the colonial encounter is a key element that shapes the autobiographical representation of the (post)colonial self, which tends to 'reflect the material effects of the histories of colonialism which often enforced fragmentation and multiplicity of identity on subjectivities' (Moore-Gilbert 2009: 14). Sara Ahmed, in *Strange Encounters* (2000), describes the impact of the colonial experience as disrupting the sense of an autonomous identity, a feature that characterises many postcolonial narratives. According to her, the colonial encounter entails a 'process of hybridization' through the meeting of two different cultures (2000: 12). However, because this encounter is conditioned by unequal power differentials, this hybridisation 'involves differentiation (the two do not co-mingle to produce one)', which yields a sense of otherness and/or in-betweenness within the (post)colonial subject (ibid.: 12).

It is crucial to establish a relationship between the effects of the colonial experience on identity formation and strategies of self-expression in Bey's texts. Bey links the heritage of the colonial history of Algeria to her perception of her (multiple) sense of identity and, ultimately, to the way this identity is self-consciously narrated. She acknowledges that national history motivates her (self) writing: 'I am a chapter of history ... a history which I interrogate in all my texts' ('Je suis un chapitre d'histoire ... Une histoire que je ne cesse d'interroger dans tous mes écrits') (2009: 12). Bey situates her personal identity within the larger historical and national context, which reflects the way

'Algeria's history and its legacy are central to much of its cultural production' (Crowley 2017: 5). Born in 1950, 'at a period of historical rupture, characterised with violence and different antagonisms' ('à une période dite de rupture historique, constellée de violences et d'antagonismes divers'), Bey states that 'the languages and the cultures of this history cohabit within me' ('en moi cohabitent des langues et des cultures liées justement à cette histoire') (2009: 13).

It is through interrogating this colonial history that Bey's texts reflect the complexity of subjectivity construction in postcolonial Algeria. The title of Bey's narrative, *L'une et l'autre* (The One and the Other), signals its central motif of otherness: it is a highly personal text but at the same time a discourse which 'has an enlarged scope that goes well beyond the borders of the self' ('[un] champ élargi va au-delà, et très largement, des frontières du moi') (Bey 2009: 12). Bey's narrative engages with otherness on two levels: the others within the self (identity multiplicity), and the others beyond the self (national/collective ethos). Such a preoccupation is shared across many Francophone Maghrebian writers, particularly those who have lived through the transitional phase between the colonial and the post-colonial periods.[17] Their life writings, specifically, as Rice reminds us:

> [tend to] attest to otherness – to their own otherness and to their desire to know the other. They tell of multiple belongings, and they speak of losses of estrangement from their family, from their native land, as well as from the language in which they have become successful writers. (2012: 3)

Indeed, Bey's text attests to her 'multiple belonging' ('appartenances multiples') on a variety of levels (2009: 13). At the onset of her monograph, Bey defines her identity in relation to four intersecting traits: nationality/ethnicity, gender, religion and age ('Nationalité. Sexe. Religion. Âge') (ibid.: 12). She conceives these identity traits as, ironically, 'incontestable'; they 'define me in the eyes of the other' because they are 'the most visible' (ibid.: 12–13). Bey identifies herself first and foremost as an Algerian woman, by birth and upbringing, from a family 'profoundly attached to Islam' (ibid.: 12). Unlike many Francophone Algerian intellectuals who chose to emigrate,[18] Bey continues to live in Algeria, in the western region of Sidi-Bel-Abbès, which strengthen her claim of belonging to the land. Bey also defines herself as Arab 'by birth, culture and language'; a descendant of 'Beni Hilal' tribes 'through my origin, history and genealogy' (ibid.: 19, 14). The author contests the orientalist, monolithic categorisation of Algerians under the ethnocentric, politically driven historical profile 'indigenous Muslims' (*indigènes musulmans*) which not only ignores the difference between 'Berbères, Kabyles et Chaouias, et les Arabes' but is also prejudicially indicative of their supposed barbarity (*barbares*) (ibid.: 18–19). Equally, she links her Arab-ness to her mother language with its dialectical and standard variations (ibid.: 20). At the same time, she presents herself as a writer and an intellectual: 'femme écrivant, écrivain' (a writing woman, and a writer) (ibid.: 45).

However, Bey outlines these broad identity traits only to show that they need to be individuated. It is within these same identity categories through which she identifies herself that she exhibits her sense of otherness and uncertainty. These characteristics of identity which frame Bey's self-definition are conflicting. Being born and brought up in colonial Algeria in an Arab, Muslim, French-educated family, Bey grew up in a milieu where 'two languages, two cultures, and two different lifestyles cohabit within me' ('où cohabitaient . . . deux langues, deux cultures, deux modes de vie'); a cohabitation which 'determined my behaviour, my view of the world, my affinities, and my taste' (Bey 2009: 23, 25).[19] However, these two worlds across which Bey thought to swiftly move came to seem irreconcilable as she realises that she belongs fully to neither. As a child, Bey thought herself to be naturally French: 'I have long and ingenuously believed that I had been French – at least until 1962 – because of my birth in a French colony' ('j'ai longtemps et ingénument cru que j'avais été française – du moins jusqu'en 1962 – du fait de ma naissance dans un département français') (ibid.: 34). It was not until she found her father's identity certificate that she discovered her true national affiliation 'indigène, musulman': a French subject but not national.[20] Only then did she realise that the French are her other (*l'autre*). Moreover, the racial profiling she encountered in school exacerbated her identity confusion. For her French teachers, her colleagues and their families, she was none other than 'the daughter of the terrorist' ('fille de fellaga')[21] and 'the little Moorish girl' ('La petite Mauresque') (ibid.: 40). At the same time, she did not fully share the lifestyle of her Algerian peers and cousins. She did accept 'gender separation' ('la separations des sexes'), she 'spoke Arabic', and 'ate on the floor' ('parlais l'arabe' and 'mangeais sur table bas') (ibid.: 23–4). Nevertheless, this was only during family gatherings because, at her parents' apartment, 'I had my books, in French . . . I slept in a bed of white wood . . ., and we all ate together, sitting at the dining room table' (ibid.: 24–5). It, thus, becomes evident that, as Anishchenkova rightly notes, 'those torn between places, cultures, and languages are destined to experience the most torrid and intricate negotiations with their inescapably fragmented, polyphonic selves' (2014: 108), which tend to materialise in different forms of self-expression.

The event that triggered Bey's persisting sense of alterity was when her pro-independence father was arrested, and later executed, by the French colonial army: 'for me, as a child, the first meeting with the other was through violence. In the sound of boots of soldiers who came one night to look for my father' ('pour moi, enfant, la première reoncontre avec l'autre s'est faite dans la violence. Dans le bruit des bottes des militaires venue une nuit chercher mon père') (2009: 39). It was the violence inherent in the colonial experience which ultimately shaped Bey's fractured sense of identity: 'It is . . . the colonisation that brought me to the awareness of my cultural and even, I would say, political identity' ('c'est . . . la colonisation qui m'a amenée à la prise de conscience identitaire, culturelle et même, je peux l'affirmer à présent, politique') (ibid.: 36–7). This discovery left Bey feeling ambivalent, yet it strengthened her sense of defiance; it motivated her to 'appropriate' the other through language and culture:

> that is what gave me an even stronger desire to become familiar with the culture of the others, to appropriate it, and therefore to better understand who they were, those who in the name of the ideals of civilisation, had taken appropriation of my country.
>
> (c'est cela qui m'a donné, encore plus forte, l'envie de connaître la culture des autres, de me l'approprier, et par là, de mieux comprendre qui étaient ceux, qui au nom d'idéaux civilisationnels, s'étaient appropriée mon pays). (Bey 2009: 41)

Bey exercised this cultural 'appropriation' primarily through the 'foreign' French tongue of her literary expression. As a Francophone writer from a transitional generation which witnessed both the colonial and postcolonial periods in Algeria, Bey's sense of alterity is predominantly shaped around her ambivalent relationship with language(s). Clearly, one of the central foci of postcolonial studies is the interrelation between language and power with the former being 'the most potent instrument of colonial control' and hence 'a fundamental site of struggle' (Ashcroft *et al.* 1989: 283). The linguistic encounter is inextricably linked to colonial history and an element that has motivated many academic discussions on its relationship to identity formation, particularly within the Francophone-Maghrebian context.[22] Bey's text offers an in-depth exploration of this lingering issue. Being an 'Arab', as she clearly defines herself, Bey reflects a great sense of reverence and affection for the Arabic language. She describes it as being 'multiple' in terms of its varieties across the standard written (*fuṣḥā*) and dialectical spoken versions (2009: 20). Equally, she ponders the cultural significance of the Algerian dialect (*dārijah*) which she describes as 'necessary' and 'familiar'. This familiarity, which suggests the sentimental value with which Bey perceives her mother tongue, is, however, simultaneously imbued with a sense of strangeness, a dichotomy which becomes inextricably related to language as an identity marker in postcolonial Algeria.

As a French-educated child, Bey was denied the right to use her mother language in the French school, a coercive regulation which distanced her from a defining element of her Arabo-Islamic identity. The Arabic language became subject to colonial violence which Bey had to endure. Likewise, in post-independent Algeria, Bey recounts a different level of restrictions related to the Arabic language. Under the Arabisation reforms of educational institutions of the 1970s, Bey describes the way the Algerian dialect was strictly prohibited in schools, and later in official institutions, in favour of the modern standard version of the language: classic Arabic, also known as *fuṣḥā*.[23] These Arabisation policies attempted to impose a unified version of a common, official language as reflective of the identity of the nation, ignoring the heteroglossic aspects and the linguistic pluralism in the Maghreb where many languages are used besides Arabic in its variations: 'Kabyle is spoken in the mountains of Kabylia, Touareg in the dessert, Mozabit in the oases – and these languages are themselves divided into dialects' (Bensmaïa 2003: 14). The dialectical and linguistic variations, thus, freed from syntactic and grammatical rules, were regarded as arbitrary, informal and inferior as compared to the sacred language of the Islamic traditions. They were perceived as threatening the homogeneity of national identity. It is to this end that the familiar language is forcefully estranged as it becomes subject to (institutional) violence. Bey ponders on how one 'can feel estranged from a language they tell you is yours' ('comment peut-on se sentir étranger dans une langue qu'on vous dit vôtre?') (2009: 23).

Conversely, Bey expresses the familiarity of French, the foreign language of the other in which she was educated and through which she became a celebrated author. She juxtaposes the sense of strangeness which came to envelop the Arabic language in colonial and post-colonial Algeria with the aura of familiarity which the language of the coloniser has acquired: 'how [odd it is] not to feel estranged from a language that is not your own' ('comment peut-on ne pas sentir étranger dans une langue qui n'est pas la sienne') (Bey 2009: 23). While Bey asserts that French is the language of the other ('la langue de l'autre'), she simultaneously exhibits a strong relationship with this tongue: 'I consider French to be my language as well', which she describes as an inevitable cultural heritage: 'language-legacy' (ibid.: 26, 23).

Bey's stance bears similarities to Djebar's position in regard to her bilingualism. Like Bey, Djebar was outspoken about her complex relationship with language. In *Ces Voix qui m'assiègent* (1999), in a section entitled 'Écrire dans la langue de l'autre' (Writing in the Language of the Other), Djebar describes French, the language of her education and literary expression, as 'la langue de l'autre' while clearly defining herself as an Arab-Berber woman ('femme arabo-berbère') (42). She laments 'the rupture of separation' ('celle de la rupture de la séparation') from the Arabic language forced by the colonial experience (ibid.: 45). However, Djebar simultaneously states that 'my tongue is French' ('ma parole est de la langue française') which she considers 'my dwelling' ('maison que j'habite') (ibid.: 41, 44). This discursive relationship with language(s) reveals the complexity and multiplicity of identity construction in postcolonial Algeria because, as Djebar puts it, 'identity is not solely identification papers and blood ties, but also language' ('l'identité n'est pas que de papier, que de sang, mais aussi de langue') (1999: 42). This ambivalent stance attends to subjects' positions 'at particular axes through the relations of power' which they 'negotiate within constraints of discursive regimes' (Smith and Watson 2001a: 145). Such a Manichean relation echoes Debra Kelly's discussion of the struggle of Francophone writers with linguistic identity that is reflected in their autobiographical discourses because 'in order to write the self, all [Maghrebi Francophone] writers of autobiographical discourse have needed to battle with their mother tongue' (2005: 33). However, in the case of Bey and Djebar, this 'battle' was necessary for the cultural encounter with, and eventually appropriation of, the French other. Djebar explains this point by stressing the power of alterity ('pouvoir d'altérité') inherent in writing in French: 'to write in the language of the other is very often to bring about, to perceive "the other" . . . and I come back to this other in all my writings' ('écrire dans la langue de l'autre, c'est très souvent amener, faire percevoir "l'autre"'; 'et j'en revien a cet 'autre' de toute écriture') (1999: 46–8). It is worth noting that while writing in French has undeniably offered both authors access to prestigious publishing networks and consequently a significant international exposure, it nevertheless persists as a marker of a postcolonial identity; 'the symptom of what has happened to their country, their people, their culture' (Bensmaïa 2003: 119).

Equally, French offered both authors a necessary distance from the social constraints of their Arabo-Islamic culture in order to write about the self. In the Maghreb, and the Arab world generally, the act of self-expression has, until recently, constituted an act of transgression because the private is associated with the Islamic cultural traditions that propagate the virtue of *sitr*, or concealment of the private, which is cherished regardless of gender. As Stacey Weber-Fève puts it, in the Maghrebian society in general, 'the metaphoric reading of the use of the "je" in literary writing [is] akin to appearing naked in public' (2010: 29). The stakes are particularly high for women: 'North African women who write autobiographical discourses, in essence, commit a double transgression. They . . . write about the private to speak to a public (assumed male) audience through their work' (ibid.: 30). Speaking to the public within a culture that traditionally denies women's oral histories constitutes a symbolic act of unveiling. Bey explains this tension in her article by stating that 'writing is evidently unveiling and, to a certain extent, a form of betrayal' ('L'écriture est évidamment un dévoilement et, jusqu' a un certain point, une sorte de trahison') (2003: 49). On another occasion, she asserts that 'for a woman, to speak about the self [is] to unveil' ('pour une femme, oser se dire, se dévoiler') (1998: 28). Similarly, Djebar elaborates that 'to write the self is to expose oneself, to appear to the sight of others' ('écrire c'est s'exposer, s'afficher à la vue des autres') (1999: 98).[24]

It is against such presumed betrayal of social norms on privacy that many Francophone Maghrebian women authors contemplate the relative protection of fictional narratives, or what Bey describes as the 'alibi of fiction' ('l'alibi de la fiction') (2003: 38).[25] Likewise, Djebar explains her recourse to (autobiographical) fiction by stating: 'writing while remaining "veiled", so writing fiction' ('écrire tout en restant "voilée", écrire donc de la fiction') (1999: 100). Equally, it is the risk of 'exposure' which led both authors to write under pseudonyms, Assia Djebar and Maïssa Bey as pen names for Fatima-Zohra Imalayen and Samia Benameur respectively, as a precaution to avoid the social, and also political, constraints on freedom of expression in postcolonial Algeria.[26] However, both authors dared to resist this imposed silence by publishing self-proclaimed autobiographical discourses through using a foreign tongue as a symbolic veil. Djebar, like Bey, emphatically states that she used 'the French language as a veil. Veil on my individual personality, veil on my female body, and I can almost say veil on my own voice' ('la langue française comme voile. Voile sur ma personne individuelle, voile sur mon corps de femme; je pourrais presque dire voile sur ma proper voix') (1999: 43).

Having said that, pursuing public self-expression exacerbates Bey's position of otherness. Through her explicit autobiographical discourses, she dares to invade the traditionally masculine arena of public speech while claiming her individuality: 'I am an other because I live in a society which aspires to obscure individualities' ('je suis autre parce que vivant dans une société qui aspire à occulter les identités particuliére') (2009: 53). Bey seizes the opportunity of writing her personal experience to touch upon the plight of women in post-independence Algeria and their struggle for self-assertion. Like in her fictional oeuvre which focuses mainly on women's issues, Bey situates women 'at the centre of identity tension' ('Au centre de la surenchère identitaire') (ibid.: 51). For her, a woman's body is 'a space for all tension, all the stakes, all the antagonistic impulses' because 'even when she is absent, even when she is silent, she incarnates desire, but also hatred of this desire' ('Lieux de toutes les crispations, de tous les enjeux, de toutes les pulsions antagoniques' parce que 'même absente, même silencieuse, elle incarne le désire, mais aussi la détestation de ce désire') (ibid.: 51). Bey speaks to and for the women of Algeria, not as a representative or a spokeswoman, but as someone who shares their predicament and traits of identity as an Arab Algerian woman: 'je suis une femme arabe. Je suis une femme algérienne' (2009: 45). Bey considers these traits of belonging to be 'non-exclusive, branches and roots with complex ramifications, and sometimes, for me, inextricable' ('non exclusifs, branches et racines aux ramifications complexes, et parfois, pour moi-même, inextricable') (ibid.: 13). By negotiating the inextricability of the subject's gendered position, Bey's discourse seems to acquire, as she asserts, 'an enlarged scope that goes well beyond the borders of the self' ('[un] champ élargi va au-delà, et très largement, des frontières du moi') (ibid.: 12). This collective aspect, as Kelly in her discussion of selfhood in North African francophone writing elaborates, is shared across many women's autobiographical practices; they tend 'to explore the social conceptions of individualism. The "I" does not necessarily "represent" a "we" but is often a vehicle to explore the relation between the "I" and the "we"' (2005: 35).

While Bey identifies with Algerian women on the basis of their gendered status and shared 'traits of belonging', it is within this same category that she feels a stranger and estranged: (*une autre*). Bey juxtaposes herself with an earlier generation of women whose only purpose in life is to attend to 'the troubles of the other' ('le souci de l'autre'), usually men; those women did not dare to 'imagine another life, other horizons beyond the walls that surround them' ('imaginer d'autre vie, d'autre horizons que les murs qui les entouraient') (2009: 48). She separates herself from these women, who are not much older than her, because 'all that seems to be very far from what I am, from what my life is' ('tout cela me semble tellement éloigné de ce que je suis, de ce que je vis') (ibid.: 48). Despite their shared sense of identity, Bey ponders whether they are, in fact, strangers: 'étrangères, elles?' (ibid.: 49). Similarly, the author contemplates the plight of the younger generation from the perspective of her own daughters. They are subject to social constraints mainly in relation to dress codes and what constitutes female modesty, which Bey and her generation of women did not experience. She describes how her daughters are surprised by the flexibility of the way she used to dress when she was their age: 'you used to go out like that?' ('tu sortais comme ça?') (ibid.: 49).

Writing in solidarity with the plight of these two generational categories of women, to neither of which Bey can completely relate, leads the author to repeatedly ponder her own identity position. She contemplates her own otherness, or what she refers to as 'solitude' by quoting Albert Camus: 'solitaire et solidaire' (2009: 58). While Bey engages in a dialogical discourse that aims to interrogate her defining relationship with the French and Algerian cultures and the women of her own country, this textual interrogation does not beget full identification with the collective; it rather prompts her to consider her own identity multiplicity by oscillating 'from one to the other' ('de l'une a l'autre'). This recalls Henderson's conception of heteroglossic dialogism in her 'Speaking in Tongues' in which she points to the ways the subject of dialogic (life)narratives reflects not only a relationship with the 'other(s), but an internal dialogue with the plural aspects of self that constitute the matrix of [marginal] female subjectivity' (1993: 344). Indeed, because of her multiple belongings, Bey attests to the plurality of her identity which positions her as other. She describes herself as *gharīb* (stranger), an Arabic term which denotes the 'unheard-of, strange, or alien' ('inouï, étrange, ou étranger') (Bey 2009: 48). Nevertheless, this knowledge eventually empowers Bey to defy her sense of subjective fragmentation as she seeks to bridge the distance that separates her from the other: 'from the one to the other. The distance is great. Yet why not the one and the other' ('de l'une a l'autre. La distance est grande. Alors pourquoi pas l'une et l'autre') (ibid.: 52). Through her practice of textual self-exploration, Bey seeks a synthetic self-definition and ultimately accepts her sense of alterity and moves towards 'meet[ing] all the others I carry in me' (ibid.: 57).

Scrutinising identity through life writing proves performative for Bey because it offers her a space to reflect on her dynamic self-formation and a way 'to liberate myself? To find myself also' ('écrit pour me libérer? Pour me retrouver aussi') (Bey 1998: 28). For her, the practice of life writing becomes 'a space of self-questioning' ('mon écriture est le lieu d'un questionnement') which, akin to spiritual and religious practices, constitutes 'a quest for making sense of one's life' ('la quête du sens que peut donner l'individu à sa vie') (2009: 56). It is to this end that Bey describes her autobiographical writing as a 'journey' (*parcours*) (ibid.: 12), not in the sense of reflecting a life's progression textually. It rather alludes to text itself as a medium through which self-knowledge and development are sought. That is, text as an ongoing quest (*ijtihād*) for self-understanding rather than a static reflection on past, well-grasped experiences. This echoes Djebar's description of 'writing as an adventure' ('l'écriture comme aventure') and a 'means of transformation' ('moyen de transformation') (1999: 42). In the same fashion, Arabophone Algerian author Ahlem Mosteghanemi, in an autobiographical essay on writing, states that 'the risks and pleasures of [autobiographical] writing lie in its being a review and continual questioning of the self' which makes it 'an everlasting adventure' (1999: 85).

The performative aspect of identity construction, as induced by autobiographical discourses, has been discussed by revisionist life writing critics who dismissed prior assumptions on the need for an absolute self-understanding to compose an autobiographical narrative. Sidonie Smith, most prominently, repudiates the conventional understanding of autobiography as a means to self-expression of an ontological interiority that is already known to the subject: '[t]here is not essential, original, coherent autobiographical self before the moment of self narrating' (2016: 262). Instead, she describes life writing as a performative practice, a medium for self-discovery, through which the subject constructs an identity processually. Smith and Watson further stress the performative aspect of autobiographical writing in the way it reveals 'self-consciousness and a need to shift through their lives for explanation and understanding' (2001a: 9). This brings to the fore an important theoretical distinction between the narrating/writing 'I' and the narrated/written 'I': the way 'the writing subject presumes to know him/herself, whereas the written subject manifests the effects of the writing process (in other words the process of coming to knowledge), which is a process of differentiation from others in language, memory, discourse, and consciousness' (Weber-Fève 2010: xxix).

Considering that Bey lives in a society 'which aspires to obscure individualities' ('une société qui aspire à occulter les identités particulières') (Bey 2009: 53), a mechanism inherent in the dominant nationalist, post-independence discourse,[27] Bey attests to the contestational nature of her life writing which resists identity homogeneity. Her textual self-analysis, she emphasises, 'liberated me from the silence'; it constitutes a means 'to discover, to unveil and to clarify what I thought I knew' ('me libérer de l'étau du silence, de découvrir, de dévoiler et de d'éclairer autrement ce que l'on croyait connaître') (ibid.: 56). It is to this end that Bey describes her autobiographical practice as 'a movement towards proximity to oneself' ('mouvement vers une proximité avec soi'), which ultimately gives 'birth, a painful birth to oneself' ('une naissance, une naissance douloureuse à soi-même') (ibid.: 53). Bey's discourse, imbued with uncertainty and self-questioning, becomes a performative practice towards self-knowledge and ultimately reconciliation:

> Writing while forgetting the self . . . but at the same time while discovering the other within the self.
> Prodigious contradiction!
> One and the Other.
> I am other because I write, carrying the words, I have gone to meet the other, all the others.
> (Écrire dans l'oubli de soi . . . mais en même temps dans la découverte de l'autre en soi.
> Prodigieuse contradiction!
> L'une et l'autre.
> Je suis autre parce, que qu'écrivant, pourtant la parole, je suis allée à la rencontre de l'autre, de toutes les autres). (Bey 2009: 56)

Through a brave and innovative enterprise of self-writing, Bey attests to the multiplicity of her identity and belonging. She gathers together a mosaic of identity fragments which speak of a woman who is unapologetically at once 'the one and the other' ('l'une et l' autre'). She embraces her diverse sense of self as a woman within whom 'two languages, two cultures, and two ways of life coexisted' ultimately without 'any incompatibility or antagonism' ('sans jamais avoir eu conscience d'une incompatibilité ou d'un antagonisme') (Bey 2009: 23). Bey closes her book by asserting her acceptance of the synthetic self-definition that her textual self-exploration has revealed; she reconciles with her otherness and decides, quoting French writer Édouard Glissant, 'to live an alterity starred with legacies and horizons' ('vivre une altérité étoilée d'héritages et d'horizons') (ibid.: 59).

Notes

1 As I outline in this book's introduction, it was in the 1950s that the genre was conceptualised and recognised in Western, mainly French, scholarship (much later in the Anglo-American scholarship due to critics like James Olney who re-introduced and translated, mainly in his *Autobiography: Essays Theoretical*

and Critical [1980], studies by the pioneers of the genre such as Georges Gusdorf's 'Conditions and Limits of Autobiography' [1956]). However, it was not until 1980 that the first comprehensive anthology of critical essays on women's life writing appeared with the publication of Estelle Jelinek's *Women's Autobiography: Essays in Criticism*, which questioned the predominant masculine focus of foundational theories of the genre.
2 While feminist critics challenge the postmodern notion of 'the death of the subject' arguing that women's autobiographies are forms of female and feminist self-validation through which marginalised subjects strive for recognition (Miller 1988: 106), postmodern scepticism about generic unity of subjectivity did usefully encourage a rethinking of the traditions and definitions of autobiography. It addresses the problematics of the genre and signalled a ground-breaking way of approaching the autobiographical by allowing the gap to emerge between the writer, the narrator and the text; see, for instance, Brodzki and Schenek (1988) and Roland Barthes's autobiography (1977).
3 This wave includes theorist such as Philippe Lejeune, Paul de Man, Paul John Eakin, Nancy K. Miller, Sidonie Smith and Leigh Gilmore, among others. See Smith and Watson (2001a: 137). On the first and second wave of autobiography criticism, see note 4 of the Introduction.
4 Moore-Gilbert argues that the fragmentation of selfhood in life writing, which he describes as 'decentred subjectivity', is not gender-determined. Through his analysis of postcolonial auto/biography, he demonstrates that this model of selfhood could be examined in auto/biographical writings by Western women and postcolonial men and women alike (see chapter one of Moore-Gilbert 2009).
5 When referring to '*Atyāf*' in her article 'Eyewitness, Scribe and Story Teller: My Experience as a Novelist' (2000), Ashour translates the title into English as 'Shadows' (91).
6 The Deir Yassin massacres took place in the village of Deir Yassin west of Jerusalem, which was occupied by the Jewish forces on 9 April 1948. Jewish soldiers occupied the village and attacked civilians leading to the murder of around 170 Palestinians (see Pappe 2006: 80–1). Ashour's *Specters* provides a detailed historical account of the atrocity and the conflicting narratives around the culpability of Israeli forces (see Ashour 2011: 64–5).
7 This point also relates to the psychoanalytic dimension of the figure of the double. Sigmund Freud argues that the use of the double suggests the subject's self-doubt and uncertainty of identity (see Freud 1948: 234–6).
8 A similar approach to life writing is adopted by the American-Palestinian author

Jean Said Makdisi in her *Beirut Fragments: A War Memoir* (1990) which chronicles her experience of living the turmoil and siege of the Lebanese Civil War of 1975. Like Ashour, Makdisi ponders the process of writing her memoir by wondering 'how to write, what form to choose' while seeking 'something uniform to hold it all, for I am one person – am I not?' (21–2). Progressively, Makdisi's narrative collapses any potential 'uniform' way of writing her experience by patching together fragments of memories, reflections, anecdotes, glossaries, and topography of a city.

9 Four-volume work published in Arabic in 2004; the English translation is an abridged edition.

10 Said briefly explores the roots of the word *ijtihād* which derives 'from the same root as the now notorious word *jihād*'. The latter, according to Said, 'does not mainly mean holy war but rather a primarily spiritual exertion on behalf of the truth' (2003a: 68–9).

11 See Chapter 1, p. 54.

12 The massacres took place in the Sabra and Shatila camps for Palestinian refugees in the south of Beirut. The atrocity, which targeted the lives of more than a thousand civilians, was believed to have been 'carried out by Lebanese Christian Militiamen . . . in an operation enabled and organised by the invading power Israel' (Llewellyn 2013: 164).

13 In *Specters*, Ashour also reflects on her process of field and archival research which contributed to the construction of her acclaimed historical trilogy *Granada: A Novel* (2003) – first part published in Arabic in 1994 (2011: 232).

14 See Chapter 1, p. 47.

15 The Algerian Civil War of 1990s was a violent period of armed conflict between the Algerian government and Islamist extremist groups. It was triggered when the results of the parliamentary elections of 1991 were cancelled as a result of the defeat of the ruling political party the FLN (Front de Libération Nationale) by the Islamist party the FIS (Islamic Salvation Front). Consequently, violence erupted between the FIS and its supporters and the army, affecting primarily hundreds of thousands of civilians. The war is most commonly known as *la décennie noire* (The Black Decade), 'a term that captures the tragedy of that decade but also the obscurity for the civilian population seemed to be caught between forces which, if identified as state and Islamism, were in practice composed of many different groups and the actual perpetrators of terror were difficult to identify' (Crowley 2017: 7).

16 In his introduction to *Postcolonial Memoir in the Middle East: Rethinking the*

Liminal in Mashriqi Writing (2012), Norbert Bugeja provides an apt analysis of the formal and thematic aspects that differentiate autobiography from the memoir genres which, he insists, 'are two patently distinct forms' (18). Bugeja rightly points out that 'autobiography would characteristically present a series of causative events and its plot is organised in a strict chronology, often with a self-justifying tone that is focused on moral experience' (ibid.: 18). A memoir, on the other hand, 'tends to focus on a founding trauma or triggering events'; it 'posits cross-temporal frames that patently differ from the episodic ones of the autobiographer' (ibid.: 19). The memoir has a more collective ethos to its construction as opposed to the purely individualistic drives of autobiography; it is 'interested in the dialectical structures of feeling that obtain from that very relation [between subjective memory and spaces of history]' (ibid.: 19).

17 The sense of the fractured self is most evidently reflected in writings by Franco-Algerian and *pieds-noirs* women authors who find themselves torn between their past and nostalgia for Algeria and their present in, the often unwelcoming, France. See, for instance, Amy L. Hubbell's article 'Dual, Divided and Doubled Selves: Three Women Writing Between Algeria and France' (2010).

18 Most prominently, contemporary authors like Leila Sebbar (b. 1941), Ahlem Mosteghanemi (b. 1953), Zahia Rahmani (b. 1962) and Kamel Daoud (b. 1970), among others.

19 In conversation with Martine Marzloff, Maïssa Bey speaks in detail of her cultural 'métissage' (see *À Contre-Silence*, 1998: 17–19).

20 This alludes to the infamous French colonial law *Code de l'indigénat*. While this law was officially applied in 1887 across the French colonial Empire, it was first implemented in Algeria as a space of 'trial' ('l'espace d'essai') from 1830 (Doho 2017: 16). Through this law, natives of the French colonies were granted an inferior legal status, by applying various legal constraints to control and 'contain' the indigenous Algerians (French subjects) who pose a potential threat to the 'civilised' (colonat local) French (ibid.: 16).

21 *Fellaga* (plural *fellagas*), from *dārijah*, literally 'bandits'. A term that was used (mainly by the French) in colonial Algeria to refer to armed militants that were active members of national anti-colonial movements.

22 The linguistic plurality debate, or one would also say confusion, in postcolonial nation states has become a defining aspect of Maghrebian countries that fall under the paradigm of the *francophonie*. Bey's discourse is reflective of this linguistic unsettlement which has persisted in the writings of many celebrated Francophone authors, most prominently Algerian-born French philosopher

Jacques Derrida and Moroccan author and critic Abdelkèbir Khatibi. Derrida and Khatibi's philosophical exchanges and reflections on issues of language(s) and Franco-Maghrebian identity shed light on the notion of linguistic otherness that is inherent in Francophone identity. In his first-hand account, *Monolingualism of the Other* (1996), Derrida expresses the possibility of the absence of a mother language by asserting his unbelonging to any language. Growing up as a French Jew in colonial Algeria, Derrida did not understand or speak Arabic but at the same time did not consider French to be his language; he famously states that: 'I have only one language, yet it is not mine' (1996: 2). At the same time, Derrida questions the 'metaphysics' of the necessity to belong to a given tongue (70). Khatibi, on the other hand, acknowledges the linguistic plurality of the Francophone world by asserting his own linguistic dualism (*bi-langue*), a marriage between the French and the Arabic languages. He writes: 'the Francophone world is *mètissage*, or mixture, with diverse bilingualisms and multilingualisms' (1999: 66).

23 This measure was mainly taken during the mandate of former president Haouari Boumediene whose presidency (1965–78) was based on the formation of an egalitarian nation through socialist policies and Arabisation reforms informed by Islamic principles (Crowley 2017: 5).

24 Fadia Faqir elaborates on self-exposure and censorship in relation to Arab women's autobiographical writing in her introduction to *In the House of Silence* (1999).

25 On autobiographical fiction by Arab women, see Chapter 1.

26 The Charter for Peace and National Reconciliation passed by former President Abdelaziz Bouteflika and enacted in 2006, which offered immunity to those who belong to extremist Islamist groups and who are willing to repent and lay down their weapons, set rigid legal constraints on the freedom of expression, especially criticising national policies. The law states that 'Anyone, who, by speech, writing, or any other act uses or exploits the wounds of National Tragedy to harm the institutions of . . . Algeria, to weaken the state, or to undermine the good reputation of its agents . . . shall be punished by three to five years in prison' (quoted in Crowley 2017: 125).

27 The dominant political-nationalist discourse in post-independence Algeria internalises and propagates a collective 'unified sense of self' (Belkaid 2017: 126), in its attempt to create a homogenous, yet 'imagined community' that is solely based on the shared historical/national struggle against the colonial domination. The shared history of the war of independence has been exploited by the authorita-

tive, single-party regime to construct a compressed, collective sense of identification. This mainly led to the creation of what Jonathan Lewis, in his exploration of Francophone literature as a site of memory, describes as collective memory. The latter, according to Lewis, evidently 'overlooks the possibility of the circulation of plural memories within and between groups and reduces an individual identity to that of the group to which s/he belongs, that group itself is defined by a certain recollection of the past: such a conception of memory ignores the fluidity of both individual and collective identities'; it rather maintains homogenised definitions of both identity and memory (2018: 11).

3

Shahādāt Nisā'iyyah: Testimonial Life Writing, Accounts of Women's Resistance

> We [Arab women] write, I write in wars and civil wars because I have no power, no strength, no weapons and no soldiers. I write because I crouch in the cellar like a rat, raising my cowardice like a child in times of hardship. I belong to the dark dampness and the forgetfulness of those who have placed history in the streets. But I also write as the rat that gnaws at foundations and pillars. I betray the establishment and give evidence against it. I write beneath the boots which stamp on my face, as if *I* were the emperor or the dictator.
>
> (Barakat 1999: 46)

Thus asserts Lebanese author Hoda Barakat (b. 1952) in a testimonial essay entitled 'I Write against my Hand' (1999), in which she evokes issues of gender, agency and female subjectivity in contexts of armed conflict. Arab women have had to endure the silence and remoteness imposed on them during historical and revolutionary moments by virtue of the inherent division of the battlefield and the home as gender-specific spheres. Women have been denied a space to make 'history in the streets' because they are socially restricted to the realm of the private and secure home. The battlefield has been historically perceived as an inherently and exclusively masculine arena in which women have no position but that of the observer, the victim and/or the weeper. Even their contribution to liberation movements and armed conflicts is generally obscured in historical records and never fully acknowledged. However, Barakat draws attention to the relationship between women's writing and active political engagement. Claiming and emphasising her identity as a writer, she contends that through performing testimonial practices, writers can redefine their position of public engagement and activism and assert Arab women's active role within contexts of armed warfare. As Barakat explains, it is through giving evidence against oppressive establishments, a crucial aspect of testimonial writing, that women authors resist dominant discourses of exclusion, challenge the stereotype of the silent passive Arab woman, appropriate stories of national struggles and write themselves into their nations' history in autobiographical narratives. While testifying against sociopolitical establishments from a gendered position of marginality might be slow and/or less visible, which Barakat evokes through the imagery of the rat, it is nonetheless accretive in its power to challenge, and even destabilise, dynamics of authoritative discourses. Testimonial writing seeks public recognition of the events it depicts and is hence strategic. It presents 'truth not previously recorded' (Barakat 1999: 44) and strives to unmute dissident voices and stories of suffering and trauma that have been traditionally obscured, which, ultimately, combats the selective historical amnesia of public authority.

This chapter approaches testimonial life writing by contemporary Arab women as chronicles of resistance and sites for asserting historical and public engagement.[1] Looking particularly at Syrian author Samar Yazbek's *A Woman in the Crossfire: Diaries of the Syrian Revolution* (2012) and *The Crossing: My Journey to the Shattered Heart of Syria* (2016), and Palestinian writer Suad Amiry's *Nothing to Lose but your Life: An 18-Hour Journey with Murad* (2010), the chapter investigates women's strategic use of literary testimony to challenge dominant discourses of participation and representation and revise the longstanding trope of the confined Arab female storyteller. It argues that the testimonial mode of writing functions as an intentional political statement of dissidence to individual and collective silencing in its production of national and historical testaments. While I consider that all the texts under scrutiny in this book reflect different aspects of bearing witness, as they are all first-hand accounts of lived experience of national struggles, the narratives I select in this chapter are both openly and deliberately testimonial. Yazbek and Amiry stress the importance of literary testimony in unearthing hidden stories of violence, social injustice and oppression as they reflect their political awareness of the forced marginalisation of women in historical records of the war story. Their deliberate use of the form creates autobiographical discourses which renegotiate the role of the woman author-activist and mediate between fighting and writing. Conscious of the historical value of the moment, they both conjure up archival materials that document and make visible women's role in the national conflict in order to dismiss the myth of the exclusive, masculine archetype of war. Their narratives thus raise important and persistent questions about the way national history should be written and remembered.

The Politics of Testimonial Writing

In his influential article 'The Margin at the Center: On *Testimonio*' (1989), John Beverley defines literary testimony as a 'direct participant account' through which the narrating 'I' bears witness to an individual experience that has a collective resonance as it speaks about, and on behalf of, a community of oppressed people (1989: 14).[2] *Testimonio* – and the genre itself – 'stands at once as a personal statement of struggle, a political indictment of oppression and exploitation, and a documentary of systematic abuses of human rights' (Harlow 1992: 46). Testimonial narratives are 'ideological practices' (Beverley 1989: 12), that are driven by the urgency of representing events that have been obscured or erased from historical and public records. The genre has a particular historical relation to slave narratives, the traumatic memory of the Holocaust and the events of anti-colonial resistance in Latin and Central America of the 1960s. Although gaining some critical attention during the 1980s and 1990s (Tagore 2009: 10), testimonial narratives are still, however, on the periphery of literary studies in comparison with more conventional forms of life writing, as they generally emerge outside of mainstream spheres of self-representation. Testimonies deviate from the luxury of recording one's extraordinary life and exemplary achievements with which the conventional autobiography is usually preoccupied; they are rather complex forms of expression that emerge from marginal communities – due to gender, ethnicity, religion and/or politics – and conflicted cultural and sociopolitical contexts. As Fiona Ross elaborates:

> [t]estimonies do not exist intact, awaiting an opportunity for expression, but emerge from interactions shaped by the complex relationships of class, race, gender and conventions of speech that are always in flux. Subject positioning is not uniform, and the social and cultural locations from which to speak

may be fraught, saturated with discomforting customs that mould patterns of speech. (2003: 163)

While conventional autobiography nurtures an image of a singular coherent subject who is speaking from an exemplary – and often exceptional and authoritative – position, testimonies are individual utterances of collective experiences and memory.[3] The narrator in a testimony is not an isolated individual with a distinctive life-long experience. He/she belongs to a collective that is 'marked by marginalization, oppression, and struggle' (Beverley 1989: 23), and their testimony is 'the means by which the disempowered experience enters the [historical] record' (Whitlock 2007: 132). In this sense, the literariness of the testimonial narrative is often considered relatively marginal when weighed against the urgency of communicating collectively experienced, traumatic and violent events. Testimonies privilege factual elements over formal considerations and authenticity over aestheticism because they are driven by the necessity to speak and remember. This is because, as Doris Sommer points out, 'autobiographers can enjoy the privilege and the privacy of being misunderstood, whereas those who testify cannot afford or even survive it' (1988: 130). Truthfulness, clarity and the urgency to scribe personal and collective memory are, therefore, the major conditions of testimonial narratives in their aim to realise social and political recognition. Hence, such narratives require the presence, and often the recognition, of an audience to reach their ends.

It is particularly the relationship between the witness of testimonial accounts and the audience they address that sets them apart from other conventional forms of life writing. Unlike autobiography, diary, memoir and letters, for instance, which might not be intended for publication and/or target a specific audience, a testimony is a text 'on the move in search of witnessing publics' (Whitlock 2015: 169). Testimonial texts are intentionally 'offered through the scribe to a broad public as one part of a general strategy to win political ground' (Sommer 1988: 109) and to conjure up a persuasive and credible narrative of resistance and survival. Unlike conventional autobiography which tends to impose 'the authority of [a subjective] experience' of its narrating 'I' (Smith and Watson 2001a: 28), the testimonial narrative solicits empathy and recognition and aims to establish a discursive relationship with its audience. The latter are not passive recipients of stories who trust the narrator's judgement on the basis of the conventional authorial authority or, in the case of autobiography, a mere contractual relationship (recalling Lejeune's autobiographical pact). Instead, the audience of a testimony and the listeners of a witness account, as Shoshana Felman and Dori Laub rightly point out, have 'to feel the victim's victories, defeats and silences, know them from within, so that they can assume the form of testimony' (1992: 58). The engagement and complicity of the audience of the testimony is invited through stimulating their senses of logical judgement and soliciting their sympathetic emotions and affect. The reader/listener, thus, must become a complicit witness, 'the enabler of the testimony' and the one who endows it with its legitimacy through recognition (ibid.: 58).

To this end, one can argue that writing in a testimonial mode is in itself a form of resistance to the prevailing, conventional strategies of literary expressions; it 'puts into question the existing institution of literature as an ideological apparatus of alienation and domination at the same time that it constitutes itself as a new form of literature' (Beverley 1989: 22). Testimonial expression calls for a new form of individual subjectivity that is enmeshed with the collective consciousness. It dismisses the aura of formal and structural literariness that characterises traditional autobiography as it attempts to revise the rigid conception of aesthetics as exclusive to a privileged few. It, hence, stands for the agency of those who would normally 'be excluded from direct literary expression, who have had to be "represented" by professional writers' (ibid.: 17), those who perhaps perceive art as an awe-inspiring, elitist practice.

In the politically fraught, violent scene of the contemporary Arab region, narratives of bearing witness have become historically urgent and imperative. They serve a persisting duty to document and remember and often act as counter-narratives to dominant discourses and, as Tahrir Hamdi notes in relation to the Palestinian context, as 'a tool of *resistance against the assassination of liberation*' (2011: 24). The relationship of testimonial writing to experiences of resistance, violence and trauma particularly materialise in narratives of women which emerge from contexts of war and national conflicts. Testimonies constitute a form of 'coming-to-voice' (Ross 2003: 27) which offers Arab women the possibility to manifest their rejection of intersectional structures of social, political and representational powers related to the postcolonial epistemological context (that includes the colonial, imperial, and/

or neocolonial states), and those imposed by patriarchal norms and cultural traditions. This is particularly relevant to Yazbek and Amiry who deploy the form to re-inscribe national history by articulating women's civil and political consciousness and engagement, and in doing so contest 'the forgetfulness of those who have placed history in the streets', to recall this chapter's epigraph.

In what follows, I foreground the element of voice and silence in my analysis of Yazbek's and Amiry's narratives and the ways in which their testimonial practices redefine the relationship between women's life writing and activism. I argue that through narratives of bearing witness, they attempt to make visible their participation in national oppositional and resistance movements as women, activists, fighters, participant and/or critical observers. Their testimonies voice an inside-out vision of marginal and hidden lives; they bring to the forefront individual and collective experiences which would not have been known otherwise, stories that are intended to linger within historical records and national memory. I also investigate the intersection of literary self-representation and sociopolitical consciousness, the archival capacity of testimony, and how violence and trauma might impede witnessing and evoke ethical questions related to historical representation.

'To Archive their Memories of the Uprising': Testimony as an Archival Practice in Samar Yazbek's *A Woman in the Crossfire: Diaries of the Syrian Revolution*

In her introduction to *Tisʿa ʿAsharāt 'Imra'ah: Sūrīyyāt Yarwiyna* (2019) (19 Women: Tales of Resilience from Syria), a collection of eyewitness accounts from the revolution, Syrian journalist and author Samar Yazbek (b. 1970) insists on the role of testimonial writing as a 'means of resistance' in the face of 'historical erasure' because it 'opens up the possibility towards revising our history and its truths' (2019: 11, 23, my translation). In this recently published collection, which is yet to be translated into English, Yazbek interviews and writes the stories of nineteen Syrian women refugees who participated in the uprising.[4] In their own words, the women featured in this book (some of whom are kept anonymous) present first-hand experiences of political activism, armed resistance, imprisonment, siege and male – including state-sponsored – violence against women. They tell stories that enact historical testaments which aim to defy forgetfulness and historically omission, expose dictatorial practices and redefine the role of women in revolutionary struggles through personal narration. Yazbek maintains that readers 'need to consider these testimonies as didactic art that sets out to teach resistance, activism and the nobility of envisioning a world that is more just' (ibid.: 23, my translation). She equally highlights 'our role, as writers and intellectuals, in taking ethical and national responsibility for ensuring justice and fairness to the victims [of the subsequent Syrian civil war] – a responsibility best manifested in our war against amnesia' (ibid.: 11, my translation), an endeavour that persists in all of Yazbek's writings on the revolution.

Yazbek has become internationally known as the feminist voice of the Syrian uprising, mainly after the publication of her outstanding account *A Woman in the Crossfire: Diaries of the Syrian Revolution* (2012). Winner of the PEN/Pinter International Writer of Courage Prize (2012), and the Oxfam Novib/PEN Award (2013), the diaries – written and published originally in Arabic as *Taqātu' Nirān: Min Yawmiyyāt al-Intifāḍah al-Sūriyyah* (2011) – document the early stages of the Syrian revolution. It chronologically charts the first four months of the uprising starting from the pro-democratic, peaceful demonstrations that took place in the city of Darʻa in March 2011, up until July of the same year, when Syria descended into a violent civil war and became 'the bloodiest of the revolutions' (Yazbek 2013b: 1), after which Yazbek was forced to flee the country and seek refuge in France. *A Woman in the Crossfire* highlights the relationship between testimonial writing and the practice of literary archiving in its intention to document and historicise the events of the Syrian revolution as witnessed by the author. The primary material of Yazbek's account comes from her own involvement in the uprising, mainly through her participation in demonstrations and interaction with revolutionaries and activists. Her testimonial narrative, as I argue, operates as a resistance strategy to individual and collective silencing, to national and Western mainstream media's misrepresentation, and to potential historical erasure particularly in relation to women's presence in, and support of, the uprising.

First, it is important to examine Yazbek's perception and representation of the 'the crossfire' in her account in order to understand the impetus behind her archiving practice and to highlight the link between testimonial writing, intersectional feminism and resistance literature. The front piece of Yazbek's diaries sets the tone of the narrative by offering the literal definition of 'the crossfire', a motif around which her story revolves: 'cross-'fire, n. Where an individual or a political or military group is within range of two or more lines of fire, from both enemy and ally alike' (2012: v). The value of *A Woman in the Crossfire* as a form of literary resistance lies in Yazbek's insistence on writing in support of the revolution against the atrocities of Bashar al-Assad's brutal regime given that she is not only an outspoken public figure but a member of the regime's Alawite (Shia Muslim) clan.[5] The way Yazbek's familial identity, religious affiliation and professional status clash with her oppositional, political stance has positioned her, literally and figuratively, in a 'crossfire' in which she, as she presents herself, is standing alone against all the belligerents of the revolution. The Alawite clan, including her family members, the regime's supporters and security forces consider her a traitor. Some of the revolutionaries, on the other hand, classify her as a member of the regime's sect while religious extremists insist that she is an unveiled *kāfirah* (unbeliever/infidel). Yazbek writes:

> [d]eath on all sides, from all the shooting. If they had got their hands on me, most of the Alawites in the demonstrators' neighbourhoods might have killed me; if the Sunni fundamentalists knew I was there, they might have done the same thing. If the security forces and the Ba'thists got wind of my presence they would have launched a military campaign against the neighbourhoods, claiming there was an armed gang there. (2012: 217)

Yazbek is disavowed by her own family and Alawite friends because she betrayed the 'ties of blood and kinship' and brought 'shame' upon the Alawite clan (Yazbek 2012: 83). Consequently, she is branded a traitor and banished from her birthplace of Jableh (ibid.: 35, 81). The author also tells us how she is constantly threatened by the adherents of the regime to cease supporting the opposition. The unexpected and recurrent visits of armed security services pressure her to move houses, to quit social media, to change her cellular number and to live in the shadows. Yazbek constitutes a threat to the pro-Assads because as an influential woman from the regime's sect, her opposition draws public attention and has gained a certain degree of credibility which the regime cannot afford. However, killing or imprisoning her would embarrass the state and eventually endow her dissidence with more appeal. Instead, she is forcefully taken to torture prisons where she is detained, beaten, harassed and humiliated. During those compulsory visits, Yazbek is exposed to horrid scenes of violence committed against young revolutionaries. She is introduced to 'snapshots of hell' where 'human beings were just pieces of flesh on display, an exhibition of the art of murder and torture that was all for show' (Yazbek 2012: 87). Yazbek's crossfire position also stems from her status as a single mother. She is torn between the dangerous anti-regime cause to which she has committed herself and the safety of her sixteen-year-old daughter, Nawara. Frightened by the constant threats her mother receives, Nawara blames Yazbek for jeopardising the safety of the family and pressures her to publicly pledge allegiance to al-Assad's regime. To this end, Yazbek finds herself in a crossfire, 'on the front line of an explosive situation . . . [in] a unique space . . . in a funny situation, one that drowns in its own blackness' (2012: 80).

However, this 'unique space' does not completely hinder or paralyse Yazbek. The author insists that 'I have no desire to change it or to incline towards one side or the other' (2012: 80). She becomes convinced that her fight for justice and dignity is more important than any social affiliation: 'and so, just like every other moment in my life when I have found myself at a crossroad, I bend towards this fate, towards my freedom' (ibid.: 51). Her self-assertive stance in relation to the uprising becomes the source of her determination; in a piece for *The Guardian* newspaper, Yazbek writes:

> I was with the revolution from the beginning, and I will stand by it until the end. I will expose its terrors, but I will not abandon it. For me, it is a testimony to the triumph of justice over oppression, the real-life expression of my own understanding of the concepts of ugliness and beauty. (2013a)

To this end, Yazbek continues her opposition activism away from the spotlight. She resists the silence imposed on her and on thousands of suppressed revolutionaries through testimonial writing. Yazbek composes a daily chronicle in order to preserve and recover the individual and collective memories of the revolution. Her aim is to 'turn my diaries into a book' when she flees the country because 'I'd never be able to do that in Syria' (2012: 258). Through writing with the intention of publication, Yazbek envisions public validation and seeks a sympathising audience who might recognise and/or reinforce her testimony. Yazbek published her survivor-witness account originally in

Arabic – the language in which she exclusively writes – and is thus primarily addressing an Arabic-speaking audience. Nevertheless, the author is well aware of the potential extended context of reception, enabled through scopes of translation and publication – and heightened by the appeal of war settings to international readers.[6] In conversation with poet and translator Stephanie Papa, Yazbek identifies her target audience stating that 'I didn't write for the people who told me their stories, because most of them are dead' (Papa 2016: 17). Instead, she declares that 'I am writing for the whole world to see what the people of Syria experience on a daily basis' (ibid.: 17).

As an active first-hand witness, Yazbek documents the course of the revolution by bringing together its personal and collective quotidian events. In addition to her own daily experience of the uprising, a large part of her diaries capitalises on various witness accounts which she secretly compiles. She goes on a self-assigned mission to expose the truth behind the massacres and mass destructions. She hops in and out of taxis to follow the events in Damascus' streets, venturing into besieged villages, and marching in mass demonstrations while trying to uncover personal narratives behind the chaotic predicament of the country. Moving in disguise across turbulent cities and towns – including Damascus, Homs, Hama, Baniyas and Jableh – Yazbek interviews Alawites from the opposition, young activists, political detainees, security officers, journalists and martyrs' family members. At the end of the day, she returns home with 'documents of flesh and blood; of wailing and bullets and the faces of murderers who don't know where they are going' (Yazbek 2012: 21). Yazbek then transcribes the stories that she witnesses and hears in order to produce a polyvocal testimonial account which aims, as she maintains, 'to smash the narrative of this criminal regime with the truth of the revolution' (2012: 230).

The personal-collective testimonial style which Yazbek chooses for her diary constitutes what Judith Butler refers to as 'a part of the general project of alternative media' (2009: 12) which aims to produce new frames of recognition and representation. In her influential discussion of the concepts of grievability and precariousness, Butler suggests that media, among other politically monitored apparatuses, is partially responsible for deciding – through processes of exclusion and inclusion – which lives are recognised as precious and deserving of grief, and which are not. This is mainly achieved through excluding certain discourses, stories and testimonies and monitoring their public exposure (Butler 2009: 10). Yazbek's account comes to expand the 'sphere of appearance' (ibid.: 1) of resistance narratives that are obscured by mainstream, international and/or regime-monitored media and eventually in national historical records. She does so by foregrounding silenced and marginalised stories of individuals who are on the periphery of representational discourses and, hence, public recognition and empathy. Yazbek's account acts as a tool of resistance to the oppressive mechanisms of mass violent silencing. It constitutes a form of bearing witness which 'can intervene – affectively, ethically, politically, critically – in situations of personal and historical violence, trauma, Othering, and collective silencing' (Tagore 2009: 7). Reporting and documenting the collective resistance and struggle for democracy allows Yazbek to give voice to the silenced stories behind prison bars, detention cells, opponents' houses and demonstrations in the street, stories which are suppressed by the regime's narrative and selective media coverage. It equally enables her to reclaim her revolutionary voice as both 'an independent writer . . . [a] critical intellectual' (Yazbek 2012: 189) and 'the Alawite woman who would not be silenced' (Yazbek and Philps 2012).

Additionally, the testimonial mode of Yazbek's diary can be attributed to the influence of her journalistic career and experience on her writing. Yazbek declares that 'my voice as a writer and a journalist must come out in support of the uprising, no matter what the cost' (2012: 230). This influence can be observed through the simultaneity and immediacy of news entries and media reports which occasionally intervene into *A Woman in the Crossfire*. In many instances, Yazbek interrupts her testimony to announce urgent violent events occurring in different parts of the country at the time of writing, often signalled by the recurrent phrase 'there is news from/about' (ibid.: 11, 23, 36, 39, 60), which in turn affects the linearity of her narrative. This immediacy of news reporting makes of her, as she describes herself, a writer of the collective 'now' who is producing 'writing forged in the present moment' (Yazbek 2013b: 2). Yazbek makes it clear that her journalistic predilection for recording dated news, collecting testimonies, stories and conversations, in Arabic and in *'amiyyah*,[7] of regime opponents belonging to varying social, educational, religious and ideological backgrounds is an attempt to debunk the obscuring, often generalising, narrative disseminated by the media on the Syrian war. While the regime-monitored mainstream media 'stirs up hatred, broadcasts false news and maligns any opposing viewpoint', international media fails to present an accurate view of life in revolutionary Syria apart from a unified narrative of violence and mass destruction (Yazbek 2012: 63, 66). The author maintains that it is the literature of bearing witness that can provide an alternative narrative due to the genre's capacity to 'provide a much-needed corrective to official versions of events as well as to the epic narratives and romantic fictions that all wars tend to inspire' (Mortimer 2018: 131).

By the same token, Nadine Gordimer, in her 'Witness: The Inward Testimony' (2006), argues that witness literature is most crucial in contexts of disasters, wars and social upheavals, especially in light of hegemonic visual media technologies. The latter have adopted the role of the incontestable witness to violent conflicts suggesting that, in light of immediate images, there is 'no need for words to describe it; no possibility words *could*' (Gordimer 2006).[8] However, Gordimer considers visual media, although important, as lacking the 'duality of inwardness and the outside world' which can only be achieved through 'the transformation of events, [along with] motives, emotions, reactions' from the immediacy of the image into witness literature. This literature is uniquely able to capture 'the tensions of sensibility, the intense awareness, the antennae of receptivity to the lives among which writers experience their own as a source of their art' (Gordimer 2006). This is what particularly distinguishes Yazbek's insider testimony from the generalising, descriptive and crudely statistical narratives of visual media reports which are often too remote from human tragedy. Yazbek's testimonial account informs the objective immediacy of the media with subjective insights through injecting personal and intimate 'meaning', 'motives', 'emotions' and 'reactions' to what the international public might already know about the Syrian revolution. In his foreword to the English edition of *A Woman in the Crossfire*, Rafik Schami describes Yazbek's diaries as 'poetic yet real' because the author succeeded in writing 'what she had experienced . . . felt and thought', which 'allows readers to truly experience the *intifada* [uprising . . .] without feeling crushed by it' (2012: vi, xi). Yazbek's diligent attention to personal and collective feelings and reactions to the revolution challenges the monolithic perspectives propagated by news reports. It enables an in-depth witnessing that makes public the hidden personal lives and experiences of the individuals involved as well as acknowledges scattered stories of courage and survival.

The value of Yazbek's testimonial project lies in its intentional endeavour to act as an archival narrative that lingers within historical records. Yazbek asserts that the main objective behind the personal-collective testimonial style of her diaries is 'to archive their [that is, the Syrians'] memories of the uprising' (2012: 104) and resist national and historical amnesia. Indeed, 'a prior condition to the use of any type of personal testimony is its survival' (Summerfield 2019: 12). Yazbek resurrects revolutionary voices to preserve a 'we-memory', as Roger Bromley rightly explains; 'in keeping the narrative alive, she has produced a document not just of the past, but for the future, one that is still fought for' (2014: 9). As the Syrian revolution slips into a multi-belligerent and brutal civil war, Yazbek's testimonies constitute a reminder that '[t]his is the people's revolution of dignity. This is the uprising of a brutalized people who wish to liberate themselves from their humiliation' (Yazbek 2012: 218). The author assumes the role of a (re)creator of the historical moment to which she is bearing witness. She contests the suppression and manipulation of the people's struggle for social justice and narratively sustains the real democratic drives of an unfinished, yet persisting, resistance.

However, the representation of the collective in a journalistic mode with an archival intention can be ethically risky. In *Soft Weapons: Autobiography in Transit* (2007), Gillian Whitlock stresses the danger of homogenising war experiences and questions the ethics of including details of other peoples' stories of trauma within personal life accounts, which is reminiscent of Yazbek's narrative mode. Whitlock reminds us that the circulation of autobiographical works from war zones are 'sharpened' by the conflict they depict. Life narratives bearing witness to violent contexts, especially from regions that are historically perceived as 'the Orient', tend to gain public appeal due to the readership's assumption of acquiring intimate and immediate access to urgent and dangerous zones that would not be possible otherwise (2007: 132). Yet, Whitlock argues that eyewitness testimonies, especially since the onset of the War on Terror (the Iraq War of 2003), have contributed to the production of 'celebrity journalism' (ibid.: 140). She explains that life writing is being used by native informants as means to 'achieve a visibility and a status as powerful individuals', intellectuals and writers and as a tool for the commodification of newsworthy stories and authentic accounts that capitalise on traumatic experiences of others that only the proxy witness, or the insider writer, can tell (ibid.: 140).

Certainly, Whitlock's argument is true and to a large extent viable taking into account ongoing debates on the ethics and politics of marketing literature. However, what she has overlooked in her analysis is the individual experience of the narrating subjects who, in many cases, are striving to work through their own experiences by portraying those of others, which I perceive as relevant to Yazbek's diaries. There seems to be more to the collective testimonial quality of *A Woman in the Crossfire* on the personal level than merely the urgency of the writing context, or the influence of the writer's journalistic drives. Testimonial writing for Yazbek is both therapeutic and cathartic;[9] her diaries are motivated by her desire to preserve collective memory and to draw strength and self-understanding from other silenced narratives. Indeed, the crossfire position influences Yazbek's emotions and affect. Throughout the text, readers are informed that she suffers from insomnia, anxiety, recurrent nightmares, daydreams and suicidal contemplations, occurring at different stages of the first four months of the uprising. Yet, she confesses that compiling stories and testimonies from the revolution helps her 'to confront fear and panic as well as to generate some hope' (2012: xii). Yazbek attests to the therapeutic benefits of her testimony and asserts: 'I soon discovered that these diaries were helping me to stay alive; they were my walking stick these days. I had to go on writing if only to keep my spirits up and to bear the pain' (ibid.: 50). She attests to the ways in which testimonial writing in times of political unrest enables women 'to understand how the war in its multiple facets forced them to see themselves and their place in the world differently, opening the way to self-understanding and empowerment' (Mortimer 2018: 158).

The different stories transcribed by Yazbek effect a shift from self-interest and temptations of retraction to daring selfless ventures in an attempt to equally unveil her own resistance and that of her compatriots, and to fathom the state of violence into which Syria has slipped. As I have explained, Yazbek's personal life in this account is enmeshed with the collective: that which is intimate or individualistic is ultimately merged with, or often put aside in favour of, immediate and collective reportage. As Miriam Cooke astutely argues, 'Yazbek has moved from being Gramsci's traditional intellectual, part of a class of thinkers, to an organic intellectual who is a part of the people' (2013:

35). In a newspaper article, Yazbek herself states that 'the Syrian revolution has changed me as a writer . . . now the relationship between my life and writing is formed by the revolution' (2013a). In *A Woman in the Crossfire*, the personal is not portrayed as isolated from the collective scene; on the contrary, it is the individualistic experience that is shaped and affected by shared national circumstances. In this sense, the inscribed collective experience in these diaries does not necessarily intend to achieve Whitlock's 'celebrity journalism'. Rather, Yazbek makes sense of her experience through the different lives she inscribes and with which she identifies. Her narrative serves as a framework which informs and gives meaning to seemingly scattered traumatic itineraries among which she experiences her own.

Yazbek reflects on the way the multiple personal narratives of resistance which she collects and inscribes empower her own dissident female voice: 'as I transcribed the stories about the uprising [she writes], I also draw strength from them' (2012: 225). Particularly, Yazbek's feminist thrust, which is evident throughout her career including prior to the revolution,[10] is demonstrated in the way she acknowledges the courage of the Syrian women and celebrates their sociopolitical consciousness. In her PEN Prize speech, she dedicates the award 'to all the women who work silently under the circumstances, dodging bullets, artillery and fighting jets to continue the revolution of the Syrian people for the establishment of free and democratic society'.[11] It is the risk of eliminating women from revolutionary discourses that motivates Yazbek's testimonies. Her diaries not only foreground its author's own engagement in the uprising but insist on women's agential role and contribution in the national fight for democracy (see, for instance, Yazbek 2012: 51–4, 130–1, 250). Yazbek's writing merges the feminine and the political, and the personal and the national histories and re-enacts new subjectivities that transform women's agency and expression from the realm of the private to the public domain of nation-building, elements which I explore further in what follows.

Contested Borders, Transgressive Testimonies

As I suggest throughout this chapter, testimonial life writing falls into the category of resistance literature which highlights the interface of literary self-representation and political activism. It resists, simultaneously, conventional forms of literary self-expression, fictionality as the quintessential literary tradition, and subordinating political and representational powers against which the subject writes and testifies. The remainder of the chapter evokes important ethical issues that are at the heart of testimonial narration: the relationship between trauma and autobiographical representation and the efficacy of *testimonio* as a comprehensive testament to the experience of women and other marginalised groups within contexts of national struggles.

Looking at accounts of illegal geographical border crossing, namely Yazbek's *The Crossing: My Journey to the Shattered Heart of Syria* (2016) and Amiry's *Nothing to Lose but your Life: An 18-Hour Journey with Murad* (2010), the following sections examine the role of testimonial narration in interrogating the border as a material frontier and as a space of literary and historical representation that demarcates gender-based participation within political conflicts. First, I examine the relationship between violence and testimony and the way traumatic memory may affect the position of the witness and result in a potential crisis of testimony. Then, I demonstrate how *testimonio* permits the transgression of political, literary and representational frontiers within which Arab women's practices of narration are conventionally framed and expected to remain. I investigate the ways in which Yazbek's and Amiry's narratives adapt the movement of the writing subject to become, in terms of both form and content, trans-border testimonies which are resistant to the gendered frames of storytelling, narration, literary (self)representation and mobility. By bringing together Yazbek and Amiry's narratives, my analysis also seeks to demonstrate the way both authors deploy *testimonio* in order to create a counter-discourse which redefines the trope of Arab woman storytellers and reinvigorates the Scheherazadian terrain of narration – from an immobile speaking agent to a border-crossing one who witnesses and inscribes.

'From Physicality into Nothingness': Border-Crossing Testimony and Borderline Persona in Samar Yazbek's The Crossing, My Journey to the Shattered Heart of Syria

After one year of involuntary exile in France, Yazbek produced a second testimonial account, *The Crossing: My Journey to the Shattered Heart of Syria* (2016), originally published in Arabic as *Bawabāt 'Ard al-'Adam* (2015), in which she reflects on her traumatic memory of the early months of the revolution and on her disenchanting diasporic experience. Readopting a similar testimonial style to that in *A Woman in the Crossfire* (2012), Yazbek's *The Crossing* details her clandestine crossings of the Turkish borders into and out of Syria which was driven by her hope to process her traumatic experience and to reconcile it with the brutal reality of the civil war. However, her hopes prove elusive as her illegal movements across borders exacerbates her personal sense of unbelonging and persistent distress. This complicates her position as a witness and puts into question the validity and truth-value of her testimony.

In *The Crossing*, Yazbek does not only cross borders; she self-consciously inhabits a borderline. Her exilic experience in France, she states, has exacerbated her sense of unbelonging to the European metropolis: 'even in Paris where beauty bursts out of the smallest of details, I still feel ugliness killing me. It nestles deep in my chest . . . [exile] means walking down the streets and knowing you don't belong there' (Yazbek 2016: 275). It has thus hindered any 'attempt to replant whatever remained of myself in fresh soil' (ibid.: 181). Her return, nevertheless, further nurtures her feelings of estrangement from war-torn Syria which has metamorphosed into 'a truly lethal place' (ibid.: 156) in which the repression of peaceful demonstrations ultimately generates sectarian feuds (*fitnah tāʾifiyyah*) and terrorism (ISIS). This sense of dislocation places Yazbek in a space she refers to throughout her narrative as 'the void'. The latter – also indicated by the title of the original Arabic text, *Bawabāt ʾArd al-ʿAdam*, which literally translates as 'gates into the land of the void'– is a recurrent motif used symbolically and literally in and beyond this specific text.[12] It describes the material vacuum created by mass deaths and destruction in (post-)revolutionary Syria. It also suggests the absence of meaning that burdens the narrator with a sense of fluid temporality and alienation, which often distorts her perception of reality and disrupts any hope of potential resolutions.

By examining Yazbek's textual persona presented in *The Crossing* against French psychoanalyst André Green's 'Borderline Concept' (1996), I suggest that she embodies the characteristics of a borderline individual. Green identifies the borderline as both a physical frontier and a state of being. He makes a distinction between having/crossing a border and being one. The border can be a physical space of division; a (im)penetrable boundary such as geographical frontiers. As a state of being, 'the borderline case is less of a frontier than a no-man's-land' (Green 1996: 74). According to Green, to be a borderline individual is to inhabit a 'void space', which is very reminiscent of, if not identical to, the image that Yazbek presents of herself in her autobiographical texts. Yazbek occupies a blank space that entails 'a feeling of non-existence and unreality of self and object-image' (ibid.: 79), which she explicitly associates with her war trauma. She writes:

> All I longed to do was to float, to swim through into boundless, white nothingness. To drift through it, under it, over it, floating ever further from geography, dimensions blurring till a skyscraper was the size of a blade of grass, colours fading in the infinite blindness of outer space, leaving behind all these bearded faces. I would merge into a flowing stream of emptiness, living nowhere, without borders to define me. (Yazbek 2016: 44)

Yazbek internalises a sense of unreality and 'lack of awareness of presence' (Green 1996: 79), which result from her traumatic encounter with recurrent scenes of death and violence. She transcends reality and presence into a void space and seeps, as she states, 'from physicality into nothingness' (2016: 270). As a way to cope with the unfathomable reality of the war, she often dissociates herself from the Syrian scene and imagines that she is 'the only fictional character' in her real-life narrative; 'an implausible figure . . . this other imaginary person' (2016: 5–6). While Yazbek attempts to process and overcome her traumatic experience, she persistently feels unhomed except in her narrative, 'uncoiled, with no solid identity apart from my language' (ibid.: 252).

Yazbek presents her narrative as the only space to which she belongs, or – more specifically – through which she is able to perceive her identity as a revolutionary, woman writer-activist. However, Yazbek's writing of her experience does not often resolve the incomprehensibility of her traumatic memory. She finds herself surrounded by 'meaninglessness' because as she writes, more '[f]utile questions lodged themselves in my throat' (2016: 132). In *The Crossing*, writing generally fails to accurately render the narrator's violent experiences and is inevitably affected by her ambivalent perception of herself as a borderline person. The narrator's feelings of alienation and unbelonging materialise in the recurrent reference to her invisibility, the void and the haunting memory of the dead, which eschews any premise of a coherent narration of which Yazbek is aware: 'it seems impossible to write . . . in any kind of sequence that makes sense. There's no way I can narrate this in any kind of order' (2016: 14). Her testimony reflects verbal insufficiency, which is evident in repetitions, interruptions and occasional lack of flow characterising many sections of the narrative.[13] Yet, putting the experience into words, although sometimes incomprehensibly, stems from Yazbek's desire to work through her experience by resisting what Abigail Ward refers to as 'the annihilation of subjectivity' (2015: 5) which comes as a direct offshoot of traumatic experiences. It allows her to reclaim, even relatively, her agency as a woman, an intellectual, a writer and a regime-opponent and hence to assert her voice and presence.

Articulating women's presence and participation in the war narrative through testimonial account is indeed a form of sociopolitical subjectivity with a therapeutic implication (scriptotherapy) (Henke 1998: xii). It gives way to 'the emergence of a new female selfhood that gains its strength from revisiting the site of atrocities committed on its body, and on the national body as well' (Al-Samman 2015: 61). However, the underlying silence (the unsaid) within these stories is equally significant in attesting to women's suffering and trauma in such violent contexts. The verbally reflected incomprehensibility of Yazbek's experience evokes the tension between trauma, (auto) biographical writing and the ethics of (self-/other-)representation. It also puts into question the efficiency, credibility and ethical value of her testimony, and ultimately problematises her position as a witness. However, it is arguably the verbal insufficiency of Yazbek's text that captures the essence of trauma in its unspeakability.[14]

In *Unclaimed Experience: Trauma, Narrative, and History* (1996), Cathy Caruth defines trauma as 'an overwhelming experience of sudden or catastrophic events in which the response to the event occurs in the often delayed, uncontrolled repetitive appearance of hallucinations and other intrusive phenomena' (11).[15] Caruth points out that 'in its delayed appearance and its belated address, [traumatic truth] cannot be linked only to what is known, but also to what remains unknown in our very actions and our language' (1996: 4). It is the temporal gap between traumatic event, its repression and its (impossibility of) comprehension that makes the experience linguistically inaccessible, and hence 'unclaimed', to echo Caruth's book title. Trauma theory has generated substantial discussions on the effect of traumatic memory on the form and language of testimony. Literary critic Lucy Brisley evokes the major debates among prominent trauma theorists who view trauma writing as generally caught between a dichotomy of unspeakability and naming. For instance, according to Brisley, while Caruth links trauma to the inexplicable, un-utterable and 'impossible saying', Judith Herman asserts the healing function of the (incomplete) articulation of trauma (2015: 100). Brisley argues that while the narration of trauma involves a textual repetition of the experience, hence reviving and maintaining it, it can also, paradoxically, serve as a mechanism of containing and coming to terms with its memory (ibid.: 100–1, 108). Brisley, with whom I align, rightly suggests that trauma's unspeakability does not hinder the testimonial text from 'inevitably [presenting] a mode of inscription' of traumatic conditions in which the un-utterable still manifests itself formally and textually (ibid.: 101). In the same way, the verbal and formal manifestation of traumatic memory in Yazbek's *The Crossing* denotes what Brisley terms 'ethical markers of remembrance', which arise 'out of trauma that cannot be named' (2015: 99, 79). In its textual inscription of trauma, Yazbek's narrative has a double function. It stems from the writing subject's attempt to make sense of, and hence contain, the experience by transcribing it. In addition, it represents 'an act of witnessing and naming' (ibid.: 101) which attests to the unspeakability of trauma that she, and other Syrians, experience.

Despite the often-incomprehensible and trauma-inducing context in which Yazbek lives and writes, she remains a vigilant observer and, as she describes herself, a committed storyteller of the collective narrative. In her dedication to the original Arabic version of *The Crossing*, *Bawabāt 'Ard al-'Adam* (2015), which is condensed in the English translation,[16] Yazbek writes:

> I write with forty fingers
> I write with blind eyes
> I live reality, when I write it, I disappear.
> I am the one through whose throat cross the dead, one by one, rowing in their godly transcendence, then fall down to my blood!
> I am the storyteller who observes your short lives, observes you with her eyes, like we did in the long nights while laughing, and wondering: whose life among ours will be taken by the next shell. I do this for you. There is

> no escape from recalling you and transforming your lives into pillars linking the earth with the sky.
> I write to you, for you, and by you: the martyrs of the betrayed Syrian revolution. (2015, my translation)

Yazbek's writing fights on behalf of the martyrs of the revolution; she conceives the collection and transcription of the uprising's buried stories as a duty from which 'there is no escape'. The narrator aims to preserve the memory of the Syrian martyrs and bring about hidden stories of individuals who are forever silenced because of their political affiliation, social status, class and/or gender. They embody a triple role in Yazbek's account – the subject, the object and the target ('I write to you, for you, and by you') – which she composes as 'one of the rights of those victims who died for the Syrians' dream of freedom and justice' (Yazbek 2016: 249). Yazbek's narrative constitutes, I would venture, a monument to the collective. As in her first chronicle of Syria, Yazbek's *The Crossing* successfully renders the intersectional individual and collective traumas through a testimonial form that transports personal experiences of violence onto national memory and permits the acknowledgement of collective suffering. She creates a polyvocal representational framework which attempts to conjure up stories of the deceased, and thus, to memorialise them while asserting her own voice as a witness and a writer.[17] Despite the unspeakability of her own trauma, Yazbek's duty to unmute the collective narrative of the civil war – which is persistently haunting 'her throat' and inhabiting 'her blood' – becomes urgent and imperative. Consequently, she reclaims her mission as a storyteller: to erect 'pillars' or literary monuments linking the words of the dead to the world of the living.

However, representing the collective and preserving the memory of the dead does not ultimately resolve the tension of Yazbek's own incomprehension, and hence unspeakability, of her own traumatic memory. It further complicates it. Although the representation of the collective narrative is relatively reassuring and proves to 'alleviate guilt and assuage the self' (Brisley 2015: 106), it does not result, in Yazbek's case, in an ultimate healing or conclusive reconciliation of trauma. If Yazbek is a god-like storyteller who transcends reality and existence through her representation of the collective story, she is one who writes with 'blind eyes' as she struggles to grasp her own role in the story. She creates narrative frames into which she attempts to demarcate her existence but when she 'write[s] it, I disappear'. She confesses that 'my life were [sic] nothing but the far-fetched plot of a novel. As I observed [and wrote] what was happening around me, I ceased to be myself' (Yazbek 2016: 6).

To this end, Yazbek becomes what Anne Cubilié terms 'the impossible witness' who observes, and testifies to, the collective narrative but fails to bear witness to her own experience, and thus occupies the position of 'the lacuna of testimony' (2005: 2). This impossibility stems from the narrator's status in the text as a borderline figure; from her inability to understand her position within this void in which death prevails, although she survives. It also explains the way trauma delimits not only the language of testimony but also its self-representational capacity. Overwhelming and violent experiences are often difficult to comprehend by the subject of trauma whose memory of the event is disrupted and fragmented. Trauma's resistance to both comprehension and representation sheds light on 'the limits of autobiography' and life narratives, to use Gilmore's terms (2001), as it raises questions in relation to the historical truth-value of witness narratives. However, the impossibility of a comprehensive account of a traumatic event does not mean the impossibility of transmitting the event as it was experienced and is perceived by the subject. It is important to recognise 'the interpretative and imaginative aspects' of subjective personal narratives as opposed to facts because eyewitness testimonies tend to reflect 'how the events felt' not report objectively 'what happened' (Summerfield 2019: 5). To this end, the truth pursued by testimony capitalises on an ethical coalition established with its audience who 'takes on, as it were, the ethical responsibility of bearing witness to what testimonial writing cannot directly represent' (Anderson 2011: 132).

Yazbek's testament to the personal and collective experiences of the Syrian uprising and subsequent civil war reflects the subjective aspect of witness testimony and attests to her commitment to assert the political role of women in the national narrative. Through revisiting the traumatic sites of her illegal border crossing in a literary *testimonio*, although often incomprehensibly, Yazbek highlights the strong relationship between women's storytelling and revolutionary action. In *The Crossing,* Yazbek doubly resists the regime's physical elimination and narrative repression through evoking the character of Scheherazade, the mythical female storyteller from *A Thousand and One Nights* (*'Alf Laylah Wa Laylah*) and the long-standing archetype of the Arab woman narrator. She deliberately redefines the traditional Scheherazadian trope in terms of restricted locales of narration, political participation and literary representation.

Scheherazade is a noble-born Persian princess and the daughter of the Vizier who offers herself as a wife to the misogynist king Shahryar. Betrayed by his wife and driven by revenge, Shahryar daily marries a virgin from the kingdom and kills her at dawn after consummation. Scheherazade, however, succeeds in postponing her own death and spares the lives of the women of the kingdom through cunning storytelling. She becomes the controller of her own fate by manipulating the curiosity of the king through her mesmerising, unfinished tales of myths and wonders. However, the critical perception of the figure of Scheherazade has been generally essentialist, inspiring romantic and exotic image of a captive storyteller and/or feminist claims on the power of narrative (Al-Samman 2015: 6). The strategic political aspect underlying the character of Scheherazade in its cultural context has been often overlooked, both in the text's earlier Western translations as well as in its critical perception (ibid.: 5–6). The political dimension of Scheherazade's narration enables her to negotiate gender-based issues of power roles, voice/silence distribution, and representational discourses; elements that are particularly negotiated in Yazbek's narrative, like in many Arab women's autobiographical voices and fictional works – including Algerians Leïla Sebbar (b. 1941) and Assia Djebar (1936–2015), Egyptian Nawal El-Saadawi (1931–2021), and more recently Lebanese Joumana Haddad (b. 1970) – whose perception of Scheherazade ranges between rejection and representational revision.[18]

For instance, in *I Killed Scheherazade: Confessions of an Angry Arab Woman* (2010), a feminist 'testimony' which consists mostly of 'revealing autobiographical notes', Jumana Haddad rejects Scheherazade's character and consider it as 'a conspiracy against Arab women in particular, and women in general' (139, 12, 142). Haddad notes that Scheherazade 'does not teach women resistance and rebellion' it rather 'teaches them concession and negotiation over their basic RIGHTS. It persuades them that pleasing the man . . . is the way to "make it" in life' (ibid.: 142). She argues for 'killing Scheherazade', or dismissing the character as representative, as a way to demystify the orientalist image of the subjugated, veiled and obedient Arab women that is persistent in the Western imagination.[19] A revisionist approach to the archetype is advocated by literary critic Hanadi Al-Samman in her book *Anxiety of Erasure: Trauma, Authorship, and the Diaspora in Arab Women's Writings* (2015), which examines literary and physical annihilation, symbolised by Scheherazade and *al-wa'd* tropes,[20] as manifested in the writings of contemporary Arab women living in the diaspora. Al-Samman argues for 'the need to dislodge Shahrazad from a fixed feminist role, to transform her contemporary [Arab women] descendants to a position more befitting their multiple locales and hybrid identities, their local and global aspirations, and their revolutionary tactics', which inform their contemporary Arab(ic) literature (252).

While Yazbek does not attempt to 'kill Scheherazade' and repudiate the political value of her storytelling, she rather redefines her role within feminist, national and revolutionary frames of representation and participation. Just like Scheherazade, Yazbek's stories of the Syrian revolution stem from her own political quest to break the silence imposed by the regime. Both women stand as 'a political hero, a liberator' (Mernissi 2001: 46) whose ammunition is stories with which they contest narratives of dominant authority. In both cases, the storyteller constitutes a threat to the power she contests through a binary of voice and silence. While Shahryar symbolically and temporarily loses his kingly authority – being enslaved by the stories which his captive fragmentally narrates and through which she controls her own moments of speech and silence – the Syrian regime is, conversely, challenged by Yazbek's unmuted narratives as she attempts to expose its brutality.

Equally, Yazbek's narrative claims a womanly space of participation in the revolution that arguably recalls Scheherazade's feminist agenda to stand for and to save the women of the kingdom. Yazbek's *The Crossing* expands the frames of representation regarding the participation of women in the Syrian uprising. Her own illegal border-crossing as the only woman in a group of nineteen men attempts to defy the socially prescribed norms to 'leave the matters of war to the men' (Yazbek 2016: 237). Her multiple crossings transgress the spatial restrictions imposed on her as an anti-regime public figure, and as a woman who is expected to remain within a specific gender-decided space of resistance and narration. In *The Crossing*, Yazbek moves beyond gender-based conceptions of war as a masculine endeavour. In addition to her, and other women's, presence in the battlefield, Yazbek portrays a range of Syrian women across the social spectrum as order-keepers who maintain the normalcy of life despite death and destruction. As Yazbek shows, the daily, domestic and 'feminine' labours with which women are conventionally associated are not rejected in revolutionary Syria; they are, rather, politicised. Women turn to alternative activities such as teaching, sewing, planting and cooking as politicised forms of resistance to the dehumanising strategies of the regime and other extremist fronts. In this sense, by 'using domestic skills for political purposes, the women give visibility to domestic labour that has often been taken for granted for its inevitability and "commonness"' (Mehta 2007: 72). These 'inevitable' activities resonate here as life-sustaining measures, maintaining a 'cycle of permanence within the cycle of war and destruction' (ibid.: 54). Yazbek presents Syrian women's mundane activities as everyday resistance strategies through which they aim to assure the continuity of life and survival. This reflects the author's consciousness that the acknowledgement of women's various roles in public and private sectors is an important criterion for pro-democratic change.

In *'Alf Laylah Wa Laylah,* Scheherazade tells stories that are indeed transcultural, transnational and translinguistic, involving geographic, characterological and epistemological crossings (Gauch 2007: 2). Her tales have various origins (such as Persian, Greek, Sanskrit and Arabic), and they tend to create linguistic and cultural tapestries in which, for example, 'Persians speak Arabic' and Chinese roam in Baghdad (Mernissi 2001: 43). However, Scheherazade remains a captive storyteller who escapes confinement only through the production of imaginary worlds. Conversely, the contemporary Scheherazade, as Al-Samman rightly notes, 'is mobile, global, revolutionary, and in print. She left her fixed position behind the walls of Shahryar's palace and embarked on several journeys that emboldened her to finally own both narrative and the body' (2015: 252). Yazbek asserts physical and interpersonal mobility. She exceeds the stereotypical image of Scheherazade through enacting physical and geographical crossings as spaces for womanly, autobiographical narration. While the captive princess, 'an intellectual wonder, who has memorised books, poetry, wisdom, and more [and who] is knowledgeable, intelligent, wise, and *adībah*' (Malti-Douglas 1991: 21), relies for her narratives on memory, orality and immobile acquisition of knowledge, Yazbek capitalises in her storytelling mission on participation rather than memorisation to acquire, produce and scribe non-fictional narratives. She negotiates the space of the woman storyteller who is, traditionally, enclosed and dependent on the knowledge of books and folk traditions to enact her agency. She claims the narrated experience through her movement across borders and cities: she is a modern Scheherazade who witnesses in order to write. In her act of bearing witness, Yazbek relies on illegal movement to collect first-hand accounts through which she attempts to break the frames of closure and silence imposed on her and on those whose stories she tells. She commits herself to a mission of meeting Syrians from different social, cultural and intellectual backgrounds, who are involved in the uprising scene, and to grant their oral stories a written, trans-border and transgressive quality. This mission, like Scheherazade's stories, has the effect of 'saving her life' through both its therapeutic function – as I outline above – and its documentary intentions to keep the personal and collective narratives alive.

By materialising the transgressive potential of Scheherazade's storytelling, Yazbek simultaneously attempts to challenge gender-based and socially distributed roles of women writers. Instead of conforming to the role of the conventional figure of Scheherazade who charms, resists and subverts through her oral stories, Yazbek intentionally and self-consciously adopts a double, self-assigned, role: the mythical princess and the mesmerised king. Yazbek is at once the narrator and the protagonist, the storyteller and the listener, the scribe and the reader. She writes:

> I would be a dual-gendered Shahryar, with a dual role: I would listen, then go back and assume the identity of Scheherazade as I passed on the narrative in turn. Sometimes I'd appear as the one and sometimes as the other; sometimes I would listen and sometimes I would create the story. (2016: 248)

Yazbek's adaptation of a dual-gendered identity, which stems from her role in the revolution as a participant, an active witness, a testifying subject and a writer, problematises gender-exclusive roles during moments of conflict and upheavals. She stands against socially constructed norms of femininity by claiming a fluid gendered role. This reflects the way gender identities can become 'malleable' in moments of political conflict in which 'women and men challenge, subvert and resignify existing gender norms often in creative ways' (El Said *et al.* 2015: 9). This gender malleability is often a response to the shared collective thrust toward democracy, equality and social justice. Yezbek's claim of 'a dual-gendered Shahryar' also implicitly rejects Scheherazade's fate. Although she is a speaking agent and a strategic saviour, Scheherazade remains a slave who restores the sanity of the murderous king and ultimately embraces the role of the confined wife and mother. The purpose of her stories is ultimately co-opted to healing the misogynist king. Thus, Yazbek's dual role attempts to create a new space of expression and agency-assertion in which a woman writer is not only the storyteller, but the listener, the first-hand witness, the scribe and the revolutionary.

Yazbek's *The Crossing* presents a testimonial account which crosses borders: between opacity and representation, narration and participation, dailiness and political activism, and from prescribed gender roles to fluid ones. This is mainly approached, as I have discussed, through the testimonial form of expression which she chooses for her book. Stepping away from the novel to embrace a non-fictional, testimonial mode of narration allows Yazbek to transgress the borders of representation between the self and the collective while physically transgressing geographical borders herself. In what follows, I examine a Palestinian woman's account that adopts a similar strategy of testimonial representation that refuses to abide by social, gendered, political, critical and literary boundaries that demarcate the representation of the personal and the collective.

Contesting Gendered Borders of Participation and Representation: Suad Amiry's Nothing to Lose but your Life: an 18-Hour Journey with Murad

Palestinian author and architect, professor at Birzeit University and the founder of Riwaq (the Centre of Architectural Conservation in Ramallah) Suad Amiry (b. 1951) undertakes an illegal border-crossing journey in which she documents one day in the lives of Palestinian illegal, migrant workers whom she joins across the borders from the West Bank seeking jobs in Israel. The outcome of this journey is *Nothing to Lose but your Life: An 18-Hour Journey with Murad* (2010), a testimonial narrative that Amiry composes to portray the effects of the Israeli 'architecture of occupation' on Palestinian mobility, national identity and sense of belonging.[21] Amiry's account interrogates physical and metaphorical borders: colonial, geospatial and representational. It also reflects on restrictive gender roles in the Palestinian resistance through the author's individual experience as a woman doubly burdened by national, patriarchal and colonial discourses.

Born to a Palestinian father and a Syrian mother in Damascus, educated in Beirut and Edinburgh, and brought up in Amman, Amiry lives with her husband, Palestinian sociologist Salim Tamari, in Ramallah where she had resided illegally for seven years (1981–8) without a *hawiyyah* (residency document). While Amiry, who describes herself as 'a pretentious bourgeois, a romantic and a leftist' (2010: 24), endures, like many Palestinians living in the Occupied Territories, the machinations of the colonial administration, she states that she remains ignorant to the sufferings of many marginal social classes. Her decision to accompany twenty-four undocumented male workers on a job-hunt across the borders stems from her desire to write and publish an eyewitness account – in English and hence targeted primarily towards an international audience – about more than 150,000 Palestinians who have lost their jobs in Israel since 2000 (Amiry 2010: 24–5). *Nothing to Lose but your Life* is a participation account that charts the dangerous, yet quotidian, ventures of a group of illegal workers who cross the colonial Israeli border seeking an unguaranteed day job. The impetus behind Amiry's testimony is indicated as early as its epigraph. Quoted from late Polish journalist and writer Ryszard Kapuscinski, it reads: 'as I see it, it is wrong to write about people without living through at least a little of what they are living through'. Amiry stresses the importance of participation, to recall Beverley's criterion, in the testimonial representation of the brutal effects of Israeli illegal colonial borders. Despite her physical and psychological lack of preparedness for the journey, the narrator puts herself forward as a disguised illegal worker in an attempt to immerse herself in the experience and to present first-hand testimony to the suffering of illegal Palestinian workers in Israel whose predicament she witnesses.

Both Amiry and Yazbek show a similar pattern in their own involvement in the events to which they testify. They highlight the importance of storytelling from an insider's position in complicating the prevailing generic, selective and biased media and distant literary representation of marginal lives. They present first-hand narratives that dissolve the borders between participation and narration and between individual and collective narratives. Through their writings, Amiry and Yazbek investigate rather than assume, look for answers rather than predict, witness rather than imagine, and document rather than tell. However, while Amiry's first-hand witnessing endows the testimony with an aura of authenticity, temporary participation proves inadequate in rendering a comprehensive representation of the daily experiences of Palestinian cross-border workers who have 'nothing to lose but their lives'.

Amiry's motivation to produce an eyewitness narrative is problematised, rather than strictly achieved, by her own participation. Throughout the text, the narrator puts into question the ethics of her representational endeavours through multiple metatextual contemplations on 'the impossible topic I had chosen for this book' (Amiry 2010: 89). Amiry is sceptical about her testimony's ability to draw a comprehensive and accurate account of the surreal and dangerous life of Palestinian migrant labourers and asks: 'why should my readers understand something I couldn't grasp?' (ibid.: 104). This evokes my earlier argument on the representational limitations of testimonial literature that emerge from traumatic, violent and life-threatening contexts. Amiry's representational quest is trivialised as she gradually realises that the experience of Palestinian migrant labourers is beyond comprehensive literary mediation. As one of the workers comments: 'she [Amiry]'ll need volumes and volumes' (ibid.: 51) to draw the full picture. Self-critically, Amiry declares: 'I'm writing a book, I confessed. My words sounded ridiculous even to me. Never in my life had I felt so guilty and so silly being a writer' (ibid.: 76). This suggests that although testimony is imperative in bearing witness to collective experiences of injustice, it may be delimited by its own subjectivity; a full comprehensive picture may never emerge. Amiry realises that different forms of colonial injustice continue to exist beyond representation, beyond the pages of books and beyond one's imagination and experiences. Nevertheless, Amiry's account demonstrates that the impossibility of a totalising testimonial narrative on a risky and violent experience does not foreclose the possibility of transmitting and conjuring up a subjective version of the events as lived and perceived by the narrating witness; while testimony remains a personal account that offers partial perspective, it is able to unearth, even relatively, hidden and marginalised stories that are otherwise unattainable.

However, participation as a prerequisite for subjective representation, as advocated by Yazbek and Amiry, is further problematised in relation to the female gender. Throughout this journey, Amiry realises that her own ignorance of the predicament of the workers she accompanies does not only stem from her position as a privileged middle-class Palestinian, but also from her own socially prescribed role as a woman which excludes her from certain masculine-exclusive sufferings of her compatriots. The corporeality of the crossings, manifested also in Yazbek's, is evident in *Nothing to Lose but your Life*. En route across the borders, Amiry's female body becomes a border that separates her from participating in an illegal job hunt; her womanly figure must be overcome to allow her to be successfully integrated into the all-male group. Eager to immerse completely into and be accepted in this gender-specific experience, Amiry relinquishes the outward appearance of her female gender in an attempt to become one of Palestine's 'Big Boys' and 'an indistinguishable member of the group' (2010: 5, 3). She disguises herself as a man by wearing her husband's clothes and covering her hair. Yet, all her efforts to pass for a male worker are thwarted due to what she comically describes as her 'wobbly chest . . . wide hips, plump tummy, big derrière, stocky legs' (ibid.: 1). Although a substantial number of Palestinian women cross borders illegally for work, mostly as helpers, cleaners and agriculture workers, they are generally socially shamed as 'vulnerable to an immoral world' (Bornstein 2002: 2).²² Sneaking though the borders in the early hours of the day remains a socially prescribed masculine form of resistance. Although, as suggested earlier, prescribed gender roles may be relatively blurred in instances of war in which 'front (male space) and home (female space) are indistinguishable' by virtue of their shared freedom, aspirations and/or position as equally oppressed (Cooke 1993: 183), certain socially distributed gender roles linger.

On her first encounter with the group of workers, Amiry's fake male appearance draws their attention. Her statement that she is job-hunting is met with hysterical laughter, scrutinising gazes and soft sexist remarks: '*[a]manet Allah*, honestly, is *she* coming with us' (2010: 48). Although Amiry is eventually accepted among the members of the group, her attempt at transgressing gender borders of participation proves to require more than just a disguise. Because of her inability to cope with the men's fitness, speed and their years of experience, Amiry compares herself to a 'cow', in her 'chubbiness and out-of-shape-ness', among gazelles (ibid.: 91). Surprisingly, gender does not ultimately prove decisive; Amiry comes 'fourth in line' and succeeds to cross the border while some of her companions are caught by the Israeli soldiers. Her determination and achievement symbolise the struggle of women in their undermined and often unacknowledged resistance against the 'double displacement of gender and nation' (Mehta 2007: 40). Unlike Yazbek whose border crossing often exacerbates her alienation, Amiry's illegal transgression of colonial borders constitutes a personal passage from unawareness to empathy and understanding. She gets a first-hand experience of the suffering of this working class of Palestinians who are very often represented by media as 'faceless illegal workers' (Amiry 2010: 45). Despite the hardships she encounters, Amiry is grateful to the workers 'for a trip that has completely changed my life and attitude' (ibid.: 160).

Amiry draws attention to the importance of political engagement in the negotiation, representation and production of life narratives that advocate, across the public sphere, the role and presence of women within national resistance movements. Amiry's narrative allows her to negotiate the traditional role and space of the female storyteller. Her mobility displaces the conventionally confined Scheherazade whom she evokes through the image of 'one thousand and one Arabian worker's nights' (2010: 56). Like Yazbek, Amiry breaks the stereotype of a woman storyteller and embodies a Scheherazade who does not rely on book knowledge for narration but rather experiences and witnesses in order to inscribe. As Al-Samman reminds us, 'the Shahrazad of today is not interested in liberating women from real or imaginary veils; rather, she is determined to demolish the walls of local and global oppression that silence Arab females and males alike' (2015: 254). Through her illegal journey, Amiry attempts to go beyond the gender-based compartmentalisation of roles during national struggles and resistance movements in an attempt to defy and demystify the normative way of perceiving them as gender-specific. However, this dissident endeavour dislocates Amiry from her own perceived femininity. Once she returns from her job-hunt, Amiry perceives herself as 'sexless'. The physical and sentimental challenges of the journey induce a lasting effect on Amiry and blurs the line between socially engraved standards of masculinity and femininity. Amiry confesses that 'I could no longer feel the innocence of the little girl in me or the playfulness of the Big Boys' (2010: 158). This gender confusion arguably occurs because Amiry dislocates herself from where she is socially expected to be; these expectations disturb her efforts to de-gender the national struggle under the banner of liberation and social justice. The narrative, however, opens up the possibility for the abolishment of gender-based exclusion that would be viable if roles during resistance movements were rethought.

In Amiry's *Nothing to Lose but your Life*, the temporal, and most importantly, spatial conditions imposed by the colonial borders are crucial in shaping the migrant workers' sense of identity and belonging. I find Derek Gregory's *The Colonial Present* (2004) particularly useful in examining the dimensions of time and space in Amiry's narrative.[23] Gregory examines the dialectics of tempo-geographical compression/expansion. He notes that capitalist globalisation has led to the compression of time and space (the notions of 'the global village' and 'the age of speed'). It has equally obscured the existence of a parallel tempo-spatial expansion. He observes that the geographical divisions of modern colonial occupation, specifically, results in the expansion of the temporal dimension of the life of the dispossessed (2004: 252). Time stretches, becomes arbitrary and ceases to function as an organisational paradigm within colonial conditions in cases of, for instance, siege, curfews, detention and imprisonment. The movement of displaced and dispossessed people – such as refugees and asylum-seekers who very often get trapped in checkpoints, airports and borders – also constitutes the condition of tempo-spatial expansion. In particular reference to the Palestinian context, Gregory observes:

> Palestinians know this [tempo-spatial extension] every time they try to make an ordinary journey that once took them an hour and now takes a day (or more), if it can be made at all; there are no longer any ordinary journeys in the occupied territories. As the modern by-pass roads compress time and space for Israel's illegal settlers, so the dislocated minor roads and dirt tracks, the checkpoints and checkpoints [sic], expand time and space for the Palestinians. (2004: 252)

Initially, the subtitle of Amiry's account, *An 18-Hour Journey with Murad*, denotes the thematic and structural relevance of temporal conditions to the narrative construction. The labourers often undertake this many threatening, often futile, hours to cross from Mezari' al-Nubani in the West Bank to Petah Tikva in Israel (which would only be a fifteen-minute drive). This stretched temporality is not only reflected through the time of the journey but also in the organisational structure of the narrative. Amiry's account expands the eighteen hours she documents across 158 pages (Bloomsbury Qatar Foundation Publishing edition). She relies on the precision of time, by hours and minutes indicated as chapter sub-titles, to narratively stage the crossing. The formal presentation of the text reflects Amiry's awareness of, and deliberate attempt to highlight, the relevance of temporal manipulation as a colonial mechanism and the importance of time to the success (or failure) of the journey undertaken by the illegal workers. Amiry's meticulous attention to the temporal dimension of the experience gestures towards the constant and ongoing effort of Palestinian cultural productions to resist 'the theft of the Palestinian time' (Moore-Gilbert 2014: 195) by highlighting the effect of colonial subjugation on the perception and the experience of time and space in occupied Palestine.

Equally, in *Nothing to Lose but your Life*, spatial conditions of border crossing are specifically important in shaping the illegal workers' sense of agency and national identity. Indeed, 'the quintessential Palestinian experience . . . takes place at a border, an airport, a checkpoint: in short at any one of those many modern barriers where identities are checked and verified' (Khalidi 1997: 01). These spaces come to define what Palestinian and non-Palestinian stand for in terms of rights, duties and identities. The freedom, mobility and agency of displaced Palestinians are demarcated by geographical borders that exist as a colonial 'mechanism of tyranny' (Bornstein 2002: 133). The physical border transgression undertaken by Amiry and the workers, thus, constitutes a form of counter-occupation that aims at reclaiming individual agency and national identity.

Border movement involving labour is an integral, yet critically marginalised, part of the Palestinian national struggle (Bornstein 2002: ix). Amiry's migrant workers not only cross borders seeking work to survive, but their passage and illegal labour are acts of dissidence which aim to resist the designated geography of occupation. While Amiry figuratively remaps parts of historical Palestine through the form of her narrative, the workers reclaim their right to the land through their daily journey and hand-labour. Their daily crossing, though illegal, reflects an 'effort to get back on the map' (Said 1986: 62) from which they have been historically erased. It constitutes a political act that puts their own right of return into practice, a concept which is at the heart of the Palestinian resistance.[24] It also challenges 'the legitimacy of Israel as an exclusive state for Jews' (Bornstein 2002: 134). Through their illegal resistance to immobility and closure – aggravated by imposed, yet often unattainable travel permits – the workers' crossing metaphorically attempts to bridge the geographical gap that was violently created by occupation and redraws the borders of pre-1948 Palestine. For the workers, earning a living in Israel, which is motivated mostly by sheer necessity, becomes a way of reclaiming ownership to the land, a form of resistance and a means of asserting their *ṣumūd* (steadfastness) and belonging. One of the labourers in the narrative, working in an Israeli construction site, asserts that he occasionally pours extra cement in the buildings to make it stronger and 'last forever' because 'the settlers will leave, and these settlements will eventually become ours' (Amiry 2010: 54). This act of contributing to the construction of 'the other side' ironically symbolises the Palestinian claim of the pre-1948 land.

Physical border-crossing as a symbolic, yet politicised, act of return evokes important issues of Palestinian identity and belonging. The narrative depicts spaces of national belonging as divergent. While Amiry feels a sense of uneasiness in modern Israel as compared to her historic homeland, her companions, notably her protagonist Murad – who has been an illegal worker for more than ten years – seems to gain more freedom. Unlike Amiry who feels 'so out of place, so out of space, so out of time, so out of history, so out of meaning, so out of logic' (2010: 135) in Israel, Murad feels 'a strong sense of entitlement to this land. He gave this place his hard work, his cheap labour, his energy and his strong muscles' (ibid.: 130). These diverse feelings of West Bankers problematise the epistemological traits of belonging and suggest that, particularly in Palestine, colonial border-division can be seen as an imaginative construct of what and where home should be, a prescribed norm to which not everyone, like Murad, subscribes.[25]

The ultimately constructed, elusive nature of the border as a sovereignty marker is, as I see it, further highlighted by Amiry's own uncertain conception of spatial belonging. She fails, partly due to darkness, to locate herself and to distinguish between which part is 'our side' (Palestine) and which part is 'theirs' (Israel). She writes: 'do you mean to tell me that we've been on "our side" all this time? And what have we been doing for the last ten fucking hours?' (2010: 106). Yet only when Amiry realises that they are in Israel, does she start to feel estranged and deterritorialised. This suggests that the border is in part an imaginary construct and that its existence depends on (articulating) one's awareness of it, which then sets the traits of the perception and definition of home.[26] On the one hand, Amiry does not easily recognise the other side of the border, but when she does, it becomes an alienating space. On the other hand, Murad and his friends perceive the border as a flexible construct that can be expanded and transgressed to accommodate one's conception of home: 'For Murad, Israel was "home". Israel was a reality; a harsh reality' (Amiry 2010: 132). Thus, for the workers, the Israeli border is but a transgressable obstacle which symbolises what Said refers to as the 'constantly postponed metaphysics of return' (1986: 150). The transgressable nature of the border is further suggested by Brinda Mehta in relation to the structure of Amiry's narrative which attempts to textually eliminate physical and metaphorical frontiers by 'enabling the writer and the protagonist to migrate back-and-forth in time, space, and history' (2012: 461). Indeed, through *testimonio*'s capacity of merging and moving across personal and collective memories, voices and experiences, Amiry's *Nothing to Lose but your Life* transgresses metaphorical and physical borders, moving textually, and fluidly, between 'their side' and 'our side', just as the workers' movement redefines the beginning and end of the borders 'separating Palestine from Palestine' (Amiry 2010: 8).

Notes

1 The phrase *Shahādāt Nisā'iyyah* used in this chapter's title is Arabic for women's/feminist testimonies. On the notion of Arab feminism(s), this book's Introduction, note 22.

2 Literally, *testimonio* refers to 'the act of testifying or bearing witness in a legal or religious sense' (Beverley 1989: 14). To testify is to provide an eye-witness account in the court of law, usually under an oath, to an event where truth is unknown or in question. Equally, testimony has a strong religious connotation; it denotes the public assertion and acknowledgement of the belief in a given religion and of its merits. Similarly, testimony in Arabic – which translates as *shahādah* – has legal and religious meanings. *Shahādah* refers both to an official

eyewitness account and to the public act of declaring oneself a Muslim. The term *shahādah* is also used to mean martyrdom: the death in the battlefield in defence of one's beliefs, family or country.

3   A testimony does not always abide by the 'auto' of the conventional 'autobiography' or solicit Lejuene's autobiographical pact. In some instances, testimonial accounts can be mediated through an external writer. The latter acts as a medium who transcribes stories of witnessing subjects that are either illiterate or unable to communicate their experiences through writing. Equally, a testimonial text does not reflect the 'bio' in its totality in the sense that it generally tells stories of violence and trauma that are fragmented, reflecting incomplete sequences of the narrator's life. It is in this sense that testimony falls into the category of life writing, rather than 'autobiography', which I theorise in the introduction of this book, see pp. 8–9.

4   Another important collection of testimonies is *Iraqi Women: Untold Stories from 1948 to the Present* (2007) by Nadje Al-Ali, which presents first-person accounts, including the author's, of the experiences of Iraqi women of war and political conflicts.

5   Alawite is used to describe a religious sect of Shia Muslims centred mostly in Syria, Lebanon and Turkey.

6   The effects of translation on the reception, truth-value, function of and expectations from the genre of testimony are indeed of paramount importance, yet they are beyond the scope of this chapter; see, for instance, Peter Davies 'Testimony and Translation' (2014) and Whitlock (2007). Also, for more details on the politics of marketing life writing, see Chapter 1.

7   Arabic for 'dialect' or 'colloquial'. '*Amiyyah,* a feminine noun, literally means that which is common and prevailing; it refers to everyday spoken language which does not abide by any rigid syntactic rules. In inscribing the testimonies that she collects, Yazbek 'made sure to pass [them] along in colloquial speech. I felt they would be truer that way than if they I translated them into modern standard Arabic' (2012: 243).

8   In *Regarding the Pain of Others* (2003), Susan Sontag provides a compelling analysis of war photography and tackles persistent issues including its (lack of) aestheticism, intrusiveness, displacement of – and often remoteness from – reality and the ethics of taking victims' pictures.

9   Suzette A. Henke highlights the therapeutic capacity of testimonial expressions by women by introducing the notion of 'scriptotherapy': a way of 'writing out and writing through traumatic experience' (1998: xii). She argues that the

inscription of trauma through a testimonial form allows the subject to reach a 'psychological catharsis' (ibid.: xix) through sharing her physical pain and psychological struggle which, in turn, lead her to reflect on her own experience and perhaps to voice the unspeakable.

10 Yazbek is known for her involvement in women's issues prior to the revolution, which is evident in the topics of her novels, newspaper articles and TV programmes all of which tend to echo the predicaments and concerns of Syrian/Arab women. Her novel *Rā'iḥat al-qirfah* (2008) (*Cinnamon*, 2015), for instance, tackles the issues of lesbianism, which is hardly, if at all, dealt with in contemporary Arab(ic) literature.

11 See 'Samar Yazbek Shares British Pen Literary Award', *Al-Arabiya*, 11 October 2012, *Youtube*, https://www.youtube.com/watch?v=luuu2ddAr7o (accessed 14 January 2017).

12 The motif of the void is also recurrent in Yazbek's *A Woman in the Crossfire* (2012).

13 Feelings of suspension, alienation, loss of meaning and the failure of language and/or speech are also characteristics of melancholia. Julia Kristeva, for instance, maintains that melancholia is characterised by 'reduplication' or 'jammed repetition' that indicates 'unstable identities, blurred by a drive that nothing could defer, deny, or signify', which 'ends up in asymbolia, in loss of meaning' (1992: 246, 42); see Kristeva's *Black Sun: Depression and Melancholia* (1992).

14 Judith Herman, most prominently, investigates the possibility of recovery through the inscription of trauma in her *Trauma and Recovery* ([1992] 2015).

15 The notion of trauma and its belated utterance goes back to Sigmund Freud's work on trauma from the late nineteenth and early twentieth centuries (see Caruth 1996: 4–7, 16–18).

16 The dedication that appears in the English version reads: '[f]or the martyrs of the Syrian revolution. I am writing for you: the betrayed.'

17 The tropes of haunting and writing to memorialise the dead are reminiscent of Assia Djebar's *Algerian White* (2003), first published in French as *Le blanc de l'Algérie* (1995a). Djebar's narrative attempts to reincarnate the memory of a group of her late friends, intellectuals and political figures who were assassinated (either by the French army or Islamic extremists) since the Algerian War of Independence of 1954–62. Similar to Yazbek's, Djebar's narrative evokes issues of memory, writing and trauma. She writes: 'I wanted, in this account, to respond to an immediate demand of memory: the death of close friends . . . I am haunted by them in full daylight . . . They never disappeared. They are

there; they sometimes come close to me, together or separately ... Whispering shadows' (Djebar 2003: 13, 17).

18 Leïla Sebbar's Scheherazade trilogy which includes *Shérazade 17 ans, brune, frisée, les yeux verts* (1982), *Les carnets de Shérazade* (1985) and *Le fou de Shérazade* (1991); Assia Djebar's *A Sister to Scheherazade* (1993b); Nawal El-Saadawi's *The Fall of the Imam* (*Suqūt al-'Imām*) (1988b); and Joumana Haddad's *I Killed Scheherazade: Confessions of an Angry Arab Woman* (2010).

19 Haddad refers to a number of Arab women authors who 'killed Scheherazade' by rejecting and/or redefining the narrative role and revolutionary character of the princess (see Haddad 2010: 138–9).

20 *Wa'd al-banāt* refers to the pre-Islamic practice of burying alive new-born female daughters because of the belief that they would bring shame and embarrassment to their families.

21 For a detailed analysis of the Israeli colonial politics of space and borders and its effects on Palestinian lives and mobility, see Eyal Weizman's *Hollow Land: Israel's Architecture of Occupation* (2007).

22 On Palestinian women's illegal labour, see Bornstein 2002: 76–81, 111–12.

23 For further discussions on the chronotopes of Israeli occupation, see, for instance, Rashid Khalidi's *Palestinian Identity: the Construction of Modern National Consciousness* (1997); Joseph Massad's 'The "Post-Colonial" Colony: Time, Space, and Bodies in Palestine/ Israel' (2000) and Samar H. AlJahdali's 'Venturing into a Vanishing Space: the Chronotope in Representing Palestinian Postcoloniality' (2014).

24 Right of Return is defined by Amiry as a reference to: 'the 1948 UN Security Council Resolution no. 194, which gives the Palestinian refugees the right to go back to their homes and/or compensation for their properties in what had become the state of Israel' (2010: 149).

25 Said writes about the different conceptions of the Palestinian notion of return: 'to some it means return to a Palestinian state alongside Israel [normalisation], yet to others it means a return to *all* of Palestine' (1986: 52).

26 National identity as an imaginary construct is, most notably, discussed by Benedict Anderson in his classic *Imagined Communities: Reflections on the Origin and Spread of Nationalism* (1983).

4

Dissident Laughter: Diaries of National Struggles and the Aesthetics of Humour

The experiences of war and armed conflicts often impose new roles and identities upon individuals and give rise to new ontological and epistemological discourses that speak to the complexity of political crises and their effects on personal and collective subjectivities. Such experiences tend to affect conventional forms of autobiographical writing. Novel and creative modes of narrating life stories emerge to capture and reflect upon the newly imposed, and often dangerous, circumstances and the way they transform and shape individual and collective everyday lives. In their introduction to *Writing War, Writing Lives* (2017), Kate McLoughlin, Lara Feigel and Nancy Martin explain that during contexts of war and political unrest, standard forms of life writing tend to be 'manipulated, stretched, broken and eschewed' as 'form-breaking, rebellious tendencies of writing lives are released' (1, 5). Indeed, as I maintain throughout this book, contemporary life writing subgenres from war-torn contexts tend to be formally experimental in a way that reflects the conditions of trauma, tempo-spatial fragmentation, identity fraction, (neo) colonial oppression and material dispossession – to name a few – surrounding the narratives' construction and production. However, literary autobiographical accounts emerging from contexts of armed conflicts and national struggles very often sustain a standard, serious register and mode of expression. They are predominantly characterised by the depiction of human suffering and tragedy which are intrinsic to the experience of war; the texts examined in McLoughlin's *et al.*'s volume are no exception. However, what would certainly strike us as 'rebellious' is the comedic portrayal of such experiences, particularly from the side of the victims. War and national struggles are not inherently funny yet representing them in a humorous frame evokes the interplay between the tragic and the comic. It draws attention to the intersection of the two paradigms – national struggles and comedy – while highlighting the potential significance of humour as a narrative of resistance.

This chapter examines the strategic functions of humour in diaries that record national struggles by contemporary Arab women, namely Palestinian author Suad Amiry's *Sharon and My Mother-in-Law: Ramallah Diaries* (2006), and Egyptian novelist and activist Mona Prince's *Revolution is My Name: an Egyptian Woman's Diary from Eighteen Days in Tahrir* (2014).[1] I argue that humour that stems from a sociopolitically gendered position of marginality and oppression is an intentional dissident strategy to concentric structures of power to which contemporary Arab women are subjected – comprising colonial/state hegemony, patriarchy and cultural/representational silencing. Both diaries by Amiry and Prince represent insiders' daily accounts of national struggles that are testimonial in essence as they stem from the writing subject's own experience as participants and witnesses of the events narrated. Although the texts are differently located, in Palestine and Egypt respectively, both are characterised by the humorous articulation of their experiences of curfews and life in militarised contexts in which restricted mobility and uneven social and political powers are forcefully maintained. The chapter explores the sociopolitical workings of humour and the ways in which the use of comedy in each diary is potentially subversive; it does not only challenge the dominant, intersectional discourses it ridicules but also unsettles the literary traditions of war (life) writing. Amiry and Prince set their narratives apart from the prevailing dichotomy within which political conflicts are often articulated: heroism and tragedy. Both diarists deliberately problematise the literary conventions of non-fictional representation of national struggles as contexts where women are traditionally expected to weep. I specifically raise questions of gender relevance to comedy through exploring how each author distinctively deploys humour to address issues of gender and make visible women's presence and participation in contexts of national conflicts.

Postcolonial Humour: Genre and Gender

The extensive theoretical conceptualisation of humour,[2] which can be traced as far back as Greek Antiquity (Carroll 2014: 6; Reichl and Stein 2005: 3), has failed to reach a consensus on the definitions and functions of this universal phenomenon. Throughout history, the function of humour has been variedly perceived as: a cognitive reaction to (perceived) incongruity (Hutcheson 1750; Beattie 1778), an emotional response to repressed energy and desires (Freud 1960), a medium for social integration (Frye 1965), a form of privileging and exclusion through derision (Hobbes 1991), a desire for (cultural) appropriation (Bhabha 2004),[3] and a disavowal of (sociopolitical) otherness and stereotypical categorisation (Barreca 1994; Bhabha 2004). While mainstream humour theorists have disagreed upon a unified category of humour (Carroll 2014: 6–7), mainly because its function depends on specific social and cultural conditions as well as variable contextual elements such as audience and context of reception (Tsakona 2020: 7–18), postcolonial and feminist theorists have generally contended that the use of humour from a sociopolitically marginalised position – by virtue of political and material imbalance, cultural difference, ethnicity and/or gender – is linked to power (Barreca 1994; Gilbert 2004; Reichl and Stein 2005; Zwagerman 2010). Structures of power motivate both a postcolonial perspective and women's humour studies because 'laughter seems to thrive in a situation of power imbalance and even oppression' (Reichl and Stein 2005: 12). While the political function of humour has been perceived as ranging from maintaining power discourses through comedic legitimisation, to challenging them through ridicule, postcolonial and feminist humour are often reactive. Postcolonial comedy primarily 'reflect[s] a struggle for agency, an imbalance of power, and a need, a desire, for release' (Reichl and Stein 2005: 9). Analogously, women's humour is 'at some level, subversive' (Gilbert 2004: 31); it is a form of 'rebellion' that 'works by bending or breaking the rules; it always has' (Barreca 1994: 21, 17).

The notion of otherness that is constructed through laughter is particularly relevant to postcolonial and feminist contexts in which the centre–margin dynamic is intrinsic. According to superiority theory of humour, laughter entails exclusion because it emerges as a reaction to the perception of differences in others as infirmities that the laughing subject supposedly transcends (Hobbes 1991: 43).[4] This process of hierarchical division poses ethical questions, especially when the target of humour is an already marginalised group. However, laughing from a position of marginality, which is structured through material power, gender and/or race, is arguably a form of resistance to otherness and sociopolitical categorisation. It empowers the laughing subject who attempts deliberately at destabilising the subjugating powers by whom he/she has historically been ridiculed. This form of marginal humour contemplates power on a variety of levels: it targets dominant discourses in an attempt to distort its authority through derision; using self-deprecation, it turns marginality into a subject of ridicule in order to address power imbalance by ridiculing none other than itself; it consciously exposes the incongruity of existing stereotypical hierarchies through laughter;[5] and it acts, in Sigmund Freud's conceptualisation (1960), as a psychological safety-value, a form of aggression-release that aims at creating a collective complicity among a given marginalised group against a shared hegemony. For Freud, the release of aggression through laughter occurs through establishing a triangular relationship: a complicity between the teller of the joke and the audience, against the 'butt', or the object of ridicule. This relationship, according to Freud, is hierarchical in the sense that it involves the degradation of one element through humour and ensures the (symbolic) victory of the other two.[6] Both postcolonial criticism and feminist studies are particularly interested in the hierarchical relations that might be distorted by, and dismantled through, humour. While the interplay between superiority and inferiority, exclusion and inclusion, tension and relief, all working on different sociopolitical and psychological levels, directly falls under the concerns of postcolonial studies (Reichl and Stein 2005: 7, 9; Ilot 2015: 135–8), it serves to extend a gendered investigation of postcolonial humour, which continues to be critically marginalised.

Whilst there has been a growing academic interest in postcolonial and feminist humour in recent years,[7] Arab humour remains at the margin of comedy scholarship, especially in existing materials in English. There is a significant paucity of nuanced critical studies that attest to the plurality and creativity of political humour as a form of resistance in contemporary Arab culture,[8] especially from a gendered (female) perspective. Known as *hazl* (farce), *tahakkum* (taunt), *hijā'* (derision), *du'ābah* (joke making), *ḍaḥik* (laughter) and *sukhriyyah* (poking fun, including forms of sarcasm and irony; hence literary humour is termed *al-adab al-sākhir*),[9] humour has always been a part of everyday life in Arabic-speaking countries. Yet, it remains largely dialectical and dependent on the specificities of national cultures in the region. The varieties of spoken Arabic complicate the existence of a unified Arab humour category. This also means that it is very difficult to critically approach much of the region's humour because it is mostly orally transmitted and hence largely unrecorded. Conversely, manifestations of humour in literature can be traced back to classical, pre-Islamic and Islamic prose and poetry (Mubeen 2008: 15–17; Damir-Geilsdorf and Milich 2020: 15). Humour is also increasingly present in modern and contemporary Arab(ic) literature.[10]

If postcolonial criticism and feminist studies are particularly interested in the hierarchical relations that might be distorted by, and/or dismantled through, humour, this can also be observed in contemporary Arab comedy of revolutions. Contemporary humour from the Arab region appears to be inherently political and, as Raoudha Kammoun asserts, transgressive: in the Arab world, 'humour and social upheavals go hand in hand' (2010: 252). Khalid Kishtainy, the author of the seminal *Arab Political Humour* (1986) – one of the few extended studies on Arab comedy – maintains that 'encouragement of the development and the widespread of political humour and satirical literature should be an essential part of any strategy of civil resistance' (2009: 54). Undeniably, the recent upheavals in the region starting in 2011, or what have been dubbed The Arab Spring, have witnessed a boom of political humour and particularly highlighted the revolutionary potential of comedy as a strategy towards possible subversion of sociopolitical norms (Cooke 2017: 39; Damir-Geilsdorf and Milich 2020: 10–11). The Arab uprisings have enabled the public emergence and disclosure of manifold forms of dissident humour, such as political jokes, cartoons, graffiti, user-generated video-clips, protest banners and stand-up shows. While, as I shall explain, humour does not have the power practically to alter sociopolitical hierarchies, it is able to disturb oppressive norms through laughter. In recent Arab revolutions, notably in Egypt, Syria, Tunisia and Algeria,[11] humour has acted as a conscious means of exposing the absurdity of everyday life under dictatorial regimes and challenging the normalisation of their rule. While, as Kishtainy notes, 'there is no record of a regime falling because of a joke . . . there is hardly any such event occurring without being preceded by a rich harvest of political jokes and satirical literature' (2009: 54). Joining the few existing works on the sociopolitical significance of contemporary Arab humour in a variety of cultural forms (Abaza and Mehrez 2016; Awad and Wagoner 2017; Cooke 2017; Helmy and Frerichs 2017; Damir-Geilsdorf and

Milich 2020), this chapter extends the available discussions to a gendered investigation of political comedy in the diary genre by contemporary Arab women while drawing on existing postcolonial and feminist theories on the subject.

'To Step out of the Frame': Mocked Occupation, Unheroic Resistance and the Daily Absurd in Suad Amiry's *Sharon and My Mother-in-Law: Ramallah Diaries*

In the preface to her diary, *Sharon and My Mother-in-Law: Ramallah Diaries* (2006), Palestinian architect and author Suad Amiry acknowledges her friend Bilal Hammad for teaching her 'how to step out of the frame and observe the senselessness of the moment' (2006: xi). This act of perceptive transgression becomes the principle around which Amiry's daily account of life under occupation is constructed. Amiry composes an intriguing account that moves away from other non-fictional Palestinian war narratives by virtue of its overwhelmingly humorous tone. When comparing Amiry's account to life writings by Palestinian women authors, such as Fadwa Tuqan, Hanan Ashrawi and Ghada Karmi,[12] to name a few, Amiry's stands apart in its thematic approaches and textual tonalities through which life under Israeli occupation is rendered. Resorting to irony, wit and sarcasm, the diarist presents a fresh perspective of daily life in the contemporary Palestinian scene by offering a new representational model that escapes the traditionally tragic/heroic frames of writing personal war accounts.[13]

Amiry's use of humour to deal with and write about everyday life in occupied Ramallah is an intentional strategic mode of frame transgression, particularly frames of (self-)representation and resistance. The intersection of humour and diary writing in *Sharon and My Mother-in-Law* offers an alternative representational framework of Palestinian reality, one which is positioned within the unheroic, the absurd and the routinely, instead of the (sometimes crudely) political and lyrical frames within which the Palestinian–Israeli conflict is generally conceived and depicted. Humour in Amiry's narrative (which covers snapshots of the years 1981–2004 with a focus on the subject's experience of the 2002 Ramallah siege) evokes different axes of resistance that move across the private and the public, the personal and the collective, the rhetorical and the physical and the heroic and the unheroic. This movement, I argue, is mainly triggered by the multiple targets of Amiry's humour that allow the mode to perform at the psychological, social and political levels.

Bart Moore-Gilbert's analysis of postcolonial life writing is of paramount importance in the field – in particular his attention to Palestinian women's auto/biography, such as Amiry's narrative. However, while his 2009 monograph offers an interesting preliminary discussion of humour in Amiry's diaries, it only briefly and almost exclusively focuses on the use of comedy from a representational point of view. Moore-Gilbert does not elaborate on the sociopolitical or the psychological uses of humour but looks at it from formal and thematic standpoints as an 'innovative construction of a "Palestinian Absurd"' which is reminiscent of authors like Harold Pinter and Samuel Beckett (2009: 126–7).[14] His interest in issues of genre in this text is further manifested in his articles in which he looks at formal autobiographical choices and their implications for selfhood and subjectivity, including questions of linearity and intergenericity but excluding humour (2013, 2014). Aware of the strategic significance of postcolonial comedy, however, Moore-Gilbert calls for nuanced analyses of the 'use of varieties of humour to produce distinctive tonalities which advance its strategic purposes' (2014: 199). This is what this chapter hopes to address; it extends the formal manifestations of humour in Amiry's text to the potential 'strategic purposes' behind its use.

The humorous quality of Amiry's diary is primarily announced through the intriguing title of her account in which Ariel Sharon,[15] former Israeli (now late) Prime Minister and an epitome of the ruthless colonial administration, is equated with Amiry's harmless yet stubborn ninety-one-year-old mother-in-law, Um Salim. While this equation between two figures who exist on two ends of a power spectrum appears incongruous, and thus laughable, it acts primarily to reflect the variant forms of oppression to which the narrator is subjected: the political and the domestic. Most importantly, this comedic equation of the political hegemony with the daily domestic skirmishes is a conscious representational strategy that is aimed at de-emphasising the effects of colonial rule on everyday life. It thus engages in a symbolic process of depriving it of its supposed power by reducing it to the daily, routinely and domestic spheres of experience. Such a perceptive process, which is carried throughout the narrative, enables Amiry to 'step out of the [established] frames' of representing the Israeli occupation of Palestine. To break out of the representational frame, for Judith Butler, 'is to show that the frame never quite contained the scene it was meant to limn'; it is to suggest 'a loosening of the mechanism of control' (2009: 8–9, 11). It is through this breakage that Amiry demonstrates that to live by and write within the conventional scope of perception that attributes certain characteristics to occupation is to conform to the authority that generates and defines it; hence, to call such a frame into question occurs only once she steps out of it. This transgressive movement allows Amiry to question the very foundations of occupation by observing the 'absurdity of my life and the lives of others' in occupied Ramallah (2006: xi).

In addition to its mocking tone, the title of the diary equally suggests the way a Palestinian personal life under occupation is inescapably intertwined with the collective experience of the political. Although Amiry describes her narrative as 'personal war diaries' (2006: ix), the subtitle of the account *Ramallah Diaries* suggests that the text engages with collective dailiness rather than the exclusively personal experience. It complicates the conventional conception and understanding of the diaristic form as one which is 'largely a private document' that exclusively records 'the thoughts, feelings, and activities of the writer' (Nussbaum 2007: 5). Amiry's diary rather suggests 'collective (self-)identifications' which particularly characterises postcolonial auto/biographical narratives (Moore-Gilbert 2009: 32). The striking difference between the individualistic nature of the diary genre and the collective ethos of the text's subtitle (suggesting a diary of a city) evokes the relationship between voice and representation. Although Amiry, the narrating subject, is a middle-class woman and a relatively privileged and mobile professional, her account reflects the collectively experienced predicament of Ramallah residents under occupation and curfew. Amiry does not claim to be the 'elite nationalist' nor the 'native informant' who embarks on an essentialist mission to represent the disempowered, to speak on behalf of the oppressed, and to give a voice to the collective, an issue with which Gayatri Spivak has been famously preoccupied in relation to her conception of the subaltern.[16] This is primarily due to the private nature of the genre of Amiry's diary which was not initially intended for publication and hence dismisses any claim of an elitist representational endeavour. However, Amiry's position as a first-hand witness and, as she describes herself, an 'observer' (2006: xi) of the communal predicament inevitably enables collectively lived, relational experiences to emerge in her narrative.

Amiry's diary, which she explicitly describes as 'personal', ultimately meets Françoise Lionnet's conception of postcolonial life writing as a genre in which 'the individual necessarily defines him – or herself with regard to a community' (1995: 22). Amiry's account does not claim to be representative of Ramallah residents, nor to depict them as a unified category sharing a homogenous experience. However, the diary's wider national frame of (self-)representation inescapably, and perhaps unintentionally, evokes a sense of relationality. The national political structure of the Israeli–Palestinian conflict engenders common experiences among the generally diverse collective category with which Amiry engages in her narrative. She conjures up a diary which reflects the temporal and spatial specificities of Ramallah by linking her private life to the public setting. The account reflects what Anna Bernard refers to as a 'national narrative' in which 'there is no private narrative without public predicament . . . [because] both [are] emblematic of and inseparable from the collective' (2013: 26). Amiry's personal narrative is made possible through, and can only be understood in relation to, the collective with which her day-to-day experiences of occupation and curfews are affiliated. Her autobiographical identity emerges as 'merging [the individualist Self] with a collective group identity' (Golley 2003: 213) because her diary reflects the unexceptionality of the narrator's experience through the lens of the communal dailiness of Ramallah under curfew.

Amiry's diary, initially written in epistolary forms (letters and emails) addressed to a selected group of relatives and friends, started as a form of therapy. In her preface, Amiry explains that writing her daily account 'was an attempt to release the tension caused and compounded by Ariel Sharon and my mother-in-law' (2006: x). While psychological relief, or healing, is a central characteristic of testimonial writings (see Chapter 3), it is particularly the use of humour in this narrative that accelerates such a cathartic process. Throughout the diary, Amiry self-consciously resorts to comedy to deal with, and sometimes escape, the arbitrary scenarios which she, as a daughter-in-law of a demanding elderly woman and as a Palestinian living under occupation, consistently encounters.

On one level, Amiry resorts to humour as a sanity-preserving strategy in order to escape the domestic pressure exercised on her by her widowed mother-in-law. After evacuating Um Salim from the militarised area where she lives, Amiry finds herself obliged to spend the monotonous days of curfews with a tyrannical president in the house. Um Salim is neither mindful of occupation nor of the successively imposed curfews. Instead, she chooses to maintain her usual routine of waking up and eating at certain hours of the day, using certain cutlery and maintaining immaculate outfits as a strategy to survive and undermine colonial effects on the course of everyday life. Additionally, Um Salim, who is overtly critical of Amiry's 'odd hours', attempts to impose her own daily schedule on her daughter-in-law. The lack of privacy which Amiry experiences for successive weeks added to the peculiar temper of the nagging elderly relative proves psychologically challenging.

As a reaction, Amiry self-consciously turns her mother-in-law into a subject of her humour; she laughs at Um Salim who is more concerned about her marmalade being spoiled than the Israeli tanks positioned outside the house. She also laughs at her immaculate outfits and attention to domestic details in an antagonistic colonial context (2006: 137, 141). Amiry's humour, being primarily addressed to her own enjoyment, comes as an act of social self-protection that allows her to elicit self-amusement from domestic tension, and hence, symbolically survive it. Her comedy thus constitutes, in the Freudian understanding, a release of repressed energy that is accumulated through social repression; it allows her to liberate domestic pressure which would only complicate her own experience of occupation. Choosing to share these scenes comedically, Amiry, again, evokes Freud's comedy triangle, by soliciting her correspondents', and later readers', laughter, sympathy and complicity against her mother-in-law, and therefore extends and enhances the relief function of her humour.

While domestic humour in the case of Amiry acts primarily to release the tension built up by her mother-in-law, her comedic attitude towards occupation bypasses the psychological function to become potentially subversive. Indeed, Amiry ridicules occupation in order to dislocate her fear and anxiety and to ease her pain and sense of oppression. Humour is used, at times, as a form of denial which seems, as she writes, 'an effective way of dealing with the unbearable encounters of life under occupation' (2006: 189). However, while the psychological function of comedy remains relevant, Amiry's humour against occupation can be understood, in Regina Barreca's theorisation of women's humour, as 'an ideological construct' that is manifested under the guise of the personal, the funny and the daily (1988: 7). Women's humour against power goes beyond the conventional theorisation of comedy 'as catharsis of desire and frustration; [and] comedy as social safety value' to constitute a medium of questioning, interrogating and challenging the legitimacy of the ridiculed authority (Barreca 1994: 18). Israeli rule in Amiry's text is a consistently mocked occupation. Such mockery does not solely aim to dismiss anxiety but to delegitimise the very foundations of occupation through laughter. While the so-called Israeli–Palestinian conflict is indeed 'a clash between . . . "two narratives"' (Bernard 2013: 6), Amiry's humour allows her not only to advocate her stance vis-à-vis the occupation and respond to its dominant narrative but also to ridicule it, and hence to attempt to destabilise existing dynamics of power discourses. By presenting the political through the personal and the serious through the humorous, Amiry raises questions concerning the mechanisms of occupation by exposing the farcical nature of its own subjugating dynamics because, as she justifies it, 'we're never sure how serious or unserious this occupation is' (2006: 59).

Throughout the narrative, the absurdity of colonial rule is consciously exposed through laughter. We follow different instances in which Amiry, a Palestinian woman living in occupied Ramallah, is the subject of colonial oppression. She is separated from her groom, denied the right to a *hawiyyah* (residency card) and subjected to racial profiling, intense interrogations and restricted mobility. These oppressive regulations are rendered by the author in a comedic disjuncture that shifts from the serious to the ludicrous. For instance, while most West Bankers need a permit to travel to Jerusalem, which they can rarely get, Amiry's dog Nura receives a Jerusalem passport after being examined by an Israeli veterinarian. Astonished by the irony of the situation, having lived *sans-papiers* in her own country for seven years (from 1981–8), Amiry decides to drive to Jerusalem and make use of the privileged dog's documentation. 'I am the dog's driver' she tells the amused soldier at the checkpoint while handing him the dog's passport, 'she is from Jerusalem, and she cannot possibly drive the car or go to Jerusalem all by herself . . . somebody has got to be her driver' (2006: 108). Such a juxtaposition between the serious and the comedic inevitably foregrounds the incongruous nature of the colonial rule which, as absurd as it may sound, guarantees the mobility of animals while it arbitrarily controls the spatial, and in effect the temporal, dimensions of the life of millions of Palestinians.[17] Surprisingly, Amiry convinces the entertained soldier and is permitted access to Jerusalem because 'all it takes is a bit of humour' (Amiry 2006: 108). Humour thus becomes, as Sean Zwagerman notes, 'a force for . . . action'; it proves to be practically reactive as it demonstrates that if humour is 'a way of speaking, it is also a way of acting and a way of moving between – and conceptualising the movement between – the mind, the word, and the world' (2010: 3, 191).

Amiry's ideological use of humour extends to collective acts of resistance. Her narrative presents instances of comedic complicity which rhetorically attempt to degrade a common enemy. Collective comedic resistance is best manifested in the chapter 'The Promised Gas Masks' (2006: 76), which takes place during the Gulf War of 1991. Threatened by Saddam Hussein's chemical weapons, the Israelis distribute gas masks to their citizens and decide to extend the distribution to Palestinians including Amiry's neighbourhood. The residents find themselves in a ridiculous predicament in which they are expected to collect the gas masks themselves but are simultaneously forbidden from breaking the curfew. This instance provides an occasion of laughter because, as Edward Said notes, 'what to many Palestinians is either an incomprehensible cruelty of fate or a measure of how appalling are the prospects for settling their claim can be clarified by seeing irony as a constitutive factor in their lives' (1991: 5). Gathering eventually to fetch the promised masks, which they never get, the neighbours start poking fun at the IDF's (Israeli Defence Forces) incongruous political rule and making jokes about the arbitrariness of their own life under occupation:

> I don't know what is it with Israeli soldiers. They have a fetish for making Palestinians stand in an orderly line. They complicate our lives with all sorts of permits, make them unbearably chaotic, then insist we stand in straight lines. (Amiry 2006: 83)

Although the collective use of humour demonstrated in this incident is initiated by a group from diverse social, educational and – often conflicting – political backgrounds, it reflects a sense of solidarity that stems from shared grievances, sociopolitical experiences and cultural knowledge. The group constitutes what Susanne Reichl and Mark Stein term 'communities of laughter' (2005: 14). Their laughter becomes a collective statement to demonstrate an image of a cohesive national identity and ultimately realises the Freudian symbolic victory through a process of identification and exclusion. The process of exclusion is further contemplated through the recurrent comedic mimicry of the Israeli Arabic accent. Amiry reports, for instance, that an Israeli soldier directs the gathering group by ordering '*wakhad, wakhad Mafkhoum* (one by one you understand)' – instead of *wāḥed* and *mafhūm* (2006: 84). The group answered '"*Mafkhoum* (We understand)" . . . imitating his distorted Arabic' (ibid.: 84). Susanne Mühleisen notes that 'the non-native speaker accent is usually a feature of non-belonging or of exclusion' (2005: 226). In the same sense, laughing at the occupiers' mispronunciation of Arabic sounds like 'ḥ', 'ḫ' and 'ḍ' and addressing them by mimicking their accent becomes a way of exploiting an image of otherness that marks and alienates the occupiers. It stresses the status of the Israelis as outsiders and illegitimate occupiers by creating a sense of intimate complicity among the laughing group. While in most cases making fun of accents would be racist and unethical, it demonstrates, in this context, the inevitability of political incorrectness in the face of the flagrant power imbalance of the Israeli–Palestinian conflict. It becomes evident that collective humour elicits solidarity. It extends from being a 'great group therapy' (Amiry 2006: 182) to become a communal strategy of resistance as 'every [collective] joke' constitutes, in George Orwell's terms, 'a tiny revolution' (1945). In this sense, collective laughter becomes a national dissidence narrative that constitutes an ideological gesture towards potential sociopolitical liberation.

However, Amiry's humour is not exclusively directed towards the tyrannical figures foregrounded in the title of her diaries. Amiry's laugher indiscriminately targets her own compatriots through unfolding social criticism which demonstrates that 'the occupation has ruined the spirit of both Israelis and Palestinians' (2006: 11). While Palestinian cultural behaviour and cases of collaboration with the occupiers on the one hand and Israeli political mechanisms on the other provide Amiry with rich materials for jokes, it is the patriarchal inclination that brings Palestinian and Israeli men under a shared banner of a ridiculed power. Amiry asserts that patriarchy 'makes the occupation doubly painful' (2006: 67) as Palestinian women find themselves eventually unable 'to define who the enemy is' (ibid.: 92). Gender-based treatment, which the author sarcastically describes as 'the only Arab tradition the Israeli seem to reinforce' (ibid.: 190), extends the targets of her humour and with it its avenues of resistance against both external and local (masculine) subjugating powers.

Amiry's consciousness of, and explicit reference to, her position as subjected to a gender-based intersectional power structure allow her to engage in different axes of resistance through self-deprecatory humour. The latter generally stems from her peripheral position constructed, as she experiences it, on the basis of her colonial status, gender and age. Feminist humour theorist Regina Barreca argues that women's humour 'derive[s] power from their exclusion' (1988: 16), and Joanna Gilbert maintains that gendered exclusion 'may ultimately serve as a powerful means of resistance to social, political, and economic inequities' (2004: 5). Similarly, using self-deprecatory humour, Amiry capitalises on and takes advantage of her stereotypical gendered position because, as Gilbert argues, 'individuals who are sociologically marginalized ... by some immutable physical reality such as sex, race/ethnicity, age, size or disfiguration/disability ... cannot help but perform their marginality' (2004: 6). In Amiry's text, the comedic performativity of gender, in the Butlerian sense of the reproduction of socially constructed conventions of gender (1990), enables the laughing subject to turn the stereotypical frame within which she is identified into a privileged position of resistance. While Butler problematises the agency of the actors who subscribe to gendered social norms,[18] Amiry, I argue, provides an agential model of gender performativity through humour. In the case of Amiry, the reproduction of gender constructs is not merely about enacting the socially expected role as much as it is about the context, setting and intended effect(s) within which this role is self-consciously enacted and reworked. Using self-deprecation, Amiry re-evokes the social constructs of her gendered profile as a middle-aged Palestinian woman as a way to foreground and experiment with spheres of liberty, restrictions and resistance that this gendered position potentially offers.

Through turning herself into a subject of humour, Amiry initially falls into the stereotypical frame of her gendered position in order to transgress it. Using self-deprecation, Amiry does not hesitate to describe herself as a paranoid, 'early menopausal woman' (2006: 67) and expose her tears, feminine vulnerability and anxieties within a comedic frame. Laughing at oneself can act as a safety mechanism; it prevents others from making you the target of their jokes as it reflects recognition of and even reconciliation with one's own supposed defects and absurdities. However, when arising from outside sociopolitical positions of power, self-mockery becomes conflated with subversion as it constitutes a means through which 'social outcasts call attention to their subordinate status' (Gilbert 2004: xi, 21). Through a powerful intersection between object and subject of humour, Amiry's self-deprecation highlights the fundamental ludicrousness of the colonial dynamics of sociopolitical categorisation and exclusion by enabling the subject laughing (at herself) to draw attention to gender-based injustice, as she experiences it.

Much of the diaries' comedy relies on gender-based self-deprecatory humour. Amiry chooses to engage with her gendered stereotypical image and turns it into a site of resistance that, I propose, reworks the conventional image of the resistance hero. Amiry's consciousness that 'being a woman helped me not to be taken seriously' (2006: 29) allows her to exploit her gendered, peripheral status and turn it into a privileged position of unheroic resistance. For example, when returning from London through Tel Aviv airport, Amiry gets heavily interrogated regarding the reasons for her trip. Because she 'was not in the mood', Amiry nonchalantly insists that she 'went dancing' (2006: 8). Infuriated by her sarcastic answer, the Israeli female officer threatens Amiry, who audaciously inverts roles and exclaims 'And do YOU have any problem with dancing' (ibid.: 8). To this end, the interrogator summons two security men in an attempt to threaten Amiry for her refusal to cooperate. Certain that any other answer will lead to further delay and hence keep the taxi driver waiting, Amiry walks insouciantly towards the exit gate to tell him to leave. She derives her confidence from her physical appearance as a harmless middle-aged Palestinian woman who might be arrested and humiliated by armed well-built men whom she threatens: 'yes, arresting me in front of these tourists will create a scene which is not favourable for tourism in Israel' (ibid.: 10). Making use of the stereotypical frame in which her gendered image is constructed, while exploiting her knowledge and consciousness of Israeli national image, Amiry is eventually, and triumphantly, allowed to leave. Her humorous resilience shifts from being a form of avoidance and ridicule to become a force for offence and eventually for action.

Similarly, Amiry takes advantage of the stigma of the weeping, emotional menopausal woman. After her 'seven-year epic' without a *hawiyyah* (residency card) (Amiry 2006: 26), for example, she decides that it is time to take action. She goes unannounced to the office of Captain Yossi from the Civil Administration where she frantically delivers an emotionally charged speech about what it means to be a Palestinian living under occupation. While Amiry melodramatically surrenders to tears, the astonished officer surrenders to her claim:

> I could see that he was capable of handling Palestinian demonstrators, rebels, stabbers, terrorists. He could handle bombs, dynamite, tanks, fighter planes and submarines. He was able to handle them all.
> BUT NOT A CRYING WOMAN.
> NOT A WOMAN FREAKING OUT. (ibid.: 43)

Amiry's strategic engagement with gender stereotypes in the previous incident is compared with the non-violent, physical and armed forms of resistance of her male compatriots. Yet, it proves more effective and eventually triumphant, allowing her to obtain her long-awaited documentation. It equally constitutes an implied critique of existing and potential restrictions on the spheres of Palestinian women's role and agency in the national struggle which continue to be perceived under a predominantly masculine nationalist banner.[19] It demonstrates that women, as subordinated actors in the resistance movement, may autonomously act to preserve and restore their dignity and may eventually prove superior to both dogmatic male nationalists and occupation. In this sense, Amiry's performativity of gender becomes a strategic form of visibility. It aims at redefining the intersectional spheres of women's resistance and participation in nationalist movements; it reflects what Anna Ball describes as '[the] interplay between their colonial oppression as Palestinian, their patriarchal oppression as women and the possibilities of agency afforded by their involvement within the nationalist cause, and indeed by their positions within "private" realms such as the home' (2012: 47).

Although the incident cited above (among others in the narrative) entails partial victory, it does not comply with the conventional understanding of the notion of heroism that is traditionally defined within the tropes of masculinity, extrinsic superiority, exceptionality, physicality and bravery. Resilience in this text, as I see it, is also manifested in the form of inaction. Amiry, for example, refuses to leave the house during the few hours when the curfew lifts. Instead, she has recourse to a self-chosen curfew as a form of refusal to submit to the colonial control and manipulation of Palestinians' mobility. She also develops a routine which mostly consists of oversleeping as a strategy to defeat 'the deadly long curfew hours' (Amiry 2006: 178). This deliberate form of (in)action ultimately reworks the image and conception of the traditional hero by highlighting the notion of *ṣumūd*.[20]

Like the notion of *ṣumūd*, Amiry's (in)action reflects her ability to 'maintain dignity, honor and a physical presence in the land despite adversity and hardship' (Ryan 2015: 300). Her unheroic dissidence is not necessarily passive or ineffective. Similar to the defining aspects of *ṣumūd*, it is a form of resilience that arises from her 'ability to remain [joyfully and triumphantly] in place in the face of indignities, injustices and humiliation at the hands of the colonial power' (El Said *et al.* 2015: 13). Resorting to 'alternative strategies' of resistance (Amiry 2006: 28), Amiry, for instance, chooses to get back at a soldier in a checkpoint who dismissively calls her '*hajjeh*' (ibid.: 67), a term that is used to address elderly women.[21] As a reaction to the sexist remark and the condescending manner in which it is made, Amiry intimidates the soldier by staring ceaselessly at him: 'I kept looking at him in the eye with an expressionless face . . . A stare, and you lose your mind' (ibid.: 71). The soldier, in turn, anxiously makes a complaint against her husband Salim for not having 'the power to force your wife to behave' (ibid.: 71). Amiry's gaze simultaneously challenges the power of occupation as well as its anchored traditions of patriarchy. Describing her behaviour as 'my passive resistance to occupation' (ibid.: 71), she draws attention to the effectiveness of unheroic resilience as, sometimes, the only avenue of resistance to which Palestinian women have access.

By stressing the potential effectiveness of unheroic dissidence, Amiry simultaneously draws attention to the volatile nature of such resistance, which may sometimes favour self-interest and individualistic survival over national/collective concerns. For instance, fearful of deportation and hopeful to obtain her residency card, Amiry finds herself signing the anti-PLO (the

Palestinian Liberation Organisation) statement and attending an Israeli official party against her own convictions. She also openly confesses that she gives up on her attempt to rescue her mother-in-law from her militarised neighbourhood because she fears for her own safety (2006: 28, 35, 133). Amiry's mock-hero representational strategy dismantles the idealised/tragic perception of the Palestinian as being synonymous with 'something mythological like a unicorn' (quoted in Moore-Gilbert 2009: 115).[22] The author engages in a representational project that attempts to demythologise the image of the Palestinian *muqāwamah* (resistance) by portraying it in its dailiness and vulnerability while inviting her readers to laugh with her at the absurdity of life under occupation.

Nevertheless, the intentional, strategic use of humour does not necessarily mean that it yields a definitive resolution. *Sharon and My Mother-in-Law* capitalises on the discursive relationship between comedy and tragedy without yielding a final denouement. This lack of resolution is enforced by the immediacy of the diaristic form of writing which is essentially 'fragmented, revisionary, in process' and the writing subject is necessarily ignorant about 'the outcomes of the plot of his [/her] life' (Smith and Watson 2001a: 193). In this narrative, humour ultimately proves limited. While readers laugh with Amiry at the Israelis' distorted Arabic, at their pride in their mud-like coffee, at Ramallah's misogynistic anti-animal vet and at the author's hallucinations and unconventional resilience, their comic amusement is often disrupted upon reflection on the underlying tragedy of the Palestinian predicament. Although constantly funny, the narrative does not dismiss the atrocities, violence, death, displacement, dispossession and other mechanisms of oppression committed against Palestinians. It rather shifts, sometimes abruptly, between the humorous and the tragic and at other times intertwines the two. Hence, this incongruity in the narrative reflects the continuous 'tragicomedy' (Amiry 2006: 81) of the Palestinian predicament in which laughter becomes only possible 'through the fears/tears' (Ilott 2015: 141, 152).

Ambivalent laughter can be observed throughout Amiry's narrative. The motifs of return and *al-Nakba*, for instance, which are recurrent throughout the diaries, are mostly comedically evoked, but the sense of bitterness which they both signify persists. The ending of the narrative is equally significant as the consistent funniness of the text gives way to a sombre note in which the author reflects on the cruelty and injustice of occupation. It becomes evident that 'smiling through an experience is different from undergoing [a definite] catharsis: the experience remains potent, dangerous and enraging despite the smile' (Barreca 1994: 19). To this end, Amiry's humour capitalises on raising the audience's consciousness of the Palestinian predicament through an accessible register and an innovative and appealing mode of (self-)representation. Her humour does not aim at practically realising an ultimate, and maybe a far-fetched, subversion of norms. It is the potentiality of such subversion that Amiry's humour contemplates. It becomes clear that what is empowering about Amiry's humour for the laughing subject and her sympathising audience is the process of laughter that may yield and maintain recognition of the idiosyncrasies of Palestinian life under occupation. It is only through stepping outside of the dominant frames of perception and representation that underpin and essentialise the Israeli–Palestinian conflict that one can observe its inherent incongruity and, perhaps, consider standing for an alternative future, one that is as humanistic as Amiry's narrative.

Carnivalesque Revolution: Comedic Resilience and the Egyptian Uprising in Mona Prince's *Revolution is My Name: An Egyptian Woman's Diary from Eighteen Days in Tahrir*

Mona Prince's *Revolution is My Name: an Egyptian Woman's Diary from Eighteen Days in Tahrir* (2014) is a predominantly funny account although, similar to Amiry's narrative, it is set within a period of national conflict, particularly during the Egyptian revolution of 2011. Reporting her experience during the eighteen days of mass peaceful protests which brought down the thirty-year rule of Hosni Mubarak, Prince's diary captures and engages with the spirit of the Egyptian uprising, which was predominantly characterised by the use of political humour. The non-violent forms in which 'the people demand[ed] the removal of the regime' ranged from sarcastic banners, satirical chants, poetry, public performances, nationalist songs, dancing, political caricatures, graffiti, social media posts to political jokes; consequently, the revolution was 'transformed into . . . a carnival' (Prince 2014: 174). Despite the regime's violent response to the people's peaceful call for *"ïsh, ḥurriyyah, 'adālah igtimā'iyyah'* (bread, freedom, social justice), the use of humour in a range of cultural media persisted as a form of protest, resistance and disobedience insofar as the uprising was critically termed 'The Laughing Revolution' (Salem and Taira 2012). This recourse to revolutionary humour, I argue, revises the conventional means of resistance and the relationship of 'the people' (*al-shaʿb*) with repressive power structures. Equally, it reworks the way non-fictional literary accounts of national struggles can be approached by writers, readers and critics. While the use of humour in a range of cultural media during the Egyptian uprising drew public attention and has been academically discussed, its literary manifestations in the narratives of the revolution have not been sufficiently examined.[23]

Published originally in Arabic (a mélange of *fuṣḥā* and *ʿamiyyah*) as *'Ismī Thawrah* (2012), Prince's diary mediates and provides a vivid example of revolutionary humour with which the author actively engages. It chronologically follows eighteen days of the author's participation in the Egyptian uprising which started as *silmiyyah* (peaceful) but as a direct result of the violent intervention of the Central Security Forces, Military Police and state-sponsored thugs became 'a war in the midan [Tahrir Square in central Cairo]' (Prince 2014: 123). Prince's narrative joins works by Egyptian women authors like Ahdaf Soueif and Radwa Ashour to constitute a part of a representational literary category which Tahia Abdel Nasser terms 'Tahrir Memoirs' (2017: 130). The term describes different forms of non-fictional participation accounts that are 'characterised by simultaneity, association, and introspection' in narrating the events and discourses of the Egyptian revolution (ibid.: 130),[24] which appropriates *Mīdān al-Taḥrīr*, Tahrir Square in Cairo, as a central, national space for revolutionary legitimacy. In comparison with Soueif, whose memoir (2014) is clearly a voice from the Egyptian diaspora, or Ashour, whose autobiography (2013) distantly and fragmentedly follows the course of the revolution from her hospital room in the United States, I regard Prince's account to be the most vivid example of Tahrir Memoirs. Her stance as an insider and her participation as a local Egyptian affects the narrative's tone, mood and structure of feeling and, hence, allows a critical approach to her diary as a literary example of revolutionary Tahrir. Prince's account chronicles her revolutionary experience while interweaving stories, speeches, social media and news reports, testimonies and jokes in a way that 'all of the stories had become one big story . . . they all completed each other' (Prince 2014: 76). While the sense of festivity and humour dominated Tahrir

Square, Prince's account draws in its tonality from the comedic resilience of the revolutionists. The immediacy of the account captures the revolutionaries as 'rocking between laughter and anxiety'; while their (un)certainty about the efficiency of the revolution fluctuates and their peaceful resilience to the regime's violence persists, they continue to exchange 'the latest [political] jokes' (ibid.: 51).

Prince actively engages with the festive spirit of the uprising. She dances to nationalist songs with men and women, holds comedic banners, exchanges political jokes and spends sleepless nights with the protestors reflecting on the trajectory of the revolution. Although Prince separates herself from any social and political categorisation, stating that: 'I am not one of the hungry or the downtrodden, nor do I belong to a political party or a particular intellectual movement. I believe in freedom of expression', she simultaneously identifies and affiliates herself with 'the people' of the *mīdān*: 'I was part of the whole' (2014: 13, 26). This 'whole', she suggests, is an inclusive category of *al-sha'b* (the people) that comprises 'real Egyptians' who 'were all one' (ibid.: 91, 154). This 'oneness' is primarily constructed on the basis of the people's national, collective aim to end their shared experience of tyranny while commonly upholding freedom of expression. However, this unified category, as I shall explain, eventually proves symbolic as it fractures at different levels to include religious conflicts, sectarian violence, ideological division and gender hierarchies, the element on which I will predominantly focus.

In its predominantly humorous tone, Prince's account chronicles a historically significant moment by constituting a part of Egypt's 'history of recent years, as represented by jokes' (Prince 2014: 9). Clearly, humour is not a new or a scarce form of expression in Egypt as the country 'continues to be recognized as the center of satire and political humour in the Arab world' (Kishtainy 2009: 54). Across the region, the Egyptian is known to be *damū khafīf* (literally, having light blood) and *ibn nuktah* (son of a joke) which denote their great sense of humour. A socio-linguistic study conducted in 2010 investigating a possible 'Arab humour' category indicates that, in general, Egyptians are regarded as 'the funniest Arabs in the whole Arab world' (Kammoun 2010: 257). This regional appeal of Egyptian humour can be mainly attributed to the prevalence, and in effect dominance, of Egyptian comedy on cinema and television industries across the Arab world, and hence, the high level of its appeal and familiarity to people across the region. Also, this can be related to the long-embedded tradition of sociopolitical humour in Egypt since the time of Pharaohs (Houlihan 2001). It can equally be attributed to the flexibility of Egyptian colloquial Arabic (*'amiyyah*) which gives way to the creation of variant forms of irony, parody, wit and sarcasm that rely on a myriad of intertextual and paratextual constructs to creatively capture the sociopolitical reality of the country (see Salem and Taira 2012).[25] However, Egyptian humour became particularly visible during the revolution of 2011 as a publicly claimed form of resistance, which persisted despite the antithetical surrounding violent circumstances.

The use of humour to communicate and address authority was instrumental in setting the Egyptian revolution in a carnivalesque mood of dissidence. Certainly, humour was not the direct factor that toppled Mubarak, but it played a crucial role in directing the demonstrations towards such a symbolically triumphant end. Prince portrays different strategies of revolutionary resistance that are predominantly humorous. For instance, some demonstrators wave red cards to announce the exclusion of Mubarak from the political 'game'; they hold school-grade panels in which Mubarak fails all the subjects including 'health services, education, industry, agriculture, commerce' (Prince 2014: 175); they use satire to reverse nationalist anthems and political poetry; and they draw offensive and grotesque political caricatures and graffiti. This myriad of comedic forms of expression is what Miriam Cooke, in a different context, calls 'crafting insults'; it entails the construction of artistic, creative discourses of offending authority which signals 'the first step in the revolutions to come . . . [because] the politics of fear [i]s transformed into a politics of insult' (2017: 42, 39). Unlike Amiry's use of humour discussed in the previous section, which is more tactical and contingent upon existing incongruities in Palestinian life under occupation, revolutionary humour in Prince's is rather 'crafted'. The plots of jokes, chants, banners and other comedic forms of dissidence are predominantly creative, improvised, imaginative, expandable and generative. For instance, banners read:

'Leave, My Arm is Aching'
'Leave, My Wife Wants to Give Birth'
'ctrl+alt+delete-Mubarak'

. . .
'Leave, I Want to Shower'
'We also want to shave' (Prince 2014: 143)

While laying the ground for the revolution, political humour was used to enforce the people's sense of entitlement to the uprising. In an opening section entitled 'A Necessary Introduction', Prince provides the backdrop of the uprising by describing the way 'we were flooded with jokes' (2014: 2). Prior to the revolution, humour was used as a tool for allaying fear and anxiety. For instance, jokes on self-immolation protests in Egypt (mainly inspired by the suicide of Tunisian street vendor Mohammed Bouazizi which triggered the Tunisian revolution in December 2010) were prevalent. Egyptians joked: 'stop setting yourselves on fire, guys; there will be no one left when the revolution begins' (ibid.: 2). Pre-revolution humour was also used to highlight the problems of everyday life under dictatorship and, therefore, to demonstrate the urgency for a popularly led political change. Jokes exposing the corruption of the regime, its manipulative dynamics, and the way the normalisation of subordination is embedded in its rule circulated widely.[26]

Similarly, during the revolution, humour was used as a form of reassurance and 'comic relief'. The protestors were eager to keep each other updated joke-wise as a way to dislocate their anxious anticipations and fear. The interplay between laughter and anxiety can be observed throughout the narrative; 'despite the injuries and the visible pain on people's faces, they were still . . . telling jokes' (Prince 2014: 135). The life-threatening violence of the regime is met with ambivalent laughter. For example, displaying the ammunition with which they are attacked, the protestors comment: '"the sons of bitches are attacking us with expired weapons!" "They don't think we're worth new canisters. Shame on the Ministry of Interior! They are doing it on the cheap!"' (ibid.: 61). This laughter is ambivalent because it arises from the fear and oppression on which the regime capitalises but at the same time challenges it by 'turning injustice and victimhood into laughable absurdity' (Cooke 2017: 51). Surrounded by death and violence, humour becomes a sign of agency, of life and (re)birth as 'the ability to laugh at the tyrant and his henchmen helps to repair the brokenness of fearful people, once bowed over in subjection' (ibid.: 51). It also highlights the role of laughter in enforcing and mobilising public dissidence movements and in bringing people together.[27]

Egyptian revolutionary humour nurtured the protester's sense of collectivity. Laughter brought the revolutionists together by virtue of their shared experiences of tyranny and common targets of humour. This created a form of solidarity, or what Bergson in his *Laughter* (*Le Rire*, 1900) describes as a 'freemasonry, or even complicity' (2005: 3). To announce their disobedience, protesters bravely, publicly, boldly and sometimes aggressively poked various jokes whose major 'butt' is the dictator, Mubarak. The sacrosanct figure of the leader is intentionally and publicly degraded through jokes that addressed three major themes: the totalitarianism of his regime, his lack of sense and judgement and the corruption of his family. As Gilbert rightly argues, 'one aspect of shared humour among marginalized groups is its tendency to unmask the unabashed hypocrisy of the dominant culture' (2004: 30). Collective Egyptian humour became a means to offend the regime, scrutinise it and expose its hypocrisy. While Mubarak showed reluctance to relinquish his position, revolutionary humour intensified and became more subtle and, as it were, aggressive. People started to poke fun at him by questioning his intellect and comprehension using more comedically explicit tone, such as: 'leave means go! In case you didn't know' (Prince 2014: 136).

In the Arab region, 'where a ruler's glorification and divinization by nationalist discourse has been so omnipresent, subverting and mocking the tyrant's hubris has offered rich – albeit dangerous – grounds for carnivalesque attacks' (Damir-Geilsdorf and Milich 2020: 25). Mikhail Bakhtin's understanding of the carnivalesque can, in fact, help us understand the sociopolitical function of Tahrir's festivity and revolutionary humour, as portrayed by Prince. Investigating the practices of the carnival in Medieval Europe and its later manifestations in (post)Renaissance literature, Bakhtin defines the carnival festival as a temporary interruption of norms during which rules are suspended, 'the official life' is reversed and people inhabit 'a second world and a second life outside officialdom' (1984b: 6). This 'second life' constitutes a space in which the incongruous is not only amusing but goes unquestioned. During a carnival, Bakhtin tells us, 'all hierarchical ranks, privileges, norms, and prohibitions' are suspended, and power norms and roles are reversed, all within a frame of entertainment (ibid.: 10). Bakhtin foregrounds the element of 'active participation' as defining of the carnival because the event 'is not a spectacle seen by people; they live in it' (ibid.: 7). The carnival involves a symbolic process of comic crowning and uncrowning in which the ruler becomes the ruled, the slave becomes the master and the crown goes from one person to another (ibid.: 11). This is particularly relevant to postcolonial humour which works towards reversing normative power order on which uneven relations between the ruler and the ruled, the occupier and the occupied and/or the margin and the centre are based. However, while the carnival enacts a reminder that power structures are mobile and can be suspended, it nonetheless implies the temporary and symbolic nature of such suspension. What I consider to be particularly relevant to the analysis of Prince's narrative is Bakhtin's views on the purpose of festive laughter, which Egyptian revolutionary humour stimulates: it is 'not an individual reaction to some isolated "comic" event [but] is the laughter of all people' (1984b: 11). This laughter is ambivalent; 'it is gay, triumphant, and at the same time mocking, deriding. It asserts and denies, buries and revives' (ibid.: 11–12). Carnivalesque laughter subverts norms, bridges social differences, challenges sociopolitical hierarchies and provides (collective) comic relief.

Humour and laughter were indeed the main emerging carnivalesque means of dissent and criticism during the Egyptian revolution. Traditionally, humour is 'inextricably linked to carnival' (Gilbert 2004: 59). It is a 'frank and free' type of communication within the marketplace (Bakhtin 1984b: 10); it denotes 'celebration of fertility and regeneration; [and] vulgar and exaggerated presentation of the familiar' (Barreca 1988: 8). Like the carnival, revolutionary humour in Egypt tests taboos through voicing what the 'official life' deems inappropriate and offensive. During the Egyptian uprising, the major functions of postcolonial humour intersect. Humour provides the protestors with a sense of reason that enforces their revolutionary movement. It also acts as a relief outlet for their accumulated anger, oppression and injustice. Simultaneously, it asserts the democratically guaranteed superiority of the people over the regime while it exposes the incongruity of its hegemonic rule.

However, the revolutionary intent behind the carnivalesque mood of the uprising, as presented in Prince's text, bypasses the playfulness of medieval festivals. It transcends the symbolic nature of Bakhtin's traditional carnival in which the actors are conscious of the impermanent revision of power norms.

The long-term, subversive intention of Egyptian revolutionary humour contrasts with the temporary and non-official functionality of carnivalesque laughter. It is directed towards realising an actual political change rather than entertaining an illusion of it – despite the disappointing long-term outcomes of these revolutionary intentions as I explain further below. Moreover, while Bakhtin's carnival necessitates 'active participation', it implicitly dismisses the situated subjectivity of the actors and their power to destabilise existing norms. As Alastair Renfrew explains, 'carnival existed not as a form of agency, but as a reminder that agency was possible' (2015: 135). The sense of freedom gained during a traditional carnival remains repressed, periodically manifested in a pre-decided time and space, expelled from the realm of seriousness and, hence, tolerated by the authorities as a safety valve. Conversely, Egyptian revolutionary carnival blurs the boundaries between the comedic and the serious, anxiety and relief, and peaceful resilience and violent oppression. Although characterised by a predominantly comedic, festive mood, the revolution aspired towards and achieved an immediate outcome by deposing a power-abusing president. Hence, it detaches itself from the restricted agency and popular symbolic intentions inherent in the traditional carnival.

Due to its prevalent festive mood, Prince describes the revolution as being 'transformed into a *moulid*, a carnival' (2014: 174).[28] *Mūlid* or *mawlid*, in colloquial and standard Arabic(s) respectively, literally translates as birth; it denotes an annual religious feast which celebrates the birth of a saint or a prophet and involves various performative rituals. While Prince equates *mūlid* with the carnival, they are not culturally equivalent. *Mūlid* is a religious celebration that capitalises on the spiritual and sacred significance of the feast whereas conventional carnivals are free 'from all religious and ecclesiastic dogmatism, from all mysticism and piety' (Bakhtin 1984b: 7). However, many affinities can be drawn between the two events. Both are annual celebrations which involve collective performances and festive ritual; both are unmonitored and unchallenged as they are devoid of rules, permanency and officiality. Like the carnival, *mūlid* is 'not only an occasion for gaiety and laughter, but also one in which there is a suspension of hierarchical boundaries and roles ... even mockery of those in high places is permitted' (Lutfi 2006: 84). Moreover, similar to the medieval carnival, *mūlid* is a liberating experience that celebrates 'renewal and a new birth' (Bakhtin 1984b: 57) which gestures towards collective mirth and social rejuvenation. In their semiotic reading of the Egyptian revolution, Sahar Keraitim and Samia Mehrez suggest that the celebratory spirit of the uprising is enforced by the protesters' familiarity with the *mūlid* festival which helps 'to nurture and maintain the utopian space that they gradually constructed in the *midan*' (2012: 31). Similarly, Ziad Elmarsafy links the uprising to the literal term of the religious festival by suggesting that 'unlike regular *mulids*, [the Egyptian revolution] really does mark the birth of something new as opposed to the birth of someone who lived in the past . . . [the revolutionaries] become Egyptian selves they didn't quite know until then' (2015: 135).[29]

Certainly, the *mūlid*-like festivity was crucial in familiarising the people with Tahrir Square as a space of free expression while sustaining the protesters' aspirations to celebrate the end of the revolution with a new triumphant beginning, a (re)birth of a democratic nation. Equally, the spiritual aspect of the *mūlid* encouraged a collective faith in a miraculous possibility for a political change that might have seemed far-fetched, beyond the power of the oppressed and dependent on the intervention of the supernatural. Performative patterns that are inspired from the *mūlid* can be observed in Prince's account. For instance, when Mubarak continues to ignore the demands of the revolutionists, one protester suggests: 'Mubarak will not leave until we have a zaar [exorcism] to dispel him . . . he's like a demon that will only leave if we get the blue jinn to drive him out' (Prince 2014: 174). The need for a ritual to exorcise evil spirits is sarcastically evoked yet politicised and collectively performed; men and women sway their bodies in circles while chanting 'leave' and 'go, go'. These *mūlid*-inspired practices are embedded in the collective Egyptian experience. Adopting them in a revolutionary context helps people to claim a sense of cultural unity despite social differences while denoting the persistence of peaceful means of resistance. Equally, drawing on folklore and cultural heritage to organise a resistance movement enabled the creation of what Bakhtin terms 'ritual spectacles' (1984b: 5) within Tahrir Square as opposed to the violence with which the regime responds. It also suggests the revolutionists' determination to overthrow the political regime by exhausting all of their nonviolent means of dissidence, even the metaphysically inspired ones.

It is important to highlight the significance of the spatial setting around which the carnivalesque atmosphere of the Egyptian revolution revolves. The

2011 uprising, as mediated by Prince, is mainly centred around and enforced by Tahrir Square (*Mīdān al-Taḥrīr*) as a politically claimed civic space of revolutionary action. While the Arabic term *taḥrīr* means liberation,[30] *mīdān* describes an urban space, usually a square, in the centre of a city that is open to all. *Mīdān al-Taḥrīr* in central Cairo, established in 1860 by Egypt's ruler Khedive Ismail, is a circle-shaped agora which is the meeting point of major military, political and cultural institutions in Egypt and is a symbol of civic engagement and revolutionary participation since the 1972 student's protests (Soueif 2014: 7–9). While Tahrir Square in central Cairo is presented in Prince's narrative as the locus of the revolution, it is by no means the only space for revolutionary protests as similar demonstrations took place in different public spaces across the country. The importance of the public square in the carnivalesque act is stressed by Bakhtin: 'carnival knows neither stage nor footlights. But the central area could only be the square' because it allows for a 'communal performance' (1984a: 128–9). Just like the carnivalesque agora, Tahrir Square becomes a symbol of 'communal performance' of dissidence in its joyful and comedic forms. Being 'open to all', it challenges differences and brings together people who 'in life are separated by impenetrable [social] hierarchical barriers' (Bakhtin 1984a: 123). Due to the egalitarian atmosphere that this space inspires, Prince refers to the revolutionists as 'strangers who were no longer strangers' as the Egyptians of the *mīdān* become, as they chanted, 'one-hand' (2014: 104). She describes the festivity as a rejuvenation of a (new-found) collective national belonging, a literal (re)birth (*mūlid*): 'we had all become Egyptians again, real Egyptians' (2014: 91).

It is the peculiarities of *Mīdān al-Taḥrīr* which enforce the collective complicity of humour. Being the locus of civic legitimacy, as the chant went '*el-sharʿiyyah mnel-Taḥrīr*' (legitimacy comes from Tahrir), the *mīdān* provides a public space of expression that is relatively free, unrestrictive and uncensored as it broke away from the regime's restrictions on freedom of speech. As a collectively claimed space with its own laws of belonging/being, the *mīdān* generates 'a new type of communication' and 'new forms of speech' that are 'impossible in everyday life' (Bakhtin 1984b: 16). It allows the expansion of the boundaries of freedom through comedically and publicly voicing, in the Freudian understanding, a previously silenced truth. The square enables political jokes to migrate from the realm of secrecy and privacy to the public sphere facilitated mainly by international media coverage and social media platforms. Consequently, being collectively adapted and fluidly transmitted, humour becomes mercurial and hence uncontrollable and untraceable as it is impossible to trace back to or attribute to an individual or a small group. Laughter becomes a medium of collectively moving beyond a category of the unspeakable that is politically constructed and normalised through fear and intimidation. Judith Herman describes the unspeakable as 'certain violations of the social [and political] compact that are too [dangerous and] terrible to utter aloud' (2015: 1). The political compact set by Mubarak's regime entails a (public) glorification of the figure of the ruler to whom ultimate obedience is unnegotiable. It is through the intersection of public, collective, degrading humour and revolution that this oppressive and monolithically set compact is dismantled and violated.

As a revolutionary setting, Tahrir Square enhances the collective comedic resilience; it also constitutes a spatial dynamic for national inclusion and exclusion. *Taḥrīr* represents a symbolic space of resistance because, similar to the carnivalesque square, it is subjected to 'the laws of its own freedom' (Bakhtin 1984b: 7). The *mīdān* becomes synecdochically 'the house of the nation' where 'the ultimately irrepressible desires of the Egyptian people' are joyfully revealed, manifested and celebrated (Moore 2018: 30). Being a collectively claimed space of revolutionary action – as Prince gloriously declares 'now, the midan is ours' (2014: 27) – Tahrir Square alienates and challenges the regime 'whose very authority is based on spatial policing and regulatory controls aimed at dispersing crowd movement and spatial negotiability' (Mehta 2014: 231–2). Moreover, it gradually becomes a feminist arena within which women's claims to public spaces are enacted. When Prince claims in her title that *Revolution is My Name*, she perhaps suggests a (re)new(ed) womanly subjectivity triggered by her presence in the *mīdān*, which also gestures towards the notion of national rejuvenation and rebirth (*mūlid*). Prince relinquishes her pre-uprising identity and adopts one that is born in and nurtured within the *mīdān* which 'had become my home' (2014: 173); an identity in which the lines between fear and persistence, anxiety and joyfulness, a revolution and a festival, and a woman writer and active revolutionary are blurred.

As I mentioned earlier, revolutionary humour is integrated into Prince's account in a variety of forms. While satire and political jokes can generally be read in the light of Bakhtin's notion, it is specifically the way Prince reports Mubarak's speeches that interestingly reflects the subversive role of the carnivalesque. During the revolution, Mubarak infamously delivers three televised speeches in a desperate attempt to contain the people's anger and stifle the protests. In her diary, Prince reports these speeches, as she witnesses them, in a comedic dialogical style. Each of the president' statements is mocked by the protestors. For instance:

> *Fellow citizens . . . This is a nation of institutions governed by a constitution and by the force of law.*
> 'Of course! The constitution you tailored to fit you and your sons.'
> . . .
> *I have taken the initiative of forming a new government . . .*
> 'A new government that brings together all the thieves and criminals!'
> . . .
> *I am a military man and would never betray what I have been entrusted with nor would I abandon my sense of duty and responsibility.*
> 'Come on, man, get on with it. Don't come begging for pity now.'
> 'Indeed! You've been glued to that chair for thirty years and you want to pass it on to your lovely son.'
> *. . . I will use the remaining months of my term to ensure a peaceful transition of power . . .*
> 'What are you talking about? You still want to stay on longer?'
> 'Leave!' (Prince 2014: 70, 115)

The agential circumstances of the revolution permit the creation of a dialogic discourse that brings together the voices of the oppressor and the oppressed, which would be prohibited, even dangerous, during the 'official life'. This conversational response is an unconventional attempt to engage with official statements in order to challenge the monolithic, patronising and exclusory nature of political speeches. It aims at interrogating and questioning the real intentions behind Mubarak's discourse through mockery while daring to 'speak truth to power'. It simultaneously signals the public's growing political agency and awareness of the hypocrisy and corruption of the regime. This multi-voiced aspect of the diary attenuates existing hierarchies and confirms the inclusive category of *al-shaʻb*, to which Prince claims to belong.

The importance of engaging with official political discourses to turn life 'upside-down' à la carnivalesque can be further demonstrated in the way the revolutionaries, as repeated by Prince, parody Mubarak's speeches. Bakhtin regards parody, what he also terms 'comic verbal compositions' (1984b: 5), as 'double-voicing' through which the speaker creates a parallel, dialogic discourse that mocks its original (1984a: 189). The protestors create and circulate a humorous video clip of 'Mubarak giving one of his previous speeches' which they call 'Mubarak's Real Speech' by changing his statements to its antithetical meaning:

> *In the Name of God, the Beneficent and the Merciful: Citizens of Egypt. As president of the republic, I have repeatedly stressed and will continue to stress my right to practice corruption . . . and my right to rob public property and to incite violence and destruction . . . as well as to foster unemployment and poverty. I work towards fulfilling these goals every day of my life . . . Once more, I repeat that I will be firm about all necessary decisions to ensure more fear, unemployment, and general setbacks. This is the responsibility I have been sworn to as a president. May God protect you all.* (Prince 2014: 155–6)

This parodic speech provides a counterpoint to the president's statement and aims at ridiculing his claims of social, political and economic reforms. It not only 'regenerates ambivalence' (Bakhtin 1984b: 21) by creating voices which are 'isolated from one another' and 'hostilely opposed' (1984a: 193). In doing so, it also deprives the speech of its political rhetoric and linguistic embellishment and hence challenges its authority and potential impact. This primarily operates to expose the disparity between the political rhetoric of the regime and its actions. Through twisting official political statements, the revolutionists provide a sociopolitical critique of the hypocritical and autocratic dynamics of Mubarak's regime. They unveil the possible intentions behind the ruler's words whose authority is then appropriated by enabling the oppressed to claim the voice of the oppressor.

As I have explained, collective humour as both repeated and actively deployed in Prince's diary is generally directed towards the hegemonic figure of Mubarak and his regime. However, as we also see in Amiry's text, Prince's targets of humour extend beyond political leaders. Prince deploys humour as a form of resistance to patriarchal norms in an attempt to dislocate and reverse gender roles and to shed light on gender issues as pivotal to the aspirations of the revolution. Comedy by women tends to draw attention to the stereotypical gendered frames within which they are often positioned. It is often a conscious strategy used 'to reflect the absurdity of dominant ideology while undermining the very basis for its discourse' (Barreca 1988: 19). For women who are excluded from the centre of power, socially and politically, 'humour attack[s] the primary norms traditionally attacked only during liminal (festive/carnival) occasions' (Gilbert 2004: 28). For instance, Prince joins citizens' checkpoints at the entrance of the *mīdān* to help check the demonstrators for security purposes. She then 'jokingly' grabs a young man while addressing him: 'finally, I get a chance to feel you up!' While he becomes 'shocked and trie[s] to protect his body', Prince declares: 'it suddenly dawned on me that I finally had the chance to harass the men and to show them how it felt when they harassed us' (2014: 105). Prince seizes the carnivalesque circumstances of the uprising to reverse the 'male gaze', which is reminiscent of Amiry's comedic staring incident discussed earlier in the chapter.

Throughout the narrative, Prince pokes fun at normative gender relations in Egypt not only to stir conversations among the revolutionaries but also as a reminder that 'the forging of alternative gender norms is integral to resisting [political] authoritarianism' (El Said *et al.* 2015: 9). On many occasions, Prince comedically, and flirtingly, harasses men and makes them uncomfortable: 'may I make a pass at you? You're really cute!', she tells an intimidated army man at Tahrir (2014: 69). In her attempt to reverse gender norms, Prince reproduces these norms instead of dismissing them, aiming to shift the standpoints of gender-assault experiences whose victims are almost exclusively women. While Prince's attempts at gender-roles subversion are enacted humorously, they permit her to shift the social perspectives regarding the dominant patriarchal culture. Equally, this humorous attempt at role subversion perhaps aims at allowing (re)new(ed) conceptions of gender paradigms and identities to emerge. Prince uses humour as an attempt to enact women's demands that are likely to be dismissed and deprioritised in favour of national interests. It becomes evident that, in Barreca's formulation, 'comedy permits, and prepares women for rebellion' that ideally exceeds the revolutionary moment (1994: 25).

Prince's humour reflects the ambivalence of gender relations during the 2011 Egyptian revolution. While the non-violent, carnivalesque resistance entailed an immediate political outcome and nurtured a utopian, egalitarian vision of the nation, Prince's diary eventually signals the fracture between permanent intentions and symbolic outcomes of the uprising; it anticipates the short-term success of the revolution, mainly in relation to gender issues. The egalitarian vision promoted by the carnivalesque resistance was eventually a liminal phase that failed to maintain permanency beyond the square, particularly regarding the creation of a homogenous nation that is able to transcend gender hierarchies.

On the one hand, the inclusive carnivalesque circumstances seem hostile to social hierarchies, particularly gender barriers. Men and women conquered the streets calling for social and economic justice. They were brought together by the euphoria of freedom, a collective quest for democracy, a common enemy and a shared utopian vision of a post-revolutionary nation. They became, as they chanted, 'one hand' as gender roles were – hindsight superficially – blurred. Mixed-gender dancing, for instance, which would be in normal circumstances unconventional, was not only tolerated during the revolution but also encouraged, giving the impression of a gender-equal atmosphere: '[women] joined the circle [of dancing], so the young men got more excited about dancing and so did we' (Prince 2014: 107).[31] On the other hand, women were caught between being simultaneously accepted and denied in the square as a public sphere, and between the collective claims for national freedom and democracy and their feminist claims for gender equality, which arguably reflects their ambivalent status in contemporary Egypt.

While the *mīdān* nurtured and promoted a sense of national unity, it simultaneously neglected serious social barriers embedded in the collective, cultural consciousness which require more than a carnivalesque revolution to be dismantled. Prince in this account stresses and celebrates feelings of national collectiveness across the revolutionaries, but at the same time, and perhaps unintentionally, relinquishes them in relation to gender. While she claims that 'there is no difference between us' (2014: 139), a gender-based difference between the protestors emerges as her narrative signals a crisis in this revolutionary sense of equality. While in post-revolutionary Egypt the prioritisation of masculine concerns proved triumphant over revolutionary claims of equality,[32] this gender imbalance had been present even during the supposedly inclusive uprising. *Revolution is My Name* reveals the limits of the carnivalesque uprising as its subversive efforts fail to extend to or entrench gender equality. This particularly emerges in the form of sexual assaults to which the narrator and other women protestors are subjected. Prince is estranged from the ostensibly 'real Egyptians' whose 'one hand' is ultimately divided when a civilian gropes her breast (Prince 2014: 91, 95). She also refers to various cases of sexual violence exercised on women outside and on the fringes of the square – by regime thugs, police, some protesters and civilians alike – where 'the enemy [are] my own compatriots' (ibid.: 131). However, Prince's estrangement, as I see it, remains implicit and often overshadowed by the euphoric, historical moment of the revolution.

The ambivalence of gender relations is symptomatic of the temporary nature of the carnivalesque revolution which eventually fails to sustain a breakage with gendered hierarchies. The carnivalesque mood of the revolution allows Prince to mockingly reverse gender relations, but this does not negate that this disruption of normative roles remains symbolic. The integration of women in the uprising scene was a liminal phase that is based on male-constructed, conditioned rules. It was governed by power discourses that were (re)producing, and often using women as the gatekeepers of, patriarchal norms. In one instance, when Prince furiously attempts to defend a male protestor who is being beaten by State Security thugs, a fellow female revolutionist comments on her behaviour: 'no manners! . . . This is between men. Women should stay out of it' (2014: 37). While this stance proves that women participants in the revolution are not a homogenous group, an element which the revolutionary demands have perhaps failed to identify (Mazloum 2015: 218), it also dismisses the very call for gendered equality by distinguishing men's 'matters' from women's.

Carnivalesque resistance enabled new conceptualisations of a possible egalitarian community; one that stressed the interconnectedness of the Egyptians' experiences under a common hegemonic rule. It also succeeded in achieving an immediate political outcome by ousting President Mubarak from office. Although Prince's humorous diary reconfigures the festive revolutionary spirit of 2011 and renews it, it also signals the unfinalisability of the sociopolitical norm-subversion to which the carnival-like uprising aspired. As in the medieval carnival, norms during the Egyptian revolution were broken only to be (re)embraced, and perhaps 'actively enforced', to use a Bakhtinian term. Arguably, the revolution failed in constructing the ideal vision of Egypt which was embodied in Tahrir Square. An inclusive Egyptian nation beyond the 2011 Tahrir Square is yet to be created. A decade later, the claims of the 2011 uprising ultimately proved to require a long-term revolutionary process in which the carnivalesque uprising is, perhaps, a symbolic first stage. Specifically, patriarchy and sexual violence against women became publicly conspicuous in post-revolutionary Egypt as a reaction to the growing visibility of women in public spaces (Hafez 2014; El Said *et al.* 2015; Allam 2018). Prince herself has suffered from gender-based bigotry and restrictions on freedom of expression. In 2013, she was temporarily suspended from her teaching position at Suez University after accusations of religious disdain regarding her openly liberal opinions during lectures. In 2017, a disciplinary procedure and legal charges were also conducted against her by the university's administration for posting a belly dancing video and bikini photos of herself on her personal Facebook account, which the university regarded as intolerable considering Prince's professional status and the reputation of the institution to which she is affiliated.[33]

Women's public presence proved threatening to a patriarchal culture that is embedded and exercised within a triangular paradigm, or what Mona Eltahawi describes as the trifecta of misogyny: the state, the street and the home (2015: 32). While the hegemony of the state was contested during the revolution, the other two patriarchal spheres continue(d) to operate unchallenged. Womanly presence in the *mīdān* has been considered an act of spatial transgression that needs to be contained. Sexual violence became 'a war tactic used by the counter-revolution to deny women their rightful access to public space by circumscribing their freedom of movement' and therefore 'their access to free expression' (Mehta: 2014: 46). It is perhaps in response to these enduring realities that Prince appropriates the feminine Arabic term for revolution, *thawrah*,[34] and defiantly asserts *'Ismī Thawrah'* (*'Revolution is My Name'*) as an act of resilience against these attempts to estrange women and distance them from public revolutionary spaces. Equally, she claims revolutionary Tahrir as a dwelling civic space of (her) womanly national engagement and visibility and her newfound revolutionary identity: 'the midan was mine . . . [it] had become my home' (2014: 27, 173).

As this chapter demonstrated, the use of humour during politically fraught contexts as a strategic, revolutionary means of dissidence can, in fact, disturb the authority of the discourses it targets. It also revises conventional ways in which we understand normative structures of power. However, humour does not instantly resolve or practically change sociopolitical realities. Amiry's and Prince's use of humour against the intersectional structure of power to which they are subjected proves limited in the short term. The consistent funniness of Amiry's text is ambivalent as it simultaneously reflects the continuous 'tragicomedy' of the Palestinian predicament (Amiry 2006: 81). Similarly, the carnivalesque mood of Prince's text is disrupted when the author is alienated from the 'real Egyptians' when she is sexually harassed by a fellow civilian; the sense of solidarity engendered by the 'laughing revolution' fractures within the narrative primarily due to gender-based violence. Since the military coup of 2013 in Egypt, restrictions on freedom of speech and political protest are ever tightening – including a large wave of arrests of regime opponents. Humour in Egypt has become, generally, a means to express disenchantment and despair in the light of life under military dictatorship. While political humour continues to act as a form of critique, it has been largely and arguably transformed from 'a self-confident, defiant, and rebellious tone into a more defensively oriented device to express the disgrace and outrage about the failure of the revolutions' (Damir-Geilsdorf and Milich 2020: 34).

Unlike violent and physical means of resistance, it is difficult 'to gauge the exact effect of humour on the social and political changes of any country or the overthrow of tyranny' (Kishtainy 2009: 54). However, humour, as used and mediated by Amiry and Prince, arguably constitutes a part of a long-term dissident process. It degrades the powers which both subjects ridicule for a period that ideally exceeds the moment of laughter. While the carnival is a momentary subversion of roles, the subversive intentions of postcolonial/women's humour extend in duration 'as once [a dominant discourse] has been degraded through laughter it somehow loses its semblance of power' (Ilott 2015: 137). Being enacted and communicated through publication, the comedic resilience of Amiry and Prince problematises norms in the long term, potentially leading to a post-laughter sense of unsettlement and contemplation of possible norm revisions. Their accounts maintain and extend the duration of laughter to constitute a part of a textual archive of dissidence. Their texts act as a reminder of the ludicrousness of power hierarchies and gender-based otherness which they ridicule. Choosing to deal with, and write, revolutionary moments in a comedic manner, both authors rework conventional literary forms of resistance. By laughing in contexts where they are expected to weep, Amiry and Prince challenge the readers' understanding of, and expectations from, autobiographical accounts from war zones and national struggles; they move elegantly and tactically beyond the traditional representational frames of war-writing by gesturing towards a literary category of 'revolutionary humour' in which comedy needs to be taken seriously.

As I argue throughout the chapter, humour can be used as an intentional strategic medium for manifesting and expressing dissent. It constitutes a revolutionary tactic that reflects what Caroline Rooney describes as an 'alternative form of consciousness' that is enacted by the people 'as solidarity, as resoluteness, as genuine *comradeship*, as collective consciousness, as revolutionary faith and [as] festiveness' (2015: 52). The strategic role of humour and laughter during revolutionary moments can also be examined during the recent Algerian protests against the regime, which started on 22 February 2019 against President Abdelaziz Bouteflika's bid for a fifth term. This pro-democratic movement (*ḥirāk*), which pressured Bouteflika to resign in April of the same year, was popularly termed 'The Revolution of Smiles' (*thawrat al-ibtisāmah*). Predominantly peaceful (*silmiyyah*), it was characterised by the dominance of political humour in different cultural forms as a strategy of manifesting dissent.[35] This highlights the role of humour as a revolutionary discourse and its relationship to dynamics of power and democracy in the contemporary Arab region, which deserve more critical attention.

Finally, it is important to note the crucial role that social media has played in enabling the circulation of revolutionary humour as a non-violent discourse of resistance. For instance, in a similar manner to the recent Algerian protests in which the Internet contributed to the creation of a national narrative of dissent, the Egyptian uprising highlighted the crucial role of social media in channelling and enhancing the people's laughter for dignity and their resistance against dictatorship. For instance, one particular joke from Prince's narrative reads:

> When Mubarak went to heaven he met Sadat and Abdel Nasser. They both wanted to know how he came to join them. So they asked him, 'Assassination like Sadat or poison like Nasser'? He lowered his head and said, 'No, Facebook'. (2014: 92)

The power and efficiency of digital and social media as emerging tools for popular resistance particularly, but not exclusively, during the Arab uprisings as used by women will be the central concern of the following chapter.

Notes

1. An earlier and shorter version of this chapter has been published in *Comedy Studies* journal under the title 'Comedic Resilience: Arab Women's Diaries of National Struggles and Dissident Humour' (10:2, pp. 183–98) (see Cheurfa 2019a).
2. While humour and comedy are often used synonymously, as I do in this chapter (as in Gilbert 2004 and Ilott 2015), the term comedy can be specifically used to describe performances – including, for example, plays, movies, sit-coms and stand-up shows – that are funny and mainly directed towards the amusement of an audience. Thus, comedy could be described as a performed humour, or humour in practice. In its literary sense, the meaning of the term comedy is extended to describe fictional narratives (Abrams 1990: 38).
3. In *The Location of Culture*, Homi Bhabha examines the notion of mimicry, which he defines as 'the sign of a double articulation' that aims to appropriate 'the [desired] Other as it visualizes power' and to represent 'a difference that is itself a process of disavowal' (2004: 122). According to Bhabha, mimicry is liable to be both a sign of admiration (and imitation) as well as of mockery, distortion and ridicule which enables the colonial subject to shift the power balance between coloniser and colonised; he writes that 'mimicry is at once resemblance and menace . . . [to] both "normalized" knowledges and disciplinary powers' (ibid.: 123).
4. Popularised by Thomas Hobbes in the mid-seventeenth century, superiority theory stresses the power of humour to exclude through creating a hierarchical division based on otherness. Hobbes perceives laughter as a 'sudden glory' that results from 'the apprehension of some deformed thing in another, by comparison whereof they suddenly applaud themselves' (1991: 43).

5   This is the view of the incongruity theory of humour. According to this theory, laughter primarily 'comes with the apprehension of incongruity' (Carroll 2014: 19) as we generally laugh when we encounter situations that do not accord with what we consider to be proper, conventional and/or realistic. Such deviation, which may be invented or reflective of existing realities, comes to disturb and undermine our prior knowledge and common perception of the orderly world and hence results in a 'subversion of expectation' (ibid.: 17).

6   This is the view of the release theory of humour, also known as relief theory. It is based on psychoanalytical approaches to comedy which stress the cathartic function of humour as being 'purgation of accumulated emotions' (Carroll 2014: 38).

7   One of the few nuanced discussions on postcolonial humour is the essay collection *Cheeky Fictions: Laughter and the Postcolonial* (2005) in which the editors Susanne Reichl and Mark Stein highlight the modest engagement of postcolonial theory with humour studies. However, an emerging academic interest in postcolonial comedy can be observed in recent publications in the field, including the special issue of *Comedy Studies* (2018), edited by Helen Davies and Sarah Ilott which pays particular attention to issues of gender, sexuality, and the body in postcolonial, feminist and disability comedies (see Davies and Ilott 2018b). Equally, an edited collection within the same scope of interest by the aforementioned scholars, entitled *Comedy and the Politics of Representation: Mocking the Weak*, was published in 2018 (2018a).

8   The most recent, and one of the few, book-length scholarly discussion on Arab political humour is *Creative Resistance: Political Humour in the Arab Uprisings* (Damir-Geilsdorf and Milich 2020). it looks at forms, functions and dynamics of comedy as a form of non-violent resistance. Although broad in its media of expression (including art, rap music, TV shows, chants, political jokes and caricatures), this edited collection – like other prior discussions on Arab humour – overlooks literary expression and does not provide a rounded discussion on its different subgenres as a means of political comedy, especially from a feminist perspective.

9   For more details on the history and etymology of humour in Arabic traditions, see Mubeen 2008: 15–27 and Damir-Geilsdorf and Milich 2020: 15.

10 Prominent examples include Francophone Egyptian writer Albert Cossery's *The Jokers* (2010) (*La Violence et la derision*, 1964), Palestinian Emile Habibi's *The Secret Life of Said the Pessoptimist* (2001 [1974]), Iraqi-American writer Sinan Antoon's *I'jām: an Iraqi Rhapsody* (Diacritics) (2007 [2004]), Francophone

Algerian Faïza Guène's *Just Like Tomorrow* (2006), Egyptian Ghada Abdel 'Aal's memoir *'Āyza 'Atgaūwiz* (2009) (*I Want to Get Married!*, 2010), Egyptian Khaled Al-Khamissi's *Taxi* (2011) and Lebanese Fatima Sharafeddine's *The Servant* (2013), to name a few. The online magazine for international literature, *Words without Borders*, has dedicated a special issue to Arab Comedy (October 2019) entitled 'The Comic Edge: Arabic Humour'; the issue, edited by Marcia Lynx Qualey, comprises a wide range of contributions (in English and in translation) including fiction, non-fiction and poetry.

11 See, for instance, Damir-Geilsdorf and Milich 2020; Cooke 2017; Cheurfa 2019b.

12 See Fadwa Tuqan's *A Mountainous Journey: An Autobiography* (1990), Hanan Ashrawi's *This Side of Peace: A Personal Account* (1995), and Ghada Karmi's *In Search of Fatima: A Palestinian Story* (2002) and *Return: A Palestinian Memoir* (2015).

13 In a more recent autobiographical essay entitled 'An Obsession' (2012), Amiry also uses humour to represent everyday life and tackle issues of identity and belonging as a Palestinian woman living under Israeli occupation.

14 The absurd (not necessarily humorous) can be also observed in Jean Sadi Makdisi's *Beirut Fragments: A War Memoir* (1990) in which she, deploying irony and satire in some instances, recounts the horror of her experience during the Lebanese Civil War.

15 The IDF (Israeli Defence Forces) reoccupied Ramallah in 2002 and put it under curfew for around forty-two days; a period that is central to Amiry's account.

16 In her 'Can the Subaltern Speak?' (1988), Spivak criticises the elite nationalists from postcolonial societies who claim to provide collective and theoretic representation of the (socially and politically) disempowered. She stresses that the supposedly representative grand narratives of privileged nationalists tend to overlook embedded differences in the local struggles of particular subaltern groups (whom she regards as denied access to political and cultural representation) and hence risk essentialism. In their attempt to represent the subaltern, the elite, for Spivak, instead silence them by framing their voice and agency within a predetermined, unified and coherent structure of – political and aesthetic – representation.

17 See Chapter 3, note 23.

18 In her *Bodies that Matter* (1993), Butler extends her discussion of the problematics of agency in relation to gender performativity initially reiterated in her *Gender Trouble* (1990) in which she controversially asserts that 'performativity contests the very notion of the subject' (33). In *Bodies*, Butler does not resolve this ten-

sion; she asserts that agency and subversion remain relative and conditioned by discourses, and gender performativity, mainly parody such as drag, does not necessarily destabilise normative gender/sex relationships.
19. For a detailed discussion on feminism and the Palestinian national struggle, see Anna Ball 2012.
20. Arabic for steadfastness. Used specifically, but not exclusively, to describe the Palestinian resistance (see El Said et al. 2015: 13). *Ṣumūd* is a form of resilience which 'relies upon adaptation to difficulties of life under occupation, staying in the territories despite hardship, and asserting Palestinian culture and identity in response to Zionist claims' of legitimacy to the land (Ryan 2015: 299).
21. *Hajjeh* is an Arabic term that is also used to describe a Muslim woman who went to Mecca for pilgrimage.
22. This is particularly reminiscent of the almost mythical images of two female figures of the Palestinian resistance: Leila Khaled (b. 1944) and Ahed Tamimi (b. 2001), whose activism has been publicly perceived as the epitome of Palestinian anti-colonial struggle. Similar to Khaled who has been caught between idealisation and demonisation for what has become known as the 1969 hijacking, Tamimi, who was detained by Israeli authorities from December 2017 until July 2018 for slapping an Israeli soldier, has gained unprecedented public attention for what is controversially considered as her bravery in the face of Israeli occupation.
23. See, for instance, critical studies on Egyptian revolutionary humour in a variety of cultural forms: Egyptian revolutionary humour and social media in Mersal (2011); semantics and translations of revolutionary humour in Salem and Taira (2012); festiveness of the revolution in Rooney (2015); revolutionary satire in Abaza and Mehrez (2016); and political cartoons of the Egyptian revolution in Helmy and Frerichs (2017).
24. Nasser points out that 'Tahrir memoirs' as a literary category marks a continuation of a tradition of Egyptian women's accounts of revolutions and national struggles: Latifa al-Zayyat's *The Search: Personal Papers* (1996) (*Ḥamlat Taftīsh:'Awrāk Shakhsiyyah*, 1992) is a prominent example (see Nasser 2017: 131).
25. This is not exclusive to Egyptian colloquial Arabic but can be the case in different non-standard forms of Arabic that have no written forms and thus are flexible and not subjected to rigid semantic and syntactic rules.
26. See Prince 2014: 2, 3, 10.
27. The notion of 'laughtivism' has been used to describe the power of humour

as a strategy of nonviolent resistance, see, for instance, Majken Jul Sørensen's *Humour in Political Activism: Creative Nonviolent Resistance* (2016) and Srdja Popovic's *Blueprint for Revolution: How to Use Rice Pudding, Lego Men, and Other Nonviolent Techniques to Galvanize Communities, Overthrow Dictators, or Simply Change the World* (2015).

28 A similar remark is made by Soueif in her memoir (2014) in which she states: 'Tahrir was like carnival' (46).

29 Caroline Rooney, in 'Sufi Springs: Air on an Oud String' (2015), also elaborates on the role of the *mūlid* festival during the Egyptian revolution. Drawing from Sufi traditions, she considers *mūlid* a cultural form of collective consciousness, and a liberating gesture.

30 Initially named Isma'iliyyah Square after its founder Khedive Ismail.

31 Also, see Prince 2014: 28, 102–3, 118.

32 Post-revolutionary Arab nations have generally re-embraced the patriarchal status quo that is relatively suspended during national struggles. While the purpose behind women's participation in national struggles might have been primarily emancipation and gender equality, their feminist demands were often discarded as their engagement tended to be perceived within predominantly nationalist frames: Algeria and Egypt are good examples; see, for instance, Mounira M. Charrad's *States and Women's Rights: the Making of Postcolonial Tunisia, Algeria, and Morocco* (2001), Sherine Hafez's 'The Revolution Shall not Pass through Women's Bodies: Egypt, Uprising and Gender Politics' (2014) and Nermin Allam's *Women and the Egyptian Revolution: Engagement and Activism During the 2011 Arab Uprisings* (2018).

33 See Prince's interview in *The Guardian* newspaper, conducted by Ruth Michaelson and entitled 'The Dancing, Beer-Drinking Woman who would be Egypt's Next President' (Michaelson 2017).

34 The notion of *thawrah* (Arabic for revolution) has drawn academic attention since the outbreak of the Arab uprisings in 2010 (see, for instance, Achcar 2016). The distinction between *thawrah* as a radical 'individual and collective *overcoming*', and *thawrah* as 'purely political, ultimately superficial *overthrowing*' is particularly highlighted by Lindsey Moore, who states that in the Egyptian context 'revolutions have been frequent, yet never particularly emancipatory' (2018: 29).

35 See Hiyem Cheurfa's 'The Laughter of Dignity: Comedy and Dissent in the Algerian Popular Protests' (2019b).

5

Arab Women's Digital Life Writing: Resistance 2.0

In *Tunisian Girl, Bnayyah Tūnsiyyah: Blogueuse pour un printemps arabe* (Blogger for an Arab Spring) (2011), late Tunisian blogger, human rights activist and Nobel Peace Prize nominee (2011) Lina Ben Mhenni acknowledges the role of resistance writing during the Tunisian revolution of December 2010 that brought down the totalitarian regime of Zine el-Abidine Ben Ali. She specifically refers to 'the audacity of certain pens – uh ... or rather certain keyboards!' ('l'audace de certaines plumes – euh ... je dirais de certains claviers!') (2011: 26). Ben Mhenni recognises the role of social media platforms in enabling and organising popular resistance movements and in advocating for social justice and democracy in the region. In so doing, she particularly reflects on her own experience, not only as an activist but as a female life writer for whom the private and the public have become intertwined in the virtual realm. This shift from 'pens' to 'keyboards' is compelling not only in relation to the changing tools, channels and formats of Arab women's autobiographical practices but also in relation to the potential avenues of resistance that are enabled by these emergent mediums of self-expression. Considering that the focus of this book is on non-fictional literary modes of dissent by contemporary Arab women, it would be remiss not to address the way contemporary autobiographical discourses are influenced by the digital culture within which they are produced.

This final chapter looks at the radical shifts in the ways witness narratives are told, autobiographical voices are mediated, and dissent is expressed within the digital culture of the contemporary Arab world. More specifically, it examines the use of social media platforms by Arab women 'typing' in times of conflict and national struggles as emerging autobiographical sites for articulating resistance. These online platforms, I argue, mediate between the virtual/personal sphere of self-expression and the physical/public world of participation and activism. The chapter also demonstrates how online autobiographical narratives contest the traditions and elitist contours of conventional (print) life writing practices and thus highlight the genre's flexibility in terms of forms and media of expression. That is, it looks at the ways in which digital culture complicates the traditional conceptions and articulation of autobiographical discourses and encourages us to think differently about the axes of resistance created by women's life writing.

In the last section, this chapter examines more closely the relationship between sociopolitical activism and women's digital life writing in Tunisia. It looks at activist Lina Ben Mhenni's use of online spaces – prior to and during the Tunisian uprising – as a site for autobiographical expression and political engagement. The focus here is on Ben Mhenni's essay-length memoir *Tunisian Girl, Bnayyah Tūnsiyyah: Blogueuse pour un printemps arabe* (2011) which recounts her experience of digital dissidence and primarily draws from her active trilingual blog *A Tunisian Girl*. Both the memoir and blog are straightforwardly autobiographical, sociopolitically informed and overtly oppositional. Clearly, Ben Mhenni – who sadly passed away at thirty-six on January 2020 (from a stroke caused by autoimmune disease) – is not the only Arab/Tunisian female blogger who used the Web to defy censorship on freedom of expression and advocate for collective social justice during the recent Arab uprisings.[1] Ben Mhenni is a compelling case because her digital platform merges collective and political concerns with daily, personal and private matters, and hence explicitly positions itself as primarily a life writing space. Surprisingly, the international visibility that Ben Mhenni has gained in the wake of the Tunisian uprising, enhanced by her nomination for the Nobel Peace Prize on 2011, has not led to any critical engagement with her texts, which could be attributed to the ongoing debates about the literary value of blogging and digital writing.[2] It is the lack of academic materials which establish the link between Ben Mhenni's sociopolitical engagements through the Web (and on the ground) and her practices of digital life writing that motivate this chapter. Ben Mhenni's texts inspire us to rethink the binaries that have historically stimulated autobiographical criticism, particularly the private/public, individual/collective and personal/political, but in a revolutionary digital context. They also call for the examination of the influential role that digital life writing has played in fostering alternative means of storytelling that potentially empower Arab women's voices and engagement in sociopolitical discussion and national debates.

Throughout the chapter, I use the term digital life writing to refer to different autobiographical discourses that are articulated through the Web. The term is used in this context to describe virtually transmitted narratives which assume authenticity, endorsing the experience that their avatars have of the events narrated through the autobiographical 'I'. Equally, I use the term resistance 2.0 in the chapter's title in reference to Web 2.0. This technology, introduced in the late twentieth century and globally adopted in 2004, has signalled the privatisation of the Internet, facilitated user-generated content and inspired new forms of autobiographical and literary creativity.

The term resistance 2.0 is used in the context of this chapter to describe different oppositional discourses that are primarily enacted within the virtual spaces of the Web and that have the potential to foster public engagement and to materialise offline.[3] In my conceptualisation of resistance 2.0, I build on Barbara Harlow's definition of resistance literature 'as immediately and directly involved in a struggle against ascendant or dominant forms of ideological and cultural production' (1987: 29). Yet, resistance 2.0 extends the fundamental oral and print focus of resistance literature, introduced by Kanafani (1966) and conceptualised by Harlow (1987), to include digitally mediated autobiographical narratives. These digital discourses are considered as a 'political and politicised activity' (Harlow1987: 29); they assume an oppositional role to dominant structures of power and reveal the popular will for freedom and reform in the context of national struggles within which they are typed. It is also crucial to consider the limitations of resistance 2.0 and to put into question issues related to the backlash, durability, fragility and ethics of relying on digital spaces as public sites for articulating and mobilising sociopolitical dissent.

However, it is important to note that the arguments advanced by this chapter are context-specific. The possibilities and the limitations of the Web as a site for the autobiographical expression of dissent remains contingent upon specific contexts of production, circulation and reception. The way the

Web operates in 2010 Tunisia and is tolerated or repressed by the authorities, for instance, is not applicable to other national contexts, or perhaps even in the same country a decade later. This is mainly due to the constantly changing workings of both the digital and the political landscapes. Thus, the lack of stability and durability are some of the limitations of digital resistance which the chapter discusses. Nevertheless, both limitations equally demonstrate the flexibility of tools, forms and media of expressing dissent autobiographically, which this book investigates closely in relation to contemporary Arab women's life writing.

Digital Life Writing and Autobiographical Criticism

Digital life writing has recently become a major area of interest within autobiographical studies. The array of new possibilities that the Web allows for episodic, instantaneous, editable, interactive and cross-cultural real-life discourses has ultimately changed the way we understand the autobiographical. In 2001, Sidonie Smith and Julia Watson described contemporary autobiographical expression as a 'rumpled bed', in reference to its formal and media flexibility (2001b: 1). They have recently gone further to refer to it as 'a messy multi-sensorium, teeming with the potential – and the pitfalls – of vibrant self-presentations across media, geographies, and worlds' (Smith and Watson 2016: xlvii). The technological shift in means, formats and cross-cultural exchange of life writing compels theoretical reconsiderations of the contemporary practices of self-representation while attesting to what Smith and Watson describe as 'the changing technologies of self' (2001b: 13). These technologies have ultimately affected how autobiographical subjectivities are constructed, expressed, channelled and consumed.

Gillian Whitlock describes contemporary autobiography as being '*in transit*' in reference to the ways in which the 'new technologies have altered the fabric of autobiographical expression [which has become] uniquely shaped by the extensive and unprecedented speed and power of cultural exchanges' (2007: 4–8). This transition in terms of the format and the global circulation of life writing has ultimately challenged and exceeded the conventional conceptions and understanding of acts of autobiographical narration and selfhood; it has also transformed the conditions of production and circulation of life narratives. Vlogging (video diaries), blogging, Twitter and Facebook posts and visual stories on Instagram and Snapchat, for instance, have altered the experience of autobiographical authorship and readership. These new tools of communication, as Philippe Lejeune suggests, 'are not only changing autobiography – the expression of a life – but also attacking life itself' as it was hitherto experienced (2014: 249). Through this range of media platforms, many of us have not only become obsessed with sharing the details of our daily lives with others, often by obligation of participation, but we have become voracious consumers of lives in different virtual formats. Today, to be online is the default; it remains debatable to what extent one participates in this virtual world by choice. The easy access to social media platforms has added to 'the communal pressure to keep producing and consuming them, . . . embed[ed] [digital] auto/biographical acts in cultural consciousness' and has consequently affected critical approaches to life writing practices (McNeill 2014: 151).

Across conventional (print) and virtual (online) modes of self-expression, the initial impetus behind constructing autobiographical narratives remains arguably unchanged. Through both media, life writers primarily aim to provide a readership with non-fictional accounts of lived experiences that are presented as credible and reliable (Arthur 2009: 82). Print and online life writings are both motivated by a desire and/or need for 'confession' (Smith and Watson 2016: 238) and aspire to inscribe similar social functions 'including self-monitoring, therapy, and meaning-making' (McNeill 2014: 145). However, the emergence of digital forms of (re)presenting lived experiences does pose certain challenges to our understanding of traditional life writing subgenres. Since the introduction of Web blogging in the late twentieth century, with the first online diary appearing in 1995, and blogging sites introduced in 1998 (Podnieks 2001: 120; Whitlock 2007: 2), the genre of autobiography has taken a new trajectory that diverts from the conventions of (the print versions of) the genre established by the founding critics of autobiographical studies. The traditional conceptions of the genre are no longer adequate to the evaluation of contemporary modes of autobiographical practices. The developmental, diachronic dimension of an autobiographical narrative/self that was established to describe the practice is no longer tenable as the defining characteristic of the genre. Interpreting 'a life in its totality' with a coherent past self and 'identity across time' as Georges Gusdorf famously asserts (1980: 38, 35), or recomposing 'a retrospective prose narrative . . . focusing on [the narrator's] individual life, in particular on the development of his personality', as Lejeune in his earlier work claims (1982: 193), are no longer essential for autobiographical narratives. The available range of digital autobiographical expression, which tends to be disunified formally and stylistically, resists the 'limits and conditions' (Gusdorf 1980) characterising traditional autobiography.

Digital life writing 'eagerly embrace[s] hybridization and fragmentation' (Lejeune 2014: 257) and is one of the most dynamic forms of autobiographical construction (Anishchenkova 2014: 11). It marries a myriad of visual and verbal media; invites – through immediate, interactive and multidirectional platforms – author/reader dialogue, often in real time; and transcends the lengthy print forms in which the presumably presented truth is non-negotiable. The form of digital life writing is partly determined by the quality of the platform in which it is mediated, including type of access to personal profiles (optimised as private or public) and media of communication (images with captions, videos and/or texts). These formal variations of self-expression also potentially affect the identity presented by the digital actor as the formation of subjectivity becomes digitally bound. As Lejeune explains, the 'I' 'expresses itself differently depending on the tools at hand . . . it is the tool that shapes the craftsman' (2014: 248). Hence, the analysis of these autobiographical performances may bypass the close reading procedures used to study traditional auto/biographical texts. It rather requires attending to new material conditions of production, reception and circulation. Equally, the easy access to an Internet connection either through mobile phones or installations at homes, institutions and public spaces – with the affordability of cyber cafés in some developing regions – has facilitated the users' access to new public means of self-expression. This has ultimately challenged the elitist contours of traditional autobiographical expression which was only the preserve of 'a great person, worthy of men's remembrance' (Gusdorf 1980: 31). Digital media has also helped evade the filtering and censorship of mainstream publication industries as it contests the privileged access to publishers of print literature within the contemporary literary market. The latter, as Graham Huggan contends, continues to be selective and contingent upon elements of popular appeal and commodification, particularly when it comes to postcolonial/ethnic auto/biography which has been, until recently, perceived through a market-oriented lens (2001: 156).

Many critical discussions attest to the development of online life writing as a field of enquiry within autobiographical studies (see Lejeune 2000, 2014; Smith and Watson 2001b, 2016; Whitlock 2007; Arthur 2009; Poletti and Rak 2014). In 2003, *Biography* journal, for instance, devoted an issue entitled *Online Lives* to the examination of emerging traditions of online autobiographical writing; the journal has also published a subsequent issue entitled *Online Lives 2.0* (2015) which rethinks contemporary practices of autobiographical expression by considering 'the way people are mobilizing online media to represent their own lives and the lives of others on the Internet' (McNeill and Zuern 2015: v). This merging of new technologies of communication with life writing practices – having no agreed-upon term but referred to diversely as, for instance, 'online diary' (Podnieks 2001), 'digital biography' (Arthur 2009), 'auto/tweetographies' (McNeill 2014), 'autoblography' (Anishchenkova 2014), 'online lives' and 'automedial lives' (Smith and Watson 2016: 226, xxxviii) – has affected the conventional experience of auto/biographical authorship. It has also altered the formal qualities of life narratives, the construction and performance of selfhood and agency and the relationship between the audience and the narrative/narrator that have characterised the conventions of life writing practices.

Just as the new communication technologies have opened up new horizons for modes of self-chronicling and life writing studies, the use of social media platforms to write autobiographically in times of conflict has altered the contours of popular resistance and activism. In the Arab world, the mobilising role of online communication platforms has been highlighted by the pro-democracy uprisings that have swept across the region since 2010. The oppressive mechanisms of the predominantly autocratic regimes in the Arab region, as Karima Laachir and Saeed Talajooy point out, 'have given way to an explosion of cultural displays of dissent in the forms of literary works, films, documentaries, media, Internet and blogging' (2013: 3). Commentators and academics have considered digital media as the major cultural tool for popular protest during the recent Arab upheavals; many of whom have argued that the uprisings would not have been the same, or even possible, without the intervention of information and communications technologies (ICT) (Howard and Hussain 2013: 33–4). Such arguments are based on the fact that the revolutionaries have primarily relied on social media in order to mobilise for sociopolitical change, to organise their pro-democracy movements, to contest state-monitored mainstream media and to gain international exposure.

In the contemporary Arab world, the Internet has altered the collective manifestation of opposition and has provided an alternative public and political space for sovereign assembly (Castells 2012: 11). Digital media has helped to make visible a culture of resistance within the region that was disguised, repressed and/or censored, and, perhaps, not possible through other cultural media. It has enabled the mediation of the repressed voices of *al-shaʻb* (the people) who have become the new actors in propagating an inclusive national narrative that contests the elitist, top-down state discourses. The Web has enabled the expression of opposition against diverse forms of oppression because of its ability to facilitate many-to-many communication and to create communities of resistance. It has equally fostered new forms of public engagement that connect the online world to the street. While contemporary demonstrations, battles, revolutions and upheavals are mostly organised in the streets and public terrains, they are also becoming increasingly enacted and mediated in the virtual spaces of the new communication technologies. Social media platforms have disrupted the presumed distance between the virtual sphere and the public sphere by creating digital discourses of dissent that also materialised offline. These virtual sites of self-expression have, thus, become inextricably linked to the material, sociopolitical context in which they are conceived.

On the other hand, the Internet has also become a parallel terrain in which oppressive regimes carry out different attempts to stifle the resistance. Digital spaces were equally used by the state to counter and contain emerging popular movements through various strategies such as digital tracking, surveillance and censorship. This demonstrates the increasing importance of ICTs as a central domain for contemporary political contestation between both the opposition and the state, as I demonstrate later. It is due to such digital contestation for sociopolitical power and legitimacy that the Arab uprisings have been, controversially, dubbed 'social-media revolutions' (Bebawi and Bossio 2014: 1), 'Facebook revolution[s]' (Jung 2016: 22) and 'Twitter Revolution[s]' (Idle and Nunns 2011: 19).

While the popular use of the Internet as a tool for voicing and structuring sociopolitical opposition in the contemporary Arab world has been discussed by many scholars, it has not been extensively approached from a gendered perspective, with only a few studies highlighting the role of Arab women as active Web users during revolutionary moments (see, for instance, Brown 2014; Khalil 2014; Hyndman-Rizk 2020; Kharroub 2021). More importantly, it has not been analysed specifically in terms of autobiographical sites of manifesting dissent against multiple forms of oppression, simultaneously within and beyond the context of the uprisings. Women around the world are increasingly using the Web to stir social and political discourses by articulating their experiences of oppression and resilience autobiographically. It is thus important to investigate the way contemporary Arab women's access to technologies of self-expression allows access to public spaces and national debates. We need to consider the possible avenues of resistance enabled by these new forms of autobiographical storytelling by highlighting the processes through which 'the [digital] form of identity expression works to give the writer access to certain kinds of power and knowledge formation, which were not available to him or her before' (Poletti and Rak 2014: 6). The Internet, I argue, permits Arab women to dismantle the public–private divide that has traditionally characterised their sociopolitical status in the region. Arab women are able to negotiate their gendered spaces of resistance and shift their activism to public and international arenas of struggle by making visible their personal experiences of national conflicts, advocating for women's rights and expressing common social grievances in digitally mediated autobiographical discourses.

Arab Women Online; Digital Voices of Resistance

The global–local divide that has been systematically contested by Web 2.0 has foregrounded both the diversities and similarities of women's experiences. While practices of self-representation on the Internet might be guided by different motives, women's digital autobiographical expressions have been argued to be generally ideological, embodying the feminist motto 'the personal is political' (Harcourt 2004: 248; Coward 2009: 237–8). Women's life stories online have 'provided both an awareness of shared grievances and transportable strategies for action' (Howard and Hussain 2013: 23). Feminist interventions for social justice and gender equality, for instance, are being increasingly carried out online. These online interventions constitute what has been termed 'cyber feminism' (Anishchenkova 2014: 183; Stephan 2020:

149) with ongoing influential campaigns such as #MeToo and #TimesUp gaining global attention and foregrounding issues of gender-based sexual and physical abuses. In the context of this chapter, the ideological dimension of online writing is specifically pertinent, mainly when digital life stories arise from conflict-torn zones by women who seek means of knowledge and power that are inaccessible, dangerous and/or impossible otherwise. Digital life writing by contemporary Arab women, in particular, constitutes a contested terrain in which the Web is a politicised space of self-expression; this space highlights the possibilities, as well as the drawbacks, of the intersectional relationship between new communication technologies, life writing practices and gender-based sociopolitical opposition.

Twenty years ago, media critic Lamis Alshejini pondered the political potential of cyberspaces that Arab women should consider; she pointed out that 'issues relevant to women's rights and democracy and subject to government suppression, can be carried on the Net and Arab women can network in order to develop their ideas and activities further' (1999: 218). Indeed, as Alshejini expected, the political realities and social challenges in the contemporary Arab region are a major concern of Arab women on the Web. While many of them are using social media platforms to recount their daily and familial lives and social aspirations (Pepe 2019: 38–9), Arab women are increasingly exploiting the digital sphere in order to enact ideological interventions by circumventing sociopolitical censorship and mobilising (inter)national feminist campaigns. Examples include #Women2Drive campaign in Saudi Arabia (2011),[4] which brought to the fore the sexism of the driving ban thanks to a viral YouTube video in which activist Manal Al-Sharif is seen driving.[5] The murder of twenty-one-year-old Palestinian women Israa Ghrayeb by male relatives in August 2019 has mobilised women in Arab states and beyond. The hashtags #WeAreAllIsraaGhrayeb and #JusticeforIsraa were widely used to protest against the so-called 'honour killing'.[6] More recently, in May 2021, twenty-three-year-old Muna el-Kurd, living and reporting from Sheikh Jarrah neighbourhood in Jerusalem, has recruited international support for the Palestinian families who are being forcefully evacuated from their homes by Israeli forces. With over 1.6 million followers on Instagram,[7] el-Kurd has become one of the most prominent Palestinian activists and social media reporters who used the widely circulated hashtag #SaveSheikhJarrah and is now a symbol of Palestinian women's *ṣumūd* (resilience). The ideological dimensions of Arab women's participation in the digital sphere have been particularly foregrounded by the Arab uprisings. Arab women have nurtured a political sense of the Web by organising dissident movements, mobilising for demonstrations and exposing the corruption of political regimes. Dissident voices of Arab women who belong to different social classes, educational backgrounds, national contexts and political affiliations received unprecedented media attention and have been internationally recognised.

For Arab women, using the Web to write personally and self-reflexively about lived sociopolitical realities in zones of conflict – while asserting one's oppositional stance – is to produce autobiographical accounts of resistance that bridge the virtual medium of self-expression with the material reality they are living. They mobilise what Whitlock describes as 'the synchronic connections between the virtual and the material worlds that can be wired through online life-writing' (2007: 3) mainly because 'self-representation on the Internet cannot be properly understood in isolation from the offline world' (Eakin 2020: 108). Arab women's digital life writing from zones of conflict not only reconfigures modes of cultural (self-)representation during revolutionary moments; their online autobiographical voices also contest the region's notorious history of gender-based political isolation and cultural silencing. The Internet has offered Arab women alternative spaces of participation and self-representation. Social media platforms 'have cracked the protective shell of somewhat inhibitive obsession with privacy and have enabled many [Arab] women to take their first steps to the outside world' (Elsadda 2010: 330). For many Arab women, access to the Internet can constitute access to public spaces. Digital spaces have become a powerful tool for advocacy which provide relatively free platforms through which they are able to contest gender-based exclusion in official discourses and decision-making in the region. At the same time, the Internet can become a contested and perilous space for Arab women who engage in the public sphere by breaking social and political barriers. Women are often subjected to intense, gender-based scrutiny that transcends the digital sphere and sometimes escalates to military repression and imprisonment, as I note further below.

Naomi Sakr rightly notes that 'contestation and parity of participation are ideals against which the actual practice of women's participation in the developing Middle East [digital] media can be assessed' (2004: 12). The use of digital media by Arab women typing from zones of conflict is potentially empowering and subversive in the sense that it can constitute a participatory space in which genuinely collective, democratic resistance to authoritarianism can be carried out. This is not to claim that contestation and subversion are inherent characteristics of social media platforms. The Web offers the possibility for opening up equal avenues for dialogic discourses and debates that are accessible, multidirectional and perhaps difficult to publicly articulate otherwise. By making their concerns and stances visible online, Arab women digital writers become more engaged in the public sphere. They assert their dissident voices against the established discourses of power by reclaiming a platform of resistance in which the private and the public/political merge. One pertinent and important example is the Arab Women Solidarity Association United (also known as AWSA United), an international feminist association founded in Egypt in 1982, which is now using cyberspaces to connect women in the Arab World – and in the diaspora – and gives them access to public spheres through the Web. AWSA allows 'Arab feminists . . . to express solidarity with other groups and assert their relevance to the feminist movement', and most importantly gives women the opportunity 'to foster their collective identity, strengthen their connectivity, and increase their [political] activism' mainly through blogging and creating websites on the Internet (Stephan 2020: 149, 152). By cultivating a political sense of their own experiences, Arab women do not merely seek visibility through the Web. They also make visible the oppressive mechanisms to which they are subjugated, and thereby solicit public and international recognition and support for their demands.

Clearly, the disclosure of life stories during war and revolutionary periods has allowed many Arab women to contest the private–public divide which has traditionally characterised their status in the region. The use of the Web to challenge the autocratic monopolies on freedom of speech and political engagement has led many Arab women to become public figures. It has given them the opportunity to gain international appeal by asserting their autobiographical agency while reflecting on current sociopolitical issues. Although the impact of language choice is crucial in terms of gaining international exposure, with English as the obvious choice being a lingua franca and the primary language of technology, non-English narratives may still gain public attention due to the urgency of the context within which they emerge. This was the case with Syrian author Samar Yazbek, for instance, who has become an international advocate of the Syrian revolution due to her literary documentations which initially started as testimonial writings mediated in Arabic through Facebook (see Chapter 3).

Other examples of digital life writers who have become public figures include Palestinian Mona Elfarra whose English-language blog *From Gaza, with Love* (http://fromgaza.blogspot.com/; beginning March 2006) is based on a digital diary she started in 2000. Elfarra's blog aspires, as she writes, to 'serve as a small window into occupied Gaza for the outside world' (22 March 2006; accessed on 10 June 2018). The blog evokes issues related to the status of women and the predicament of children under occupation through the author's own position as an insider and a witness. Also, Tunisian journalist and author Soumaya Ghannouchi who started blogging – in French, English and Arabic – in June 2004, has become an international writer concerned with sociopolitical realities of the Arab world and particularly with Arab women's rights, publishing in leading international newspapers such as *The Guardian* and *Huffington Post*. Ghannouchi is now the editor of *Meem Magazine*, an online socio-cultural platform which is primarily concerned with Arab women's issues. However, it is important to note that gaining international prominence through autobiographical narratives from zones of conflict is not a haphazard process. While the urgency of such contexts increases the public demand for first-hand narratives, especially from women whose experiences are often more complex, and hence reader-tempting and empathy-provoking, the production and circulation of such testimonies can risk becoming a commodity and a tool for propaganda, a point to which I shall return later.

The potential for anonymity that the Internet offers has particularly encouraged many Arab women to talk about their lives and experiences in ways that were not available to them before. It allows them to avoid the fear of being socially shamed and pressured. This emerging desire for disclosure in Arab culture is mainly resistant to the persisting notion of *sitr* (concealment), a cultural virtue that encourages secrecy and decency, as opposed to the idea of *faḍḥ*, which denotes exposure and scene-making. In *Leaks, Hacks, and Scandals: Arab Culture in the Digital Age* (2019), Tarek El-Ariss explores 'the intersection between the digital and the subversive in Arab traditions' (7).

He points out that the notion of *faḍḥ*, 'a visual and affective exposure' which 'shames, makes a scene, causes a scandal, and reveals in the process of new codes of writing', has become one of the main drives behind the use of digital networks as writing and political practices in the Arab world (ibid.: 2). The digital age, as El-Ariss points out, has introduced a new generation of Arab bloggers, activists, leakers and hackers who confront authoritarian regimes and oppressive social systems thorough the power of images, videos and digital writing to expose and divulge, which is pertinent to the context of this chapter. However, as I see it, Arab women typing from contexts of national struggle who choose to remain anonymous online occupy an intersectional space between *sitr* (concealment) and *faḍḥ* (exposure). Traditionally, Arab women have been subjected to a culture of secrecy; they are often shamed, disgraced and even threatened for using different forms of self-disclosure, including literary ones.[8] By choosing to remain anonymous online, Arab women participate in an ideological process of unveiling (*faḍḥ*) through digital storytelling while simultaneously ensuring a safe, confident and self-filtered expression of public and private matters that would preserve their social image (*sitr*). Interestingly, refusal to disclose one's identity in the digital world, specifically in contexts that lack democracy and freedom of expression, can project what Smith and Watson describe as 'an aura of authenticity' (2016: 116), because it attests to the restricted and dangerous contexts in which autobiographical voices are made visible online.

The politicised character of digital self-expression in the Arab region has transformed social media outlets into a 'platform for ideological movements' (Anishchenkova 2014: 172). It has particularly emerged in the wake of 9/11 and the US military intervention in Iraq and Afghanistan (Kahn and Kellner 2005: 78). One of the earliest Arab women blogs was launched by a young Iraqi woman who goes by the pseudonym Riverbend. Blogging in English between 2003 and 2007, in her online platform *Baghdad Burning* (https://riverbendblog.blogspot.com/), Riverbend reflects autobiographically on her own position as a young woman living in war-torn Baghdad by providing political commentary and inner insights into the details of her daily life under occupation. Despite the fact that her identity remains anonymous, she has gained an international appeal. This is partly because she speaks to English-readers while maintaining an 'aura of authenticity' that her anonymity projects.⁹ While Riverbend insists on remaining anonymous – 'I shall remain anonymous. I wouldn't feel free to write otherwise' (24 August 2003) – she asserts the important role of the blogosphere for Arab women who are living under attack, whose identities are marginal, whose voices are stifled, and whose access to public, free forms of self-expression has been restricted by the circumstances of the war. On 1 December 2005, she writes: 'I've lost my voice. That's not a metaphor for anything, by the way. I've managed to literally lose my voice . . . and that's why blogging is a wonderful thing right now: it gives voice to the temporarily voiceless' (accessed 26 July 2018). Riverbend's digital voice, personal and private but equally socially and politically informed, offers an alternative to conventional journalistic reporting; it provides a candid and first-hand portrayal of the impact of siege and war on her life and the lives of those around her. Due to its international appeal, a selection of entries from Riverbend's blog was subsequently published as a book entitled *Baghdad Burning: Girl Blog from Iraq* (2005), which was shortlisted for the Samuel Johnson prize in 2006.¹⁰

Riverbend's account from war-torn Iraq, which won the third place in the Letter Ulysses Award for the Art of Reportage (2005), highlights the rise of alternative journalism in the Arab region or what is known as 'citizen journalism': a digital practice through which ordinary people become the source of news production and dissemination by using amateur reportages of real-life experiences (see Bebawi and Bossio 2014; Douai and Ben Moussa 2016). Online testimonies and life stories from zones of conflict have altered the conventional frames of understanding, perceiving, producing, disseminating and consuming news in times of crises. This has also come to be known as 'autobiographical journalism' which constitutes a 'part of a wider cultural phenomenon concerned with investigating and assimilating the emotional and experiential, into the range of social and political concerns' (Coward 2009: 243). The peculiar temporal and spatial dimensions of digital accounts from zones of conflict (being immediate, personal and internationally accessible) have allowed digital life writing to function as an up-to-the-minute testimony to the realities it mediates. Such journalistic testimonies emphasise 'overt advocacy, first-person and eyewitness accounts, collective organisation and reporting practice and populist styles of presentation' (Bebawi and Bossio 2014: 5). Virtually mediated accounts of bearing witness resist not only the traditional conventions of autobiographical authorship, publication and circulations but also the power and the authority of mainstream media. While digital testimonies might also be judged as fragmented, simplistic and inadequate syntactically and aesthetically, those seeming formal and linguistic limitations are not only the norm of digital writing (because of its speed, instantaneity, and character-restricted space such as on Twitter) but can be markers of urgency in contexts of conflicts. They signal the subject's status as positioned within restricted and perhaps life-threatening circumstances, and hence can be considered as signs of authenticity. As Anne Cubilié notes, 'plain language conveying "the truth" of horrific experience is one of the authenticating aspects of testimonial in whatever form' (quoted in Smith and Watson 2016: 122).

Similar to the experience of Riverbend, for example, sixteen-year-old-girl Farah Baker used digital platforms of self-expression to provide first-hand stories from besieged Gaza to an international audience. Baker, an eyewitness living under the Israeli military attack on Gaza in 2014, used Twitter as a digital diary to report, in English, the conflict as she experienced it and to record her daily plight as a young woman under the atrocities of war. Baker's young age and her use of the digital diary form in a context of military mass destruction has triggered comparison with the German-born female icon of the genre as she was publicly, and controversially, called (the modern) Anne Frank of Palestine.[11] Seven years later, in May 2021, when Israel launched a military campaign against Gaza – after escalation of the ethnic cleansing of the Sheikh Jarrah neighbourhood in Jerusalem – Baker was reporting online again. She used the same hashtag, #GazaUnderAttack, to provide accounts of her experience of the persistent violence and brutality of Israeli occupation. Other personal accounts on Instagram and Facebook by Palestinians living in the occupied territories also reported the events, attracting hundreds of thousands of viewers, despite claims of systematic censorship of Palestinian content by major social media platforms (Lewis 2021). Baker's Twitter account (@Farah_Gazan), which is now officially verified with more than 190,000 followers,[12] has gained the attention of international media outlets and became a reference for exclusive, otherwise-unmediated news. This can be attributed to the subject's position as an insider source of exclusive and newsworthy stories as well as to the immediacy of digital writing, which enables the instantaneous diffusion of events.

Digital life writing has equally altered the politics of reportage as it is no longer restricted to 'writing' but manifests itself in different multimedia of cultural self-representation. The Internet has enriched accounts of first-hand experiences with visual-textual elements, hyperlinks (Riverbend's blog, for instance, links major relevant news outlets such as the *BBC*, *Al-Jazeera* and *Iraq Today*) and discursive spaces. Although digital (autobiographical) journalism might be judged as lacking the professionalism, objectivity, organisation and credibility of mainstream media, being often unmonitored and non-filtered, it uncontestably enables the negotiation of a sociopolitical space of engagement that breaks the boundaries between the personal and the public while putting pressure on the authority and monopoly of print and traditional media. In this sense, Baker's digital practices of reporting, for instance, gained popularity because it constituted a fresh, up-to-the-minute, reachable and non-authoritarian perspective. It provided an insider's point of view that is often inaccessible to other media and whose subject is grounded in their social realities. Today, twenty-three-year-old Baker identifies herself as a 'social media activist and influencer'.[13]

In addition to providing insider-exclusive news that is often disseminated instantaneously, digital life stories from zones of conflict may constitute archival documents of historical significance. Indeed, to write a testimony, in any form, is 'not just to duplicate or record events, but to make history available to imaginative acts' (Whitlock 2015: 169). Arab women's digital life writing has the potential to enable their stories to act as documentation and historical evidence. Interestingly, *tadwīn*, Arabic for blogging, is used to refer to the act of recording, archiving and/or preserving important information through writing. Equally, the plural feminine word *mudawanāt*, Arabic for blogs, signifies transcripts of historical merit that can also be considered as references. Certainly, immediacy and global reach are the most empowering characteristics of the Web when it comes to reporting from war zones. Of equal importance is the possibility of preserving experiences of victims and survivors whose accounts not only embody their autobiographical agency but constitute significant historical interventions. However, it is important to note the element of contingency that governs the archival value of digital writing. Life stories and reports on blogs and social media can be hacked and/or censored and are contingent upon the author's willingness to keep them online. Equally, while digital stories and reportages are searchable through various tools such as hashtags and keywords (for instance, Baker using #GazaUnderAttack for her Tweets), their visibility might be obscured by the constant flow of digital content.

We need to consider the limitations of digital life writing and what is at stake when the Internet becomes an autobiographical site for mediating acts of sociopolitical opposition and resistance by Arab women. While, conventionally, the truthfulness of autobiographical writings is relative and mostly tied by an author–reader pact that promises non-fictionality, digital spaces of self-expression are notorious sites for hoaxes that often remain unverifiable and unexposed. Take for instance the blog *Gay Girl in Damascus*, which claimed to document the life of a gay Syrian woman, Amina Abdallah Arraf al-Omari, in war-torn Syria. The blog gained worldwide attention in June 2011, when Amina, who mobilised activists and international news agencies after claims of being arrested, was revealed to be Tom MacMaster, an American student blogging from Scotland.[14] This incident shows the ways in which the Internet further complicates the fundamental notions that have been at the core of controversies in autobiographical studies: fact versus fiction. It also demonstrates that, unlike traditional autobiographical discourses, the pact between the author and the reader of digital life narratives is unclear, if not non-existent. The difficulty of verifying the credibility of sources of stories and testimonies on social media makes Lejeune's pact fluid, as authenticity is no longer measured by the name of the writing subject. Truthfulness is rather measured through other elements including historical accuracy, photographic evidence, external endorsement of public figures and experts and material evidence, to name a few. Nevertheless, ethical reading of testimonial writing from conflict-zones should not be based on specific 'metrics of authenticity' (Smith and Watson 2016: 116) because assessment of truthfulness is often subjective and never absolute. Over-investment in the truthfulness of accounts from zones of conflict risks falling into a 'crisis of suspicion' which would ultimately underestimate 'the validity, and the moral suasion, of those testimonial projects' (ibid.: 149).

We need to acknowledge that digital life writings are sets of personal observations whose authenticity is relative and subjective. Such autobiographical avatars remain of importance nevertheless as they draw attention to and solicit support of historically obscured human experiences and voices that are often unchannelled and unrecognised otherwise. As Penny Summerfield, in her elaborate study of personal narratives as historical practices, rightly argues: 'subjectivity has become a legitimate matter for historical enquiry and a route to understanding the past' (2019: 14). Stories by Arab women typing from zones of conflict yield urgent and relevant models of digital life writing through which we can examine practices of online self-representation and documentation that rework the relationship between the autobiographical subject and the audience. They also provide alternative media through which marginal discourses of resistance are potentially channelled. They contest the assumptions that the ensemble of women's visual and textual self-representation is 'merely personal' and 'narcissistic' (Smith and Watson 2016: 346) but might stand as an autobiographical practice which solicits alternative platforms of sociopolitical engagement.

It is also worth noting that Arab women's engagement in political debates and their ability to produce cultural and social commentary through digital media is not spontaneous and unconstrained. It remains generally dependent on a position of social and educational privilege, mainly technological accessibility and literacy. In 2019, only 44.2 per cent of Arab women had access to and used the Internet.[15] Access to the new communication technologies by uneducated, non-literate and poor women, for instance, remains largely limited; they continue to be excluded from these new spaces of public participation and dissent. Similarly, the potential for international exposure of digitally mediated voices remains to a great extent contingent on the use of the English language which is more or less elitist. Additionally, the unstoppable flow of digital narratives from zones of conflict may cause a traffic of discourses of dissent which can obscure some at the expense of others; this leads to a process of selection and prioritisation whose criteria are often dependent not solely on urgency but on popular appeal. Such cross-cultural movement and selective appeal, as discussed by Whitlock, makes digital testimonies from war zones vulnerable to becoming 'soft weapons' (2007). That is, they potentially constitute commodified tools for propaganda that are used to maintain particular ideologies and to reify or dismiss certain stereotypes at the expanse of the subject's authenticity and truthfulness.

As I have mentioned, the Web as a site for expressing and mediating dissent is one way of escaping state censorship. However, it can be simultaneously used as a counter tool of surveillance and monitoring. Tracking the locations of bloggers, anticipating activist movements, stifling demonstrations, shutting social media websites, limiting access to the Web and repressing and imprisoning digital activists are among the states' counter-movements in the face of the political and oppositional use of the Internet (Castells 2012; Howard and Hussain 2013). For instance, in November 2009, Tunisian blogger and theatre teacher Fatma Riahi, who blogs as Fatma Arabicca, was charged with defamation for her satirical and political writings on Ben Ali's regime; she was arrested and detained for almost a week (Lutz 2009). In Egypt, thousands of activists have been tracked down and imprisoned since the removal of elected president Mohamed Morsi from power in July 2013, including leading Egyptian blogger and software developer, Alaa Abdel Fattah, who rose to prominence during the uprising of 2011. In February 2015, Abdel Fattah was sentenced to five years in prison for organising a popular protest without official permission (Malsin 2015). When released in March 2019, he was re-arrested in September of the same year and accused of using social media to spread fake news undermining national security; he was given another five years sentence and is still in prison. Similarly, the ever-tightened control over digital media can be examined in Algeria where, after the *ḥirāk* (social movement) of February 2019 that brought down the twenty-year rule of Abdelaziz Bouteflika, the newly elected government launched fierce campaign of arrests against humourists, actors and journalists who used online platforms to protest against the new regime.[16] In September 2020, independent journalist Khaled Drareni, for instance, was sentenced to two years in prison for reporting on opposition protests on his personal social media accounts.[17] Prior to this, Algerian cartoonist Amine Benabdelhamid, known as Nime, was charged for allegedly insulting the state. He served one month in prison for posting a cartoon on social media questioning the legitimacy of the presidential election of December 2019.

Virtual spaces are also marked by patriarchal practices. Women expressing different forms of dissent through online life stories might be dismissed as trivial and non-constructive and their subjects are very often liable to become targets of gender-based harassment, shaming and censorship. Such reactions are mainly motivated by the stereotypical perception of women in the region who are traditionally expected to remain reserved; unabashed display of their personal lives online and their active involvement in the public sphere are often considered socially inappropriate. In post-uprising Egypt, most notoriously, the authorities' crackdown on freedom of expression have been targeting women, mainly for posting videos and visual stories that are deemed too personal and culturally inappropriate. In January 2020, five female social media influencers were fined and sentenced to two years in prison for posting video clips of themselves dancing, fully clothed, which, allegedly, violates Egyptian conservative values and promotes indecency (Farouk 2020). However, online harassment, digital censorship and surveillance are among the oppressive mechanisms against which many Arab women digital activists and life writers have been fighting. In this case, the experience of Tunisian blogger Lina Ben Mhenni is particularly pertinent; her politically engaged digital life writing has contributed to challenging the state's manipulation of, and control over, cyberspaces and freedom of expression.

A 'Tunisian Girl': Blogging the Resistance

The nomination list of the 2011 Nobel Peace Prize was remarkably characterised by its inclusion of figures connected to the Arab uprisings. The reward was co-received by Tawakkol Abdel-Salam Karman, a prominent activist in the Yemeni uprising, a human rights advocate and the first Arab woman to be awarded this prize. The nominees also included Arab digital activists who have demonstrated an outstanding ability in using the Web to mobilise for social justice and political change in their countries, such as the Egyptians Wael Ghonim and Esraa Abdel Fatah. Nomination for such a prestigious prize is in effect an international recognition of the role of youth generally and digital spaces particularly in enabling pro-democracy movements and in striving towards peace-building in the region. The list also included twenty-eight-year-old Tunisian blogger Lina Ben Mhenni, one of the leading figures of the Tunisian uprising.

What is particularly interesting about Ben Mhenni, who had been blogging since 2009 on her digital platform *A Tunisian Girl* (http://atunisiangirl.blogspot.com/), is that her blog constitutes an intersectional space in which her online journalism, on-the-ground sociopolitical activism, oppositional political views and private life come together in the virtual world. She rose to prominence after blogging the Tunisian revolution by defying the regime's monopoly on local media outlets and its restrictions on international media organisations. As a trilingual space of self-expression (in Arabic, English and French), Ben Mhenni's blog *Tunisian Girl* reflects the subject's status as a reachable, educated millennial woman; it solicits a wide range of readership as it escapes some linguistic constraints that might impede accessibility. The blog has been consulted by over half a million visitors from various countries.[18] Although the topics she tackles reflect her own personal perspective as a young Tunisian woman, they are generally politically informed and confront issues of social justice that are of interest to the Tunisian public. Ben Mhenni's blogging experience inspired her short memoir *Tunisian Girl, Bnayyah Tūnsiyyah: Blogueuse pour un printemps arabe* (Blogger for an Arab Spring) published in France in 2011. Written in French, this essay-length book (thirty-two pages) constitutes a testimonial reflection on the subject's personal life and challenges in relation to her digital experience, prior to and during the revolution. Expanding upon some entries from the blog, the memoir presents a first-hand commentary on the importance of digital activism and self-expression as an empowering space for the articulation and performance of sociopolitical dissent.

Despite being an internationally recognised blogger and a celebrated figure of the Tunisian Revolution, Ben Mhenni's experience of digital dissidence as presented in her memoir/blog remains critically under-examined, especially from an autobiographical perspective. I examine Ben Mhenni's monograph, with reference to her blog, as dissident life writing platforms in which the public/political and the private/personal intertwine to express sociopolitical opposition. Ben Mhenni's experience illuminates what is potentially empowering about dissident digital writing for a woman blogger in the face of state censorship and repression of freedom of speech. My analysis of her texts highlights the way the Web permits access to new ways of self-expression and representation that are closely tied to engagement in the public domain and participation in national oppositional movements. It also considers instances in which the virtual world becomes a hostile space for Arab women who make their private stories and oppositional voices visible online.

Ben Mhenni opens her short memoir with a clear assertion of her digital subjectivity: 'I am a blogger, and I will always be' ('[j]e suis une blogueuse, et je le resterai') (2011: 3). Although she defines herself as a 'blogger for an Arab Spring' (*Blogueuse pour un printemps arabe*), her engagement with digital dissidence and blogging started prior to the Tunisian Revolution of 2010–11. The daughter of a left-wing militant, Sadok Ben Mhenni, who was imprisoned from 1974 to 1980 for his outspoken oppositional views under the rule of President Habib Bourguiba,[19] Ben Mhenni had been actively and publicly engaged in exposing the corruption of the regime of the infamous 'ZABA' (Zine el-Abidine Ben Ali) since 2008,[20] and, until her death, her writing continued to be critically engaged in the Tunisian sociopolitical scene. Claiming that she is a blogger for an Arab Spring, which is now a problematic appellation, was due to the euphoric spirit of the revolutions and the optimism for change which they engendered across the region. It reflects a pride in her contribution in raising consciousness and encouraging social action. Her claim can be also regarded as a marketing strategy for the book which was published in a period during which the uprisings were urgent and/or still ongoing.

Ben Mhenni overtly dissociates herself from any political affiliation by asserting that 'I am an independent [free] blogger' ('je suis un électron libre') (2011: 3). Similarly, in her blog, she defines herself as 'a Tunisian blogger with no political affiliation' (27 May 2010).[21] For Ben Mhenni, such a political dissociation, indicated by the French adjective '*libre*' which denotes her independence as an activist and also depicts the subject as politically unconstrained, does indeed offer her some form of freedom of engagement that is lacking in political-party activism. Ben Mhenni contrasts digital activism with traditional political-party engagement by acknowledging the flexibility and the discursive, democratic qualities of the Web:

> In a political party, time becomes limited, we are enlisted, bound, chained by a political agenda that needs to be followed, we stop reacting live, in the immediacy. There are rules, protocols, and limits. By contrast, an independent cyber-activist has no limits. A blogger is a thousand times faster and more efficient. There's no leadership. Everyone can participate in the process of decision-making.

(Dans un parti, le temps devient limité, on est embrigadés, ligotés, enchaînés, on a un agenda politique à suivre, on cesse de réagir en direct, dans l'immédiateté. Il y a des règles, des protocoles, des limites. Un électron libre n'a pas de limites. Un blogueur, une blogueuse, c'est mille fois plus efficace, plus rapide. Personne n'est leader. Tout le monde peut participer au processus de prise de décision). (2011: 3–4)

While immediacy is often cited as the most important quality of cyber-activism, Ben Mhenni highlights the advantages of the lack of leadership. According to her, it enables an inclusive, participatory environment that permits egalitarian interactions among users: 'the Web is [a space] where everyone can participate in the process of decision-making, where every single person can have an effect on reality' ('[l]a Toile est . . . où tout le monde puisse participer aux prise de décisions, où chacun puisse avoir un effet sur la réalité') (2011: 31). That is, cyber activists, or what Mohamed Kerrou identifies as the 'new actors' in the Tunisian political scene, 'do not obey a pyramidal and hierarchical organization. They have, therefore, an unequalled margin of flexibility and freedom of thought' due to the user-dependent character of social media (2012: 85). The latter enables 'mass self-communication' which open a space for many-to-many interaction while simultaneously guarantees the autonomy of the social actor whose message is self-produced (Castells 2012: 7). The absence of leadership in digital dissidence helps eliminate embedded social hierarchies among citizens and stresses the collectivity of all Tunisians who share similar concerns, grievances and aspirations. Ben Mhenni notes that in the Tunisian Web-sphere of resistance 'there is no leader, everyone had the same objectives, dreamed of the same horizon, held on to the same sky' ('il y'a pas de leader, tout le monde avait le même objectif, rêvait du même horizon, tenait au même ciel') (2011: 23).

This sense of relationality, where individual subjectivity is constructed around inter-personal relations and understood in connection to – national – collectivity, is further stressed by the title of the blog/book. *Tunisian Girl, Bnayyah Tūnsiyyah* reflects Ben Mhenni's sense of self-fashioning as a young, active and engaged subject who belongs to the national Tunisian collective. It also invites trust and proximity by appealing as a conspiratorial space. The assertive use of the term 'girl' – *Bnayyah* in the Tunisian dialect, which is often used to describe a youthful, unmarried woman – also suggests the independence of its subject who is only bound by her national affiliation. Through the title *Tunisian Girl, Bnayyah Tūnsiyyah*, Ben Mhenni asserts her gendered, feminist identity but only as emphatically grounded within and encompassed by the collectively shared national one. This collective relation is also suggested by the cover image of the memoir (Indigène édition) which depicts an upper-face portrait of Ben Mhenni blurred into a background image of a chanting crowd of Tunisian demonstrators. On one occasion, she writes: 'I blended with them: I felt more Tunisian than ever, and I screamed with them, I shouted their slogans, my anger and my thirst for justice' ('je me suis mélangée à eux: je me sentais plus Tunisienne que jamais et j'ai hurlé avec eux, j'ai hurlé leurs slogans, ma colère, ma soif de justice') (2011: 20). Therefore, this sense of relational national belonging can be understood as a marker of identity which fosters Ben Mhenni's dissident life writing and activism.

While oppositional cyber writing in Tunisia, as in the rest of the Arab world, has been foregrounded by the latest political movements in the region, Ben Mhenni's blog and book invite a rethinking of the role of political cyber activism prior to the uprisings, particularly as building up towards these social movements. While almost all observers and critics have considered street vendor Mohamed Bouazizi's self-immolation on 17 December 2010 as the starting moment of the Tunisian revolution, Ben Mhenni provides a new perspective on its backdrop. She suggests that the revolution was triggered by the first public call for demonstration against the regime's restrictions on freedom of speech and digital censorship, with Bouazizi's suicide as the final straw. She traces the seeds of the revolution back to bloggers' first street protest.[22] She writes: 'it has not been said enough: the Tunisian revolution was precipitated on May 22, 2010' ('[o]n ne l'a pas assez dit: la révolution tunisienne a basculé le 22 mai 2010') (2011: 30–1).[23] On that day, Tunisian bloggers called for a demonstration in the capital Tunis against what they have dubbed 'Ammar 404'. The latter is a humorous label – with Ammar as a traditional, masculine name which denotes authoritarianism – that is used to personify and mock the infamous message on censored websites 'Not Found Error 404'. This popular call for protest, sarcastically labelled *Nhār ʿala ʿAmmār* (a bad day for Ammar), was a response to the wave of censorship that targeted various digital platforms of oppositional bloggers undertaken by governmental entities, mainly the Ministry of Communication and the Tunisian Internet Agency (ATI) (Ben Mhenni 2011: 8), which reminds us that the Web is not a space of absolute freedom. On May 2010, Ben Mhenni posted a letter on her blog addressed 'To Ammar' indicating that most topics, including art, students' issues and even cooking are censored; she sarcastically pleaded: 'by the name of God and by your mother's life, Ammar, explain and clarify to me which topics am I allowed to discuss [online]?'[24]

Prior to and during the revolution, Ben Ali's regime monopolised traditional media outlets while diligently monitoring virtual spaces, so as to control political and non-political sites that could be used to express dissent (Khamis and Vaughn 2016: 49). The state's diligence in repressing cyber activists and digital dissidence is, in fact, a measure of their efficacy in threatening the semblance of authority of dictatorship. Such restrictions on cyber activism and freedom of expression did not only attack virtual spaces but targeted individuals. This is because, as Philip Howard and Muzammil Hussain remind us, 'Tunisian bloggers had, for several years, been among the most critical opponents of Ben Ali's regime' (2013: 51). Ben Mhenni, for instance, tells us that her parents' house, constantly under surveillance, was stormed by the political police who seized her personal computers, cameras, hard disks and DVDs (2011: 8). Moreover, as a university lecturer, she was denied a one-year salary for her oppositional activism. Ben Mhenni also recounts the way her fellow bloggers Slim Amamou and Yassine Ayari were followed, kidnapped and obliged to release a video in which they announce the cancellation of the May 22 demonstration (2011: 9). It is against such mechanisms of oppression that cyber activists and oppositional bloggers in Tunisia called for several peaceful demonstrations to denounce the regime's infringement on freedom of digital expression. This ongoing process of digital contestation between the state and the opposition demonstrates that the new technologies are central to the contemporary struggle for political power. Mechanisms of popular resistance and state repression are becoming increasingly shaped by the race for a superior possession of and control over technologically sophisticated means of communication. As Miriyam Aouragh notes, in the context of the Arab revolutions, 'Internet activists rely on the same tools as their oppressive authorities' (2012: 530). Social media rivalry between the state and the people is materialised in the dynamic relation between defiance and repression. This reflects the Foucauldian view of the interactive and confrontational relationship between oppressive power and resistance which, in this case, takes digital means of communication and representation as its terrain.[25]

While the gatherings and demonstrations of digital activists were prohibited, monitored and thwarted by the regime, Tunisian bloggers sustained an online presence by continuing to strengthen their community and assert solidarity through the Web. They have resorted to alternative strategies to escape censorship mainly by creating online private chat groups and using unmonitored international blogging spaces, such as Global Voice Online, VPN (Virtual Private Network) and public cyber cafés, in order to avoid tracking. Ben Mhenni posted various entries, like 'You Can't Stop us from Writing' and 'Hacked buStill Writing!' [sic], and launched online campaigns encouraging the public to engage in digital dialogues such as '7ellblog' (launch a blog).[26] The online platform nawaat.org,[27] for instance, launched in 2004, provided a supportive, collaborative space which brought together Tunisian journalists and bloggers (such as Yassine Nabli, Sami Ben Gharbia, Amamou and Ben Mhenni) against different mechanisms of silencing and suppression. Such online social platforms become 'virtual space[s] of assembly' (Khamis and Vaughn 2016: 42) which constitute an alternative to the public and virtual spaces controlled and ceased by Ben Ali's regime. By maintaining a virtual continuity of acts of resistance, Tunisian cyber activists demonstrate that the Web is not only a tool for expressing opposition but can be a public space where resistance is mediated, manifested and exercised, despite technological advancements in repression mechanisms. Consequently, the resort to the virtual world to compensate for the lack of freedom of expression in public spaces has induced Tunisian popular curiosity and participation in digital dialogues; as Ben Mhenni notes, between October 2009 and February 2011, the number of Tunisian Facebook users increased by 200 per cent (2011: 28).

The virtually constructed sense of togetherness and solidarity among digital dissidents conforms to Aouragh's argument that the Web can constitute, in Benedict Anderson's phrase, a space for the creation of 'imagined communities'. She argues, in a different context, that 'mass media and communication strengthen national awareness . . . fuel a sense of community and make it possible to experience the nation's territorial contours' (2012: 25). This sense of community is possible due to the Internet's ability to shape a collective imagination that is socially and historically constructed through the national symbols it mediates. That is, mediating collective experiences and grievances online increases users' sense of national awareness, identification and belonging. In the same sense, Tunisian dissident cyberspaces, according to Ben Mhenni's experience, (re)construct shared national and political expressions that engender a sense of collective identity and affiliation. These online spaces allow *al-sha'b* to identify a communal desire for self-determination. They also forge inclusory national values and interests that are different from and often contradictory to the autocratic discourses propagated by state officials and mainstream media. By nurturing a national collective sense among social media users and blog-followers, Tunisian bloggers have made it possible to form virtual communities of resistance that break the barrier of fear and silence in the face of dictatorship. It is to this end that Ben Mhenni assertively states: 'for me, the decisive moment for our [Tunisian] revolution is the day of 22 May 2010' ('à mes yeux le moment décisif de notre révolution, cette journée du 22 mai 2010') (2011: 7).

During the course of the Tunisian revolution of 2010, the regime's attempts to suppress the demonstrations on the streets coincided with its attack on digital spaces of dissidence. This dual mechanism of political repression was in response to the way both forms of dissidence operated simultaneously and complementarily. While social media was a catalyst to popular street protests, public spaces of demonstrations, in turn, provided rich materials that circulated in different social Web pages. Platforms like Facebook, Twitter and YouTube buzzed with images and videos from public spaces of protest. This abundance of digital documentation provided the audience with a rich, multifaceted perspective on the movement. Ben Mhenni was one of the bloggers who operated simultaneously on the ground and in the virtual world, acting often as an active intermediary. During the revolution, she blogged from the towns of Sidi Bouzid and Kasserine as an active protester and witness. She notes that 'I myself became a source of news' ('Je suis devenue moi-même une source d'information') (2011:12). She instantaneously reported events on her social media platforms as well as provided reports to leading international news channels such as *France 24* and *Al-Jazeera*. Her reportages helped to widen public access to the events of the movement which were ignored and/or misrepresented by state-sponsored television and were often inaccessible to international media. Ben Mhenni's experience, thus, attests to the role of online spaces in democratising journalistic practices and their capacity to disseminate in-depth, first-hand accounts of social movements that travel beyond their national territorial spaces.

Driven by her desire to 'divulge the horrors and the crimes of ZABA's regime' ('divulger les horreurs et les crimes du regime de ZABA' (2011: 19), Ben Mhenni enacted a movement back and forth between virtual dissidence and street resistance. She was the only blogger and activist who visited Regueb, a turbulent small town near Sidi Bouzid, where the police killed five demonstrators. Although alienated and traumatised by the atrocities committed against innocent Tunisians, Ben Mhenni bravely covered the events and obtained and published the names of those who were killed by the regime to honour their memory. Persuaded by the family of one of the victims, she took a picture of the martyr's body and posted it on her blog (10 January 2011).[28] The photograph fuelled a wave of outrage and sympathy across the country and beyond. In her reading of Susan Sontag, Judith Butler points out that in the digital age 'the contemporary notion of atrocity requires photographic evidence: if there is no photographic evidence, there is no atrocity' (2005: 824). This is true not only because of the power of images to induce affect in viewers and create a 'sense of moral obligation' (ibid. 824) by vivifying the regime's atrocities, inducing sympathy and condemnation, fuelling anger against the perpetrators and/or giving moral legitimacy to the revolutionaries demands. Photographs also have the ability to travel across media, appealing to different social categories of viewers. Sontag, in *Regarding the Pain of Others* (2003) in which she reflects on images of violence and brutality from contexts of conflict, points out that '[i]n contrast to a written account – which, depending on its complexity of thought, reference, and vocabulary, is pitched at a larger or smaller readership – a photograph has only one language and is destined potentially for all' (17). It is due to the ability of (digital) images to widen the scope of exposure to human suffering and to provide a compact way of apprehending calamities that Ben Mhenni captions the martyr's photograph (in English) with 'I'll let the picture explain everything' (10 January 2011). Providing digital evidence of atrocities is a pressing mission of which Ben Mhenni was conscious and to which she was committed: 'I understood my true role as a blogger: I was there to take pictures, to film video footage, to testify against the insanities that ZABA's proponents did not fail to propagate' ('je comprenais mon vrai rôle de blogueuse: j'étais là pour prendre des photos, filmer des séquence vidéo, témoigner de façon à contrer les insanités que les loyaux de ZABA ne manqueraient pas de déverser') (2011: 17). Through video documentation, photo-sharing and event reporting, Ben Mhenni was among those who used social media to mediate popular resistance as well as to give a face to dictatorship.

Coordination between virtual spaces and the street was fundamental to the materialisation of the Arab uprisings. The possibility of an active, public engagement against political oppression which digital dissidence permits is what particularly threatens to expose the misdeeds, and potentially shake the power, of totalitarian regimes. Freedom of (digital) assembly and speech facilitated by the Internet may encourage individuals to adopt more democratic values outside the virtual realm and possibly attempt to change the normative workings of autocratic rules. A study conducted on the Tunisian blogosphere has shown that between November 2010 and May 2011 the topics discussed in Tunisian blogs were closely tied to the political events occurring on the street (Howard and Hussain 2013: 50). This is one of the reasons why the Web constitutes a threat to the regime. The attention that is given to digital activism and social media networks by the state denotes the potential efficacy of digital dissidence in threatening the stability and continuity of non-democratic powers.

However, it is important to note that the efficiency of social media as sites of dissent and potential trajectories toward democracy remains contingent upon public engagement and more traditional forms of resistance. Such platforms can be directed towards potential change only when enforced by simultaneous engagement in the real public sphere. As identified by Ben Mhenni, ICTs tools offer multiple possibilities for information diffusion, social solidarity and political mobilisation (2011: 30). Nevertheless, change remains dependent on human agency. As Howard puts it: '[n]ew information technologies do not topple dictators; they are used to catch dictators off-guard' (2011: 12). Exposing the misdeeds of a regime or a political figure is not always a way to mobilise people towards change. It can only be a step towards change when enforced by a wide, national public engagement and a collective will to end dictatorship. Ben Mhenni, an active participant, a witness and a reporter of the Tunisian public scene, asserts that 'a real cyber-activist does not hide behind his/her screen, he/she goes to the field' ('[u]n vrai cyberactivist ne se contente pas de rester assis derrière son écran, il va sur le terrain') (2011: 30). Like Ben Mhenni who emphasises on-the-ground mass engagement as a source of power that lends legitimacy to the testimonies and cases made by cyber activists and bloggers, Aouragh reminds us that in times of revolution, 'many forms of online politics are rendered meaningless – unless organically related to offline street politics' (2012: 518).

While social media platforms do not autonomously alter sociopolitical realities as they are not inherently subversive, they do provide new venues to publicly scrutinise political actors and hold them accountable. This perhaps explains why Ben Ali's presidential decision to end digital censorship in his infamous speech on 13 January 2011 coincided with his resignation the following day. This suggests that a ruling power that capitalises on coercion and intimidation is unable to survive when oppositional voices are made visible. By legitimising such oppositional stances, Ben Ali legitimised their claims for a free, democratic nation, which is antithetical to and cannot coexist with the dictatorial rule of his regime. The potential parallel operation of the virtual world and the public, physical engagement attests to the ability of the new communication technologies to enact a collaborative resistance movement between the screen and the street. Digital dissidence, thus, has the potential to mobilise an active engagement in sociopolitical change and even decision-making. This was the case with prominent Tunisian dissident blogger Slim Amamou who was appointed Secretary of State for Sport and Youth for the transitional Tunisian (post-revolution) government in 2011. He resigned very shortly afterwards.

While, as I have demonstrated, the relationship between Ben Mhenni's digital writing and public engagement can be examined through her blog and book, both platforms are equally grounded in her personal life and experiences. For instance, while Ben Mhenni celebrates the transformative possibilities of blogging at the collective and political levels, she simultaneously acknowledges the effects of digital writing on her personal life. She recounts her journey on the Web starting from the first computer she received as a child to her adolescent years during which 'I discovered the concept of blogging by a mere coincidence' ('[j]'ai découvert le concept de blogging tout à fait par hasard') (2011: 25). The latter has opened new horizons to network with like-minded individuals and helped her to 'overcome my timidity' ('dépassé ma timidité') (2011: 30). Ben Mhenni's memoir is also an illness narrative. She shares details about her health crisis in 2007 during which she underwent a kidney transplant surgery (ibid.: 27). She competed twice in the World Transplant Games for athletes who have received transplants – in Thailand and Australia – and won a silver medal in athletic walking in 2009. She writes:

> Six months after my kidney transplant, I participated in the first World Transplant Games in Bangkok, and I obtained a silver medal in the 3km walk category. Two years later, I obtained a second in Australia. I often made the connection between my struggle in the Tunisian revolution and the physical ordeal that I endured with my kidneys.

> ('Six mois après ma transplantation, j'ai participé à mes premiers Jeux mondiaux des transplantes d'organes à Bangkok et j'y obtenu une médaille d'argent dans la discipline des 3km marche. Deux ans plus tard, j'en obtenais une seconde aux jeux d'Australie. J'ai souvent fait le rapprochement entre ma lutte dans la révolution tunisienne et le calvaire physique que j'ai endure avec mes reins'). (ibid.: 27–8)

Such personal details, which indeed lose their semblance of privacy once made publicly accessible on the Web, give Ben Mhenni's digital life writing an intimate, humane contour. It endows her narrative of resistance with familiarity and grounds it in its social and national conditions, hence legitimising her struggle for social and political justice.

The public and the private merge in Ben Mhenni's blog and memoir to constitute a coherent life narrative that reflects her autobiographical performance of subjectivity. The memoir itself is marked by a topical transition through which the subject moves subtly, and sometimes abruptly, from the collective, political environment in Tunisia to her familial and personal life. This merging of the public with the personal can equally be observed in the acknowledgement of the book which she simultaneously dedicates to the martyrs of the revolution, her family members, her fellow bloggers and digital activist, her friends, prisoners of conscience and her illness (2011: 1). Such an intersectional web of people and conditions has allowed Ben Mhenni to construct an autobiographical avatar that is a hybrid of private, social and political relations and is positioned in a given historical context. Smith argues that a coherent self-identity does not pre-exist the autobiographical act of telling: 'there is no essential, original, coherent autobiographical self before the moment of self narrating' (2016: 262). Nor is an autobiographical identity representative of an uninterrupted, true and interior self. Identity, Smith argues, is autobiographically performed through which subjects assign meaning to their life (ibid.: 261). In the same sense, Ben Mhenni's platforms of self-expression entail performative elements that construct an autobiographical identity in which 'the political is not only personal but also collective' (McNeill and Zuern 2015: xii). Marketing herself as an approachable 'girl', fostering a trilingual blog, moving between the highly public sphere and private matters (such as her health crisis) and engaging pervasive political discourses, are all performative means of representing an autobiographical identity that is conditioned by the cultural and historical contexts of autobiographical production and reception.

It is this politically fraught and technologically sophisticated context of production and reception which allows Ben Mhenni to create an autobiographical assemblage of the personal and the collective. I agree with Valerie Anishchenkova, in her discussion of Arab blogs, that 'there is something very paradoxical about rendering the highly individual, private narrative accounts in the highly public space of the World Wide Web' (2014: 173) mainly because the personal loses its character when positioned as a public affair. However, I regard this enacted movement between the private and the public spheres in Ben Mhenni's case to be a strategic shift that presents the subject as grounded in the sociopolitical conditions which she observes, evaluates and criticises. For politically engaged digital life writers, 'being private in public' (McNeill and Zuern 2015: viii) is not essentially a form of digital narcissism or attention-seeking. It rather enables new relations between the individual subject and the collective to emerge as it solicits a sense of togetherness and intimacy with one's audience. In order to mobilise online spaces to configure sociopolitical reforms, Ben Mhenni engages her personal life to enact an autobiographical narrative which eliminates the distance between her virtually constructed oppositional voice and the people (*al-shaʻb*). She infuses her narrative with a sense of credibility by confirming her identity as the ordinary citizen, the typical 'Tunisian girl'.

Equally, Ben Mhenni's experience evokes persisting issues of gender that are relevant to her digital activism. In her life writing platforms, she, generally, indiscriminately advocates for collective human freedom and against repression of speech exceeding her explicit feminist position, particularly during the revolution. This can be also observed in the way the author does not often mark a feminine subject in her memoir but rather uses the default masculine form which is – problematically – used in the French language to de-gender the collective. Ben Mhenni, for instance, often uses the singular masculine form (deploying the article '*un*' and/or the pronoun '*il(s)*') to refer to cyber dissidents, including herself. For example, she refers to 'un électron' (2011: 3), and 'un vrai cyberactivist' (ibid.: 30). In her discussion of the role of Tunisian women during the revolution of 2011, Andrea Khalil rightly notes that gender equality and feminist demands during the revolution were subordinated to the collective nationalist demands for social dignity and justice for all Tunisians (2014: 188). Gender-specific and feminist agendas were temporarily relinquished because national aspiration for justice under authoritarian regimes and patriarchal societies have been recognised as fundamental to the realisation of women's/feminist demands. Instead, collective subjectivities emerged due to the rise of what Khalil describes as 'gender-neutral crowds' whose demands were predominantly in favour of the nation regardless of any social divisions.[29]

However, although Ben Mhenni had been an advocate for the rights of all Tunisians, regardless of social categorisation, her feminist stance persists. She acknowledges her gendered position as shaping her digital self-expression and struggles against the repression of speech. Being a woman makes her online engagement in the public sphere more challenging as she is constantly subjected to gender-based shaming and harassment. The democratic principles of digital life writing do not make the Web a safe space for self-expression, especially for women; as in the real-life public domain, social media remains a space where ideological differences clash. Digital media provides sites for evoking gender issues and renegotiating gender relations. Nevertheless, it is equally liable to constitute sites in which gender-based exclusion is exercised. This can be inflicted by restricted accessibility, male and elite monopoly and governmental censorship (Howard and Hussain 2013: 63).

While blogging for Ben Mhenni offers an alternative space for political engagement and self-reflection, it also positions her as a direct target of gender-based harassment. Ben Mhenni's online platform is also a personal space in which she posts various entries on her daily life, personal reflections on social and cultural issues, excerpts of her favourite Arabic poetry, quotations from the novels she reads, and selfies and pictures from international events and family gatherings. She also does not hesitate to evoke controversial topics such as sexual assaults and sex work and is open about her body image. However, she receives many gender-based, bigoted comments from some of her followers, many of whom accuse her of cultural and religious disdain. For instance, in an entry in which she criticises Islamic fundamentalism and openly discusses the topic of sexual frustration among Tunisian men (posted on 30 June 2012), a follower named Iheeb Racheeddi comments: 'I pity a revolution that gave prominence to people like you' (my translation from Arabic). Another who goes by the pseudonym i.think writes in English: 'u have nothing to do with the Tunisian revolution! . . . the problem is that u r too ugly to work as a prostitute'.[30] Moreover, the regime took advantage of her gendered position in an attempt to suppress her dissidence. According to Ben Mhenni, a website called *Putes Tunisiennes* (Tunisian prostitutes) was created by the regime using the personal life of female bloggers to tarnish their reputation and thwart their cyber activities (2011: 31). This demonstrates that if the Web is a relatively free site for expressing and manifesting sociopolitical dissent, it can also be used as a space for national division and a site for counter-movements which capitalise on social norms to weaken and suppress the resistance of users. Whether such counteractions are successful or not, the Web remains a public space of providing conditions for political incorrectness as much as it enables social movements and marginal voices of dissidence to be heard.

Clearly, the outcomes of the Tunisian uprising were not satisfactory for Ben Mhenni, as they did not fully answer the revolutionaries' call for social justice and equal fundamental rights for all (bread, freedom and social justice). The night of her death, Ben Mhenni posted an entry on her Facebook page criticising political leadership for failing the aspirations of those who lost their lives during the Arab uprisings.[31] However, before her tragic demise, she had continued to assert that it is censorship of freedom of expression that hinders any possibility for a successful democratic transition: 'nothing will change if information does not circulate, if the truth is not communicated, if we do not connect' ('rien ne changera si l'information ne passe pas, si la vérité ne se diffuse pas, si nous ne nous connectons pas') (2011: 30). Hoping to push for a new law in the Tunisian Constitution which guarantees unfiltered cyber-expression and non-restricted Internet access and usage (ibid.: 31), Ben Mhenni insisted that the role of Tunisian dissident bloggers did not begin with the revolution and will not end with the deposition of Ben Ali; it remains 'an on-going process' ('le role d'un blogueur ne s'arrête jamais') (ibid.: 30).

Notes

1 Other compelling examples of Arab women digital activists include Egyptian Esraa Abdel-Fattah and Asmaa Mahfouz, two politically committed activists who have gained public appeal due to their online political engagements during the Egyptian Revolution of 2011. However, unlike Ben Mhenni, Abdel-Fattah's and Mahfouz's activism on the Web have gained considerable academic attention for being straightforwardly political and oppositional. Emnaa Ben Jemaa and Neila Kilani are two other Tunisian Web activists who advocated for democracy and social justice during the Tunisian Revolution. However, Jemaa and Kilani did not establish the wide reach and impact as well as the international visibility of Ben Mhenni.

2 The literariness of Arab(ic) digital writing, mainly blogging, has been stirring controversies among critics and scholars, some of whom consider digital writing as easy, non-aesthetic writing practices that threaten the merits and values of Arabic literature (Elsadda 2010: 330), while others attest to the new models of engagement and literary expression that digital platforms offer (El-Ariss 2019: 25). Scholars who look at the Arab(ic) blogosphere and its relationship to literary aesthetics and production include Hoda Elsadda (2010), Valerie Anishchenkova (2014), Tarek El-Ariss (2019) and Teresa Pepe (2019).

3 A similar term is used by prominent Egyptian activist Wael Ghonim in his memoir of the Egyptian uprising *Revolution 2.0: The Power of the People is Greater than the People in Power* (2012). Ghonim contrasts the past 'Revolution 1.0 model', which 'have usually had charismatic leaders who were politically savvy and sometimes even military geniuses' with 'the Revolution 2.0 model' in which '[p]eople who would only post comments in cyberspace became willing to stand in public . . . made the great leap to become marchers and chanters, and

grew into a critical mass that toppled a brutal and tyrannical regime' (2012: 293). He concludes that the recent Arab uprisings fit into 'the Revolution 2.0 model: no *one* was the hero because *everyone* was a hero' (ibid.: 294).

4   See United Nations Human Rights Office of the High Commissioner, 11 January 2013, https://www.ohchr.org/EN/NewsEvents/Pages/ManalAl-Sharifadriving forceforchange.aspx (accessed 28 August 2021).

5   Manal al-Sharif has authored a memoir on her experience entitled *Daring to Drive: A Saudi Woman's Awakening* (2017).

6   See *BBC News*, 12 September 2019, https://www.bbc.com/news/world-middle -east-49682115.

7   Accessed on 18 August 2021. Also see, for example, Charlotte Edwardes's 'The Gen Z Activist Twins of Sheikh Jarrah, Jerusalem', in *The Times* (17 July 2021).

8   See Chapter 1, pp. 50–1.

9   Riverbend chooses to be selective regarding the information she reveals about her identity; she writes: 'I'm female, Iraqi, and 24. I survived the war. That's all you need to know. It's all that matters these days anyway' (2005: 5).

10 Riverbend's book, a collection of blog posts and comments covering the period from August 2003 to September 2004, is also reminiscent of a subsequent Iraqi, blog-based monograph entitled *Iraqi Girl: Diary of a Teenage Girl in Iraq* (2009) (edited by Elizabeth Wrigley-Field; developed by John Ross). The subject of *Iraqi Girl* is an anonymous sixteen-year-old girl from Mosul who chooses to go by the pseudonym Hadiya. Through her blog, which she started in July 2004, Hadiya reflects autobiographically on the effects of the war on her family, friends and school by mediating the daily details in a simple language which subtly reflects the prevailing political scene.

11 The association of Baker, a Muslim Palestinian, with Frank, a Jewish figure, has sparked a public controversy. Although the comparison is based on the genre of life writing and the age/gender that both subjects share, many have perceived it as an inappropriate association of the victims with the – now – perpetrators (see Wolf 2017).

12 Accessed 18 August 2021.

13 From Baker's Twitter bio (accessed 18 August 2021).

14 See, for example: 'Syria Gay Girl in Damascus blog as a Hoax by US man', *BBC News*, 13 June 2011, https://www.bbc.co.uk/news/world-middle-east-1374 4980 (accessed 11 August 2019), and Teresa Pepe's introduction to *Blogging from Egypt: Digital Literature, 2005–2016* (2019).

15 See International Telecommunications Union's 'Measuring Digital Development'

(2019) at https://www.itu.int/en/ITU-D/Statistics/Documents/facts/Facts Figures2019.pdf.

16 For more details on repression of freedom of speech, particularly humour, in post-*ḥirāk* Algeria, see Hiyem Cheurfa's 'Controversial Humour in Algerian TV: Ramadan Comedies and the Limits of Laughter' (2020b).

17 See, for instance, 'Algerian Journalist Khaled Drareni Jailed for Two Years on Appeal', *France 24*, 15 September 2020, https://www.france24.com/en/2020 0915-algerian-journalist-khaled-drareni-jailed-for-two-years-on-appeal (accessed 26 December 2020).

18 Statistics retrieved from Ben Mhenni's blog (accessed 3 July 2018).

19 Ben Mhenni's father, Sadok Ben Mhenni, has published a prison memoir entitled *Sāriq al-Tamātim: Aw Zādani al-Ḥabsu ʿUmra* (The Tomato Thief: or Imprisonment has Aged Me) (2017).

20 ZABA is the acronym used by the Tunisian opponents of the regime to refer to Zine el-Abidine Ben Ali. It is used as a form of degrading the official resonance and authority of the late ex-President's name. The acronym is often deployed by Ben Mhenni throughout her book/blog.

21 See the post on Ben Mhenni's blog at http://atunisiangirl.blogspot.com/2010 /05/may-22nd-story.html (accessed 3 September 2020).

22 Ben Mhenni also recounts her participation in a preceding demonstration, Free Arabicca campaign (November 2009), which called for the release of a fellow blogger Fatma Riahi (whose avatar is Arabicca). The campaign brought international media attention to the issue of censorship in Tunisia and succeeded in putting an end to Fatma's unjust arrest (Ben Mhenni 2011: 6–7).

23 The full story is entitled 'May 22nd: the Story', which can be found on Ben Mhenni's blog at http://atunisiangirl.blogspot.com/2010/05/may-22nd-story .html, posted on 27 May 2010 (accessed 3 September 2020).

24 My translation from Tunisian *dārijah*. Entry 'To Ammar' could be found at http://atunisiangirl.blogspot.com/2010/05/blog-post_08.html (accessed 3 September 2020).

25 See this book's Introduction, p. 27.

26 Entries posted by Ben Mhenni on 3 January 2011.

27 nawaat.org was awarded a number of international prizes including The Reporters Without Borders Netizen Prize of 2011, and The Index on Censorship Award of 2011.

28 Ben Mhenni's entry on Regueb can be found at http://atunisiangirl.blogspot .com/2011/01/erregueb-january-9th-2011.html (accessed 2 July 2018).

29 Amal Amireh discusses the prioritisation of national concerns over feminist demands in contexts of national liberation, particularly in relation to the Palestinian case. She notes that this 'prioritisation paradigm' of nationalist agendas over women's issues is either because national liberation is 'more pressing' and, thus, 'have priority', or because 'high political risks of legitimacy and influence are involved in bringing them [feminist concerns] up when "society" is not ready' (2014: 196).

30 The entry with the comments can be found at http://atunisiangirl.blogspot.com/2012/06/blog-post_30.html (accessed 14 July 2018).

31 See Ben Mhenni's Facebook page at https://www.facebook.com/atunisiangirl (accessed 3 September 2020).

Conclusion

Arab(ic) Resistance Non-fiction: Critical Trajectories

Throughout this book, my aim has been to examine Arab women's life writings as cultural sites of expressing and manifesting resistance to an imbrication of power discourses. I have demonstrated that the importance of Arab women's autobiographical literature lies in the way the genre provides an unmediated literary access to personal voice and narratives – as compared to other literary genres like fiction. This autobiographical literature, therefore, offers intimate insights into the political, cultural and ideological mechanisms of national struggles as experienced by the narrating/writing subject. Life writing by Arab women embodies the intertwined relationship between resistance, (self-)representation and self-determination and captures a convergence of feminist, literary and historico-political issues. It highlights the interplay between literary production and power discourses as well as how forms of self-expression can engage with, interrogate and challenge dominant social, political and representational narratives. Through using the genre deliberately and creatively, Arab '[w]omen coerce the multiple limitations of their traditionally ascribed domestic roles to raise their voices and assert their own priorities in the public forums of ideological debate and public struggle' (Harlow 1992: 33). By assuming and asserting the position of the speaking agent, Arab women life writers examined in this book attempt to dismiss representational mediation, or what Moroccan author Laila Laalami describes as 'the surrogate storytellers' (2020: 155), and to depict the political and cultural landscapes from the personal lens of experience. Driven by the desire to make their stories visible in their own terms, they use the genre as a space of agency to 'speak truth to the power(s)' against which their narratives emerge. Their stories are first-hand personal testaments that also constitute political statements. They speak against tyrannical regimes, exploitative and oppressive constructions of gender in the region, and prevalent – often monolithic – discourses of cultural representation that tend to demarcate Arab women's life and participation in the public arena of political struggle.

My main purpose in this book has been to demonstrate that life writing subgenres are not merely concerned with voice and representation or challenging the long-standing stereotype of the passive and submissive Arab woman. They equally represent a cultural form of revolutionary engagement that deliberately complicates any straightforward thinking around forms and conventions of non-fiction. The sociopolitical contexts of national struggles within/about which Arab women write inspire and allow for various formal and aesthetic experimentation with(in) the genre. Women authors examined in this book enact their active involvement within revolutions and resistance through diverse literary approaches – often entailing creative elements which challenge formal conventions – that assert their own voices, personal experiences and unique literary aesthetics. In doing so, these authors make critical interventions into scholarly fields of knowledge production and consumption. They revise literary representational frameworks that tend to homogenise Arab women's writing, thematically and stylistically. Having said this, we should not assume that experimentation with the genre means that the texts are more politically engaged, and/or represent better forms of cultural resistance, than those which conform to generic rules and conventions. Instead, I hope to have illustrated that the range of literary strategies discussed in this book highlight some of the new and emerging literary approaches that Arab women enact in order to write autobiographically during moments of conflict. These literary trajectories reflect the aesthetic diversity in life writing forms through which resistance is both sought and articulated.

In the rapidly changing context of the contemporary Arab world, life writing continues to be an important form that penetrates and provides alternatives to official discourses, especially with the tendency of essentialist narratives to dominate. Indeed, autobiographical narratives reflect a specific historical reality that is circumstanced to its particular moment of articulation and narration. However, while the political landscape in the region seems to be in a perpetual flux, and hence the meaning and means of resistance are often changing and/or developing, looking at personal accounts of specific contexts of national struggles is crucial in understanding and in evaluating the role of Arab women as women, as citizens, as writers, as critics and as revolutionaries in particular historical moments. The processes of retrospection and reflection that go into the writing of non-fiction help recapture these historical periods and make their impact more narratively visible and sustainable – mainly through the genre's archival capacity. These autobiographical discourses, thus, constitute politically engaged, historically embedded and culturally persisting acts of resistance which demonstrate and redefine the relationship between writing and fighting. Additionally, while autobiographical works provide competing histories to dominant narratives on Arab women and resistance, they simultaneously sustain the notion of the collective. As I have demonstrated through my textual analysis, the nexus between the individual and the collective particularly emerges through the writing of the self. While each autobiographical text examined in this book is positioned in its individual author's specific social, cultural, institutional and historical contexts, I have also noted the relationality of these context and the overlapping historical circumstances and material conditions of the Arab region that inform these narratives. Arab women articulate their experience of resistance, not as an exclusive or isolated event but as part of a collective narrative, by writing themselves into the national history discourse.

However, life witing as a literary form of resistance has its limitations. Autobiographical writing is not an immediate and/or natural form of resistance. It is often deliberate, strategic and tactical and targets an educated, often intellectual, audience who is aware of the significance of historical referencing and the sociopolitical conditions of writing. That is, autobiographical narratives may not be as accessible to a wider public as, say, film, graffiti, oral chants and popular poetry. Life writing generally depends on channels of publication and circulation to exist, and hence can be selective regarding the readership it targets and reaches. This also affects the scopes of (self)representation as stories and testimonies of less privileged Arab women may remain unknown. Additionally, like all forms of cultural resistance, the impact of life writing on inducing an actual change at the sociopolitical level remains limited and contingent upon external factors such as on-the-ground activism and engagement. This, however, does not dismiss the important role that this literature, in its different forms, plays in mobilising liberation movements and the ways in which culture continues to be an intrinsic part of political agendas (Kanafani 1966; Harlow 1987).

Moreover, resistance literature, like other oppositional cultural discourses, has historically engendered counter-resistance from the oppressive powers and authorities it contests. Political writers and intellectuals are potential targets of various forms of censorship, silencing, interrogation, imprisonment (as we have seen in Chapter 1) and, in some extreme cases, assassination. The death of the writer/activist at the hand of oppressive colonial powers and/or dictatorial regimes, such as the case of, most prominently, Palestinian author Ghassan Kanfani and cartoonist Naji al Ali, proves the threatening power of culture – that arises from conditions of resistance – to oppressive systems and consequently its significant role in the national liberation struggle (Harlow 1996: 26). The assassination of the writer/activist is thus politically motivated and, as Tahrir Hamdi puts it, 'has a broad historical, political and cultural dimension in which an attempt is made to silence the witness and extinguish the flame of resistance . . . hoping not only to erase the history of the dispossessed but to kill their defiant will and their story' (2011: 23). The cultural projects of these writers/activists, however, continue to live to redefine and highlight the role of resistance literature in motivating political dissidence. They ultimately open up new critical trajectories on the fundamental relationship between cultural and political engagements, an endeavour that was central to this monograph.

Contemporary Arab Women's Life Writing and the Politics of Resistance has examined Arab women's autobiographical writings that speak to and/or emerge as part of national liberation struggles and/or revolutionary movements as cultural sites for the articulation of resistance. Surveying works published in the twentieth century (Chapter 1) was crucial to my argument because it allowed us to examine how the genre has engaged with histories of (post)colonialism, national movements and independence struggles. The survey therefore contextualised women's life writing within an earlier tradition of autobiographical resistance writing. The following chapters examined selected thematic and formal modalities of resistance in more recent (twenty-first-century published) autobiographical works. Chapter 2 examined the representation of decentred subjectivities in life narratives by Egyptian Radwa

Ashour and Algerian Maïssa Bey. Both authors reflect an awareness of mainstream critical conceptions of the genre. They produce texts which do not fall into predominant patterns of non-fictional writing about gendered postcolonial selves. Instead, they undertake a deliberate – and in each case unique – bricolage of genre (relying on multiplicity of forms and voices, metatextual approaches and historical references). Their writings problematise the adequacy of predefined aesthetic and critical approaches to autobiographical writing when the subject is burdened by an enduring colonial heritage, gendered identity, sociopolitical marginalisation and representational homogenisation.

Devoted to testimonial writing, Chapter 3 assessed eye-witness accounts by Syrian Samar Yazbek and Palestinian Suad Amiry. It demonstrated that these authors' use of the form of testimony – to bear witness to the Syrian revolution and the ongoing Palestinian occupation respectively – highlights the capacity of life narratives to perform as historical references and archival materials, putting into question ways in which collective memory and national history should be inscribed and remembered. Equally, Yazbek's and Amiry's transborder testimonies present a politically revised model of the Arab woman storyteller who is not a distant narrator but an active actor in the war story which she scribes.

In Chapter 4, I explored the strategic use of comedy in diaries that record national struggles by Palestinian Suad Amiry and Egyptian Mona Prince. The chapter argued that the use of comedy to write autobiographically about national conflicts revises the conventional image of the female war victim and enacts a subject who is capable of daily laughter in the face of atrocity. Amiry's and Prince's humorous diaries reinvigorate our understanding of women's non-fictional accounts from conflict zones. They foreground the instrumental role of the comedy of dissent in the contemporary Arab world as a strategic revolutionary discourse for voicing the desire of the people for liberation, democracy and social justice.

Chapter 5 examined social media platforms as emerging autobiographical sites for the articulation of dissent, or what I referred to as resistance 2.0. Focusing its analysis on the case of Tunisian digital activist Lina Ben Mhenni, the chapter provided insights into ways in which digital media has altered critical conventions of autobiographical writing and broadened the available channels for sociopolitical engagement and resistance.

As I point out in my Introduction, no elaborate study of this length has been conducted to examine Arab women's life writing as sites of voicing and exercising dissent, in different linguistic and sub-generic channels, and with such up-to-date historical and contextual frameworks as those I pursue here. At the same time, I acknowledge that this book is not a comprehensive study of the available autobiographical approaches to resistance literature by contemporary Arab women. Such a project is beyond the scope of the present work. Equally, I do not claim that oppositional life writing that is contextualised in national struggles and revolutionary movements is a new phenomenon among Arab women or exclusive to the authors under scrutiny. The limited selection of texts included here highlight some specific literary forms of cultural dissent that are relevant to the frameworks of my analysis: postcolonial Arab literature, resistance literature and contemporary women's life writing. This book, however, highlights the need for a nuanced development of a critical field of Arab auto/biography studies.

This monograph has sought to initiate and hopes to encourage new networks of postcolonial research on life writing forms as part of revolutionary and dissident culture, as expressed and advocated by women in the Arab region. Each chapter in this book suggests some exciting trajectories for future research, including book-length biographies and biographical fragments and non-fiction on political detention (Chapter 1), autobiographical writings from the Maghreb in Arabic and in French (Chapter 2), oral stories and mediated testimonies from war-torn areas (Chapter 3), the diary genre in modern and contemporary Arab culture (Chapter 4), digital diaries in vernacular Arabic (Chapter 5) and the politics of paratext and translation of Arab women's auto/biographies and memoirs.

Chapter 2 of this book, for example, sheds light on the use of metatext in Arab autobiographical writings as a venue of inquiry that emphatically needs more critical examination. The chapter suggests that the use of metatextual elements in life narratives provides useful models of understanding the construction of autobiographical subjectivity and its relationship to reality outside the text. The use of metatext in autobiographical narratives gives as much importance to the text/language as to its speaking subject/her life. It draws attention to the linguistic and structural frames within which the 'life' in life writing projects is being represented; it thus questions the notion of totality in writing autobiographically and acts as a reminder of the frames of literary artificiality within which this mediated life is necessarily reduced. While this chapter provides a brief examination of the use of metatext in selected examples within a particular gendered, postcolonial and regional context, it demonstrates the clear critical gap in the intersectional frame of metatext and autobiography. Hence, it urges further critical exploration of pressing inquiries including: how does the use of metatext negotiate the relation between autobiographical and theoretical writing? Does it act to confirm, or contest established distinctions between theoretical writing on the one hand, and individual and personal writing on the other? Is the use of metatext in postcolonial women's autobiographical texts always subversive of dominant creative and critical approaches to the autobiographical?

Autobiographical essays and short creative non-fiction by Arab women are forms of life writing that deserve critical attention for their exploration of the intertwined relationship between women's self-expression and persisting issues of gender, class, sexuality and politics. Since the publication of Fadia Faqir's edited collection, *In the House of Silence* (1999), several edited volumes have been published which bring together diverse experiences and voices of Arab women authors, public figures, activists and journalists. A recent example is *Our Women on the Ground: Arab Women Reporting from the Arab World* (2019), a collection of autobiographical essays by nineteen Arab female journalists reporting from the war-torn Arab region. The editor of this collection, British Lebanese journalist Zahra Hankir, writes in her introduction that each of the essays autobiographically confronts 'issues surrounding gender, nationality, tradition, and authenticity' in order to 'help ensure that the voices of the women who are striving to shape and document Arab history now are amplified' (2019: xx). This anthology, a powerful and efficient combination of memoir, journalistic reportage, socio-cultural commentary and historical documentary, provides important insights into the experiences of women who are writing in moments of social and political upheaval. The book foregrounds the importance of first-hand accounts for Arab women who are writing about and against intersectional power discourses to which they are subjected as politically committed female writers and activists in contexts of political unrest. It also illustrates the range of literary autobiographical forms that Arab women deploy in order to make visible their voices and experiences as active agents in the war story; concerns that were central to my book. Other relevant examples that appeared in the last few years include *Ḥaflah li Thā'ira: Falastīniyāt Yaktubn al-Ḥayāt* (2017) (A Party for The Revolutionary: Palestinian Women Writing Life), a collection of non-fictional creative essays by former Palestinian women prisoners edited by Iraqi author Haifa Zangana; *Sex and Lies: True Stories of Women's Intimate Lives in the Arab World* (2020), collected by Franco-Moroccan author Leila Slimani (published originally in 2017 in French as *Sexe et mensonges – La vie sexuelle au Maroc*); and *Beyond Memory: An Anthology of Contemporary Arab American Creative Nonfiction* (2020), edited by Pauline Kaldas and Khaled Mattawa.[1]

A distinctive form of life writing in which I am particularly interested as a cultural vehicle for sociopolitical expression and a salient form of representational, formal and ideological resistance is Arab graphic life writing. Graphic life writing, also called 'autographics' – a literary form that investigates the 'conjunctions of visual and verbal text in this genre of autobiography' (Whitlock 2006: 966) – is a growing form of self-expression in contemporary Arab culture that has flourished in the last decade. The form has become part of Arab subversive culture (Høigilt 2019: 2), and is available in English, Arabic and French, and increasingly in translations.[2] The most common themes explored in contemporary Arab autographics are questions of identity and belonging, refugee crises, issues of displacement and political upheavals especially since the Arab uprisings. Some of the available works (by men and women authors) that provide excellent examples of resistance literature in autographics form include Lebanese author and illustrator Zeina Abirached's *A Game for Swallows: To Die, To Leave, To Return* (2012) and *I Remember Beirut* (2014), originally published in French in 2007 and 2008 respectively; French-Syrian author Riyadh Sattouf's account of his childhood in the Middle East *The Arab of the Future* (2015) (a series of five volumes originally published in French as *l'Arab de future*); and Lebanese Mazen Kerbaj's *Beirut Won't Cry: Lebanon's July War: a Visual Diary* (2017), originally published in Arabic in 2007. Graphic memoirs by women of Arab origins include, most recently, Lebanese Lamia Ziadé's *Bye Bye Babylon: Beirut 1975–1979* (2011) (published originally in French in 2010), Palestinian American artists Iasmin Omar Ata's *Mis(h)adra* (2017) and Marguerite Dabaie's *The Hookah Girl: And Other True Stories* (2018), American-Egyptian-Filipino artist Malaka Gharib's *I Was Their American Dream* (2019) and British (of Iraqi origins) Carol Isaacs's *The Woolf of Baghdad* (2020), to mention a few. New works keep appearing across the region and in the diaspora. My work on *Contemporary Arab Women's Life Writing and the Politics of Resistance* has, thus, made it appropriate for me to expand the scope of my research to include non-fictional comics,[3] an area on which I look forward to seeing more robust scholarly investigation.

Autobiographical literature by women living in and/or originally from the Gulf region (Bahrain, Kuwait, Iraq, Oman, Qatar, Saudi Arabia and the United Arab Emirates) and Jordan is a category that is missing in this book, but I recognise it as a subject of research that lacks a sustained critical interest in Anglophone scholarship. Gulf literature by women is increasingly gaining international attention especially after the translation of many fictional works that have received considerable critical acclaim – such as Saudi writers Rajaa al-Sanea's *Girls of Riyadh* (2008) and Raja Alem's *The Dove's Necklace* (2016), Kuwaiti author Bothayna al-Essa's *All That I Want to Forget* (2019) and, arguably most prominently, Omani author Jokha al-Harthi's *Celestial Bodies* (2019), which won the Man Booker International Prize 2019 with its translator Marilyn Booth – and the rise of a new generation of women authors writing in English like Kuwaiti writers Mai Al-Nakib and Layla al-Ammar and Qatari American artist and writer Sophia Al-Maria. Available autobiographical works by women from this region are not abundant but have been, in recent years, proliferating. Some of these works include Saudi author Fadia Basrawi's *Brownies and Kalashnikovs: A Saudi Woman's Memoir of American Arabia and Wartime Beirut* (2009), Qatari American artist and author Sophia Al-Maria's *The Girl Who Fell to Earth: A Memoir* (2012), Saudi activist Manal al-Sharif's memoir *Daring to Drive: A Saudi Woman's Awakening* (2017), and Jordanian American author Diana Abu Jaber's *The Language of Baklava: A Memoir* (2005). Abu Jaber's narrative, a fascinating combination of life stories and food recipes, in which the author tells us about her experience of growing up as an Arab American in 1960s–70s USA through stories from her family's kitchen, also encourages us to investigate what has been labelled 'culinary memoirs' (Nyman 2009), or 'cookbook-memoirs' in modern and contemporary Arab literature and culture.[4]

I look forward to seeing new research on Arab literary non-fiction in different forms and modes of expression. Arab life writing continues to be an under-theorised form of cultural resistance which requires postcolonial analysis sensitive to its varied and rich literary and artistic forms. As Barbara Harlow famously maintains, 'this [resistance] literature, like the resistance and national liberation movements which it reflects and in which it can be said to participate, not only demands recognition of its independent status and existence as literary production'; it also 'presents a serious challenge to the codes and cannons of both the theory and the practice of literature and its criticism' (1987: xvi). The enduring effects and the unfulfilling outcomes of the Arab uprisings, the persisting oppression of Palestinians by Israeli occupation, the ongoing popular desire for sociopolitical change in the region, the longstanding gender inequality and the systematic oppression of freedom of speech have inspired a range of autobiographical writings in different forms that speak to, testify against and record the predicament of the individual and the collective in different Arab states, often in creative and experimental ways. The critical consideration of Arab autobiographical voices as central to revolutionary movements is, thus, both historically and politically urgent and compelling, especially in the light of the renewed, and ongoing, pro-democratic movements (*ḥirāks*) across the region – particularly in Algeria, Sudan, Iraq and Lebanon – and the substantial rise in life writing production and publication that emerge thereof. Future scholarship can examine the genre's political imprints and the relationship between experimental modes of non-fictional writing and sociopolitical activism in diverse autobiographical forms and media of self-expression from less known authors and critically marginalised Arab countries – which I did not have the space to address here but some of which I suggest in this conclusion. The way this literature revises and reinvigorates theoretical and critical conventions on the practice of life writing also begs for meticulous studies. Such new routes of research would help us understand the range of aesthetic models of non-fictional writing that Arab authors choose for enunciating dissent and can ultimately inform ways in which we understand, critically approach and consume Arab autobiographical literature.

Notes

1. In their introduction to *Beyond Memory* (2020), a collection of creative non-fiction by Arab American authors, Kaldas and Mattawa refer to the included essays as 'memoir essays' which are vehicles 'to witness selves broadening their horizons – expending their, and our, potential for empathy and solidarity'; they describe 'the impulse to experiment with the form of the essay itself, compelling it to accommodate explorations that stem and go beyond one's experiences and memories' (xi).
2. In *Comics in Contemporary Arab Culture: Politics, Language and Resistance* (2019), Jacob Høigilt distinguishes between comics from the Middle East/Arab countries and comics about the Middle East/Arab countries in the sense that, according to the author, the former 'are comics written in the Arab world, by Arabs, in Arabic (for the most part), and published in the Arab world' (3).
3. See Cheurfa 2020a.
4. The literary magazine *ArabLit Quarterly* has an issue entitled *The Kitchen* (Summer 2021), edited by Nour Kamel and Marcia Lynx, which discusses food and culinary practices in Arab literary traditions.

Bibliography

Abaza, Mona and Samia Mehrez (eds) (2016). *Arts and the Uprising in Egypt: The Making of a Culture of Dissent?* Cairo: The American University of Cairo Press.

Abdel ʿAal, Ghada (2009). *ʿĀyza ʾAtgaūwiz* (*I Want to Get Married!*, 2010). Egypt: Dār al-Shurūq.

Abirached, Zeina (2012). *A Game for Swallows: To Die, To Leave, To Return.* Minneapolis: Graphic Universe.

— (2014). *I Remember Beirut.* Minneapolis: Graphic Universe.

Abou Rached, Ruth (2021). *Reading Iraqi Women's Novels in English Translation: Iraqi Women's Stories.* Abingdon: Routledge.

Abouzeid, Leila (1989). *Year of the Elephant: A Moroccan Woman's Journey Towards Independence and Other Stories* (*ʿĀm al-Fīl*, 1979), trans. Barbara Parmenter. Austin: University of Texas Press.

— (1991). *Amrīkā al-Wajh al-Ākhar* (America: The Other Face). Casablanca: Maṭbaʿat al-Jadīdā.

— (1993). *al-Rujūʿ ila-l-Ṭufūlah.* Casablanca: al-Madāris.

— (1998). *Return to Childhood: The Memoir of a Modern Moroccan Woman,* trans. Leila Abouzeid with Heather Logan Taylor. Austin: University of Texas Press.

Abrams, M. H. (1990). *A Glossary of Literary Terms,* 7th edn. Massachusetts: Heinle & Heinle.

Abu Jaber, Diana (2005). *The Language of Baklava: A Memoir.* New York: Anchor Books.

Achcar, Gilbert (2016). *Morbid Symptoms: Relapse in the Arab Uprising.* Stanford: Stanford University Press.

Ahmed, Leila (1999). *A Border Passage: From Cairo to America, A Woman's Journey*. New York: Farrar, Straus, and Giroux.

Ahmed, Sara (2000). *Strange Encounters: Embodied Others in Post-Coloniality*. New York: Routledge.

Al-Ali, Nadje (2007). *Iraqi Women: Untold Stories from 1948 to the Present*. London: Zed Books.

Al-Ali, Nadje and Nicola Pratt (eds) (2009). *Women and War in the Middle East: Transnational Perspectives*. London: Zed Books.

al-Barghouti, Tamim (2015). 'Cracked Cauldrons: The Failure of the States and the Rise of New Narratives in the Middle East', in Raja Shehadeh and Penny Johnson (eds), *Shifting Sands: The Unravelling of the Old Order in the Middle East*. London: Profile Books.

al-Essa, Bothayna (2019). *All That I Want to Forget*, trans. Michele Henjum. New York: Hoopoe.

al-Ghazali, Zaynab (1989). *Days from My Life* (*Ayyām min Ḥayātī*, 1972), trans. A. R. Kidwai. Delhi: Hindustan Publications.

al-Harthi, Jokha (2019). *Celestial Bodies*, trans. Marilyn Booth. New York: Catapult & Sandstone Press.

al-Hassan, Hawra (2020). *Women, Writing and the Iraqi Ba'thist State: Contending Discourses of Resistance and Collaboration, 1968–2003*. Edinburgh: Edinburgh University Press.

Al-Khamissi, Khaled (2011). *Taxi*, trans. Jonathan Wright. Doha: Bloomsbury Qatar Foundation Publishing.

Al-Maria, Sophia (2012). *The Girl Who Fell to Earth: A Memoir*. New York: Harper Perennial.

Al-Samman, Hanadi (2015). *Anxiety of Erasure: Trauma, Authorship, and the Diaspora in Arab Women's Writing*. Syracuse: Syracuse University Press.

al-Sanea, Rajaa (2008). *Girls of Riyadh*, trans. Rajaa al-Sanea and Marilyn Booth. London: Penguin Books.

al-Sharif, Manal (2017). *Daring to Drive: A Saudi Woman's Awakening*. New York: Simon and Schuster.

al-Zayyat, Latifa (1996). *The Search: Personal Papers* (*Ḥamlat Taftīsh:'Awrāk Shakhṣiyyah*, 1992), trans. Sophie Bennet. London: Quartet Books.

— (2000). *The Open Door*, trans. Marilyn Booth. Cairo: American University in Cairo Press.

Alem, Raja (2016). *The Dove's Necklace*, trans. Katherine Hals and Adam Talib. London: Overlook Duckworth.

AlJahdali, Samar H. (2014). 'Venturing into a Vanishing Space: the Chronotope in Representing Palestinian Postcoloniality', *Journal of Postcolonial Writing*, 50:2, pp. 216–29.

Allam, Nermin (2018). *Women and the Egyptian Revolution: Engagement and Activism During the 2011 Arab Uprisings*. Cambridge: Cambridge University Press.

Alshejini, Lamis (1999). 'Unveiling the Arab Woman's Voice through the Net', in Wendy Harcourt (ed.), *Women@Internet: Creating New Culture in Cyberspace*. London: Zed Books.

Amin, Ahmad (1978). *My Life: The Autobiography of an Egyptian Scholar, Writer, and Cultural Leader* (*Ḥayāti*, 1950), trans. Issa J. Boullata. Leiden: E. J Brill.

Amireh, Amal (1996). 'Publishing in the West: Problems and Prospects for Arab Women Writers', *al-Jadid*, 2:10, https://www.aljadid.com/content/publishing-west-problems-and-prospects-arab-women-writers.

— (2014). 'Liberation Struggles: Reflections on the Palestinian Women's Movement', in Jean Said Makdisi, Noha Bayoumi and Rafif Rida Sidawi (eds), *Arab Feminisms: Gender Equality in the Middle East*. London: I. B. Tauris & Co. Ltd.

Amireh, Amal and Lisa Suhair Majaj (2000). *Going Global: The Transnational Reception of Third World Women Writers*. New York: Garland.

Amiry, Suad (2006). *Sharon and my Mother-in-Law: Ramallah Diaries*. London: Granta.

— (2010). *Nothing to Lose but your Life: an 18-hour Journey with Murad*. Qatar: Bloomsbury Qatar Foundation Publishing.

— (2012). 'An Obsession', in Penny Johnson and Raja Shehadeh (eds), *Seeking Palestine: New Palestinian Writing on Exile and Home*. Northampton, MA: Interlink Books.

Anderson, Benedict (1983). *Imagined Communities: Reflections on the Origin and Spread of Nationalism*. London: Verso Books.

Anderson, Linda (2011). *Autobiography*, 2nd edn. London: Routledge.

Anishchenkova, Valerie (2014). *Autobiographical Identities in Contemporary Arab Culture*. Edinburgh: Edinburgh University Press.

Antoon, Sinan (2007). *I'jām: an Iraqi Rhapsody*, trans. Rebecca C. Johnson and Sinan Antoon. San Francisco: City Lights.

Aouragh, Miriyam (2012). 'Social Media, Mediation and the Arab Revolutions', *Triple C*, 10:2, pp. 518–36.

Arthur, Paul Longley (2009). 'Digital Biography: Capturing Lives Online', *a/b: Auto/Biography Studies*, 24:1, pp. 74–92.

Ashcroft, Bill, Gareth Griffiths and Helen Tiffin (1989). *The Empire Writes Back: Theory and Practice in Post-Colonial Literature*. London: Routledge.
Ashour, Radwa (1981). *Al-Ṭarīq Ilā al-Khaymā al-Ukhrā* (The Road to the Other Tent). Beirut: Dār al-Ādāb.
— (1983). *Al-Riḥlah: Ayyām Ṭālibah Miṣriyyah fī Amrīkā*. Beirut: Dār al-Ādāb.
— (1993). 'My Experience with Writing', trans. Rebecca Porteous, *Alif: Journal of Comparative Poetics*, 13, pp. 170–5.
— (1999). *Aṭyāf*. Cairo: Dār al-Hilāl.
— (2000). 'Eyewitness, Scribe and Story Teller: My Experience as a Novelist', *The Massachusetts Review*, 41:1, pp. 85–92.
— (2003). *Granada: A Novel*, trans. William Granara. Syracuse: Syracuse University Press.
— (2011). *Specters*, trans. Barbara Romaine. Northampton, MA: Interlink Books.
— (2013). *Athqal min Radwā: Maqāṭiʿ min Sīrah Dhātiyyah* (Heavier than Radwa: Fragments of an Autobiography). Cairo: Dār al-Shurūq.
— (2014). *The Woman from Tantoura: A Novel of Palestine*. Cairo: The American University in Cairo Press.
— (2015). *Al-Ṣarkhah: Maqāṭiʿ min Sīrah Dhātiyyah* (The Scream: Fragments of an Autobiography). Cairo: Dār al-Shurūq.
— (2018). *The Journey: Memoirs of an Egyptian Woman Student in America*, trans. Michelle Hartman. Northampton, MA: Interlink Publishing.
Ashour, Radwa, Ferial Jabouri Ghazoul and Hasna Reda-Mekdashi (2008). *Arab Women Writers: a Critical Reference Guide, 1873–1999*. Cairo: The American University in Cairo Press.
Ashrawi, Hanan (1995). *This Side of Peace: A Personal Account*. New York: Touchstone.
Atiya, Nayra (1982). *Khul-Khaal: Five Egyptian Women Tell Their Stories*. Syracuse: Syracuse University Press.
Awad, Sarah H. and Brady Wagoner (eds) (2017). *Street Art of Resistance*. London: Palgrave Macmillan.
Badran, Margot (ed.) (1986). *Harem Years: The Memoirs of an Egyptian Feminist*. New York: The Feminist Press at the City University of New York.
— (1996). *Feminists, Islam, and Nation: Gender and the Making of Modern Egypt*. Princeton, NJ: Princeton University Press.
— (2005). 'Between Secular and Islamic Feminism/s: Reflections on the Middle East and Beyond', *Journal of Middle East Women's Studies*, 1:1, pp. 6–28, http://www.jstor.org/stable/40326847 (accessed 21 May 2021).

Badran, Margot and Miriam Cooke (eds) (1990). *Opening the Gates: A Century of Arab Feminist Writing* (London: Virago)
— (eds) (2004). *Opening the Gates: A Century of Arab Feminist Writing*, 2nd edn. Bloomington: Indiana University Press.
Baker, Farah (2021). 'Twitter account', 18 August, 10 a.m., https://twitter.com/Farah_Gazan.
Bakhtin, Mikhail (1984a). *Problems of Dostoevsky's Poetics*, trans. Caryl Emerson. Minneapolis: University of Minnesota Press.
— (1984b). *Rabelais and his World*, trans. Hélèn Iswolsky. Bloomington: Indiana University Press.
Ball, Anna (2012). *Palestinian Literature and Film in Postcolonial Feminist Perspective*. New York: Routledge.
Ball, Anna and Karim Mattar (eds) (2019). *The Edinburgh Companion to the Postcolonial Middle East*. Edinburgh: Edinburgh University Press.
Barakat, Hoda (1999). 'I Write against my Hand', in Fadia Faqir (ed.), *In the House of Silence: Autobiographical Essays by Arab Women Writers*. Reading: Garnet.
Barreca, Regina (ed.) (1988). *Last Laughs: Perspective on Women and Comedy*. Amsterdam: Gordon and Breach Science Publishers, Inc.
— (1991). *They Used to Call me Snow White . . . but I Drifted: Women's Strategic Use of Humor*. New York: Viking Penguin.
— (ed.) (1992). *New Perspectives on Women and Comedy*. Amsterdam: Gordon and Breach Science Publishers.
— (1994). *Untamed and Unabashed: Essays on Women and Humor in British Literature*. Detroit: Wayne State University Press.
Barthes, Roland (1977). *Roland Barthes by Roland Barthes*, trans. Richard Howard. London: Macmillan.
Basrawi, Fadia (2009). *Brownies and Kalashnikovs: A Saudi Woman's Memoir of American Arabia and Wartime Beirut*. Reading: South Street Press.
Beattie, James (1778). 'Essays on Laughter and Ludicrous Composition', in Beattie, *Essays on Poetry and Music*. Edinburgh: Creech.
Bebawi, Saba and Diana Bossio (eds) (2014). *Social Media and the Politics of Reportage: the Arab Spring*. London: Palgrave Macmillan.
Belkaid, Meryem (2017). 'Writing beyond Trauma: Assia Djebar, Maissa Bey, and New National Identities after Algeria's Civil War', *The Journal of North African Studies* 23:1–2, pp. 125–39.
Ben Mhenni, Lina (2011). *Tunisian Girl, Bnayyah Tūnsiyyah: Blogueuse pour un printemps arabe* (Blogger for an Arab Spring). Paris: Indigène édition.

— *A Tunisian Girl*, http://atunisiangirl.blogspot.com/.
— *Tunisian Girl*, بنية تونسية *Lina Ben Mhenni*, Facebook page, https://www.facebook.com/atunisiangirl (accessed 3 September 2020).
Ben Mhenni, Sadok (2017). *Sāriq al-Tamātim: Aw Zādani al-Ḥabsu 'Umra* (The Tomato Thief: or Imprisonment has Aged Me). Tunis: Cérès éditions.
Bensmaïa, Réda (2003). *Experimental Nations: Or the Invention of the Maghreb*, trans. Alyson Waters. Princeton, NJ: Princeton University Press.
Benstock, Shari (1988). *The Private Self: Theory and Practice of Women's Autobiographical Writings*. Chapel Hill: University of North Carolina Press.
Bergson, Henri (2005). *Laughter: An Essay on the Meaning of the Comic* (*Le Rire*, 1900), trans. Cloudesley Brereton and Fred Rothwell. Mineola: Dover Publications.
Bernard, Anna (2013). *Rhetorics of Belonging: Nation, Narration, and Israel/Palestine*. Liverpool: Liverpool University Press.
Berque, Jacques (1978). *Cultural Expression in Arab Society Today*. Texas: University of Texas Press.
Beverley, John (1989). 'The Margin at the Center: On *Testimonio*', *MFS Modern Fiction Studies*, 35, pp. 11–28.
Bey, Maïssa (1998). *À Contre-Silence*. Paris: Parole D'Aube.
— (2003). 'Faut-il aller chercher des rêves ailleurs que dans la nuit?' (Should We Go Looking for Dreams Somewhere Other than the Night), in M. Bey *et al.*, *Journal intime et politique: Algérie, 40 ans après*, ed. Martine Picard. Paris: L'Aube.
— (2009). *L'une et l'autre*. Paris: L'Aube.
Bhabha, Homi (2004). *The Location of Culture*. London: Routledge.
Booth, Marilyn (1983). 'Farida al-Naqqash, Barred from Writing in Egypt: The Experience of a Journalist who was Critical of the Government', *Index on Censorship* 12:3, pp. 20–1, https://journals.sagepub.com/doi/pdf/10.1080/03064228308533533.
— (2001). *May Her Likes Be Multiplied: Biography and Gender Politics in Egypt*. Berkeley: University of California Press.
Bornstein, Avram S. (2002). *Crossing the Green Line between The West Bank and Israel*. Philadelphia: University of Pennsylvania Press.
Brisley, Lucy (2015). 'Trauma Theory, Melancholia and the Postcolonial Novel: Assia Djebar's *Algerian White/Le Blanc de l'Algérie*', in Abigail Ward (ed.), *Postcolonial Traumas: Memory, Narrative, Resistance*. London: Palgrave Macmillan.

Brodzki, Bella and Celeste Schenck (eds) (1988). *Life/Lines: Theorizing Women's Autobiography*. Ithaca: Cornell University Press.

Bromley, Roger (2014). '"Giving Memory a Future": Women, Writing, Revolution', *Journal for Cultural Research*, 19:2, pp. 221–32.

Brouillette, Sarah (2007). *Postcolonial Writers in the Global Literary Marketplace*. Basingstoke: Palgrave Macmillan.

Brown, Sophia (2014). 'Blogging the Resistance: Testimony and Solidarity in Egyptian Women's Blogs', *Contention: The Multidisciplinary Journal of Social Protest*, 2:1, pp. 41–55.

Bugeja, Norbert (2012). *Postcolonial Memoir in the Middle East: Rethinking the Liminal in Mashriqi Writing*. Abingdon: Routledge.

Butler, Judith (1990). *Gender Trouble: Feminism and the Subversion of Identity*. Abingdon: Routledge.

— (1993). *Bodies that Matter: on the Discursive Limits of "Sex"*. Abingdon: Routledge.

— (2005). 'Photography, War, Outrage', *PMLA*, 120: 3, pp. 822–7.

— (2009). *Frames of War: When is Life Grievable?* London: Verso.

Carroll, Noël (2014). *Humour: A Very Short Introduction*. Oxford: Oxford University Press.

Caruth, Cathy (1996). *Unclaimed Experience: Trauma, Narrative, and History*. Baltimore: Johns Hopkins University Press.

Castells, Manuel (2012). *Networks of Outrage and Hope: Social Movements in the Internet Age*. Cambridge: Polity Press.

Charrad, Mounira (2001). *States and Women's Rights: the Making of Postcolonial Tunisia, Algeria, and Morocco*. Berkeley: University of California Press.

Cheurfa, Hiyem (2019a). 'Comedic Resilience: Arab Women's Diaries of National Struggles and Dissident Humour', *Comedy Studies*, 10:2, pp. 183–98.

— (2019b). 'The Laughter of Dignity: Comedy and Dissent in the Algerian Popular Protests', *Jadaliyya*, 26 March, https://www.jadaliyya.com/Details/38495 (accessed 23 October 2019).

— (2019c). '12 (Auto)biographical Narratives by Algerian Women', *ArabLit*, 20 May, https://arablit.org/2019/05/20/12-autobiographical-narratives-by-algerian-women/.

— (2020a). 'Testifying Graphically: Bearing Witness to a Palestinian Childhood in Leila Abdelrazaq's Baddawi', *a/b: Auto/Biography Studies*, 35:2, pp. 359–82.

— (2020b). 'Controversial Humour in Algerian TV: Ramadan Comedies and the Limits of Laughter', *Jadaliyya*, 13 May, https://www.jadaliyya.com/Details

/41099/Controversial-Humour-in-Algerian-TV-Ramadan-Comedies-and-The-Limits-of-Laughter.

Civantos, Christina (2013). 'Reading and Writing the Turn-of-the-Century Egyptian Woman Intellectual: Nabawiyya Musa's Ta'rikhi Bi-Qalami', *Journal of Middle East Women's Studies*, 9: 2, pp. 4–31, www.jstor.org/stable/10.2979/jmiddeast womstud.9.2.4 (accessed 4 May 2021).

Cooke, Miriam (1993). 'WO-men, Retelling the War Myth', in Miriam Cooke and Angela Woollacott (eds), *Gendering War Talk*. Princeton, NJ: Princeton University Press.

— (2013). 'Tadmor's Ghosts', *Review of Middle East Studies*, 47, pp. 28–36.

— (2017). *Dancing in Damascus: Creativity, Resilience, and the Syrian Revolution*. New York: Routledge.

Cossery, Albert (2010). *The Jokers* (*La Violence et la derision*, 1964). New York: New York Review of Books Classics.

Coward, Ross (2009). 'Me, Me, Me: The Rise and Rise of Autobiographical Journalism', in Stuart Allan (ed.), *The Routledge Companion to News and Journalism*. Abingdon: Routledge.

Craps, Stef (2012). *Postcolonial Witnessing: Trauma out of Bounds*. London: Palgrave Macmillan.

Crowley, Patrick (ed.) (2017). *Algeria: Nation, Culture and Transnationalism 1988–2015*. Liverpool: Liverpool University Press.

Cubilié, Anne (2005). *Women Witnessing Terror: Testimony and the Cultural Politics of Human Rights*. New York: Fordham University Press.

Dabaie, Marguerite (2018). *The Hookah Girl: And Other True Stories*. College Park, MD: Rosarium Publishing.

Damir-Geilsdorf, Sabine and Stephan Milich (eds) (2020). *Creative Resistance: Political Humour in the Arab Uprisings*. Bielefeld: Transcript Verlag.

Davies, Helen and Sarah Ilott (eds) (2018a). *Comedy and the Politics of Representation: Mocking the Weak*. London: Palgrave Macmillan.

— (eds) (2018b). 'Gender, Sexuality and the body in Comedy: Performance, Reiteration, Resistance', *Comedy Studies*, 9:1.

Davies, Peter (2014). 'Testimony and Translation', *Translation and Literature*, 23:2, pp. 170–84.

de Man, Paul (1979). 'Autobiography as De-Facement', *MLN*, 94, pp. 919–30.

Derrida, Jacques (1996). *Monolingualism of the Other or The Prosthesis of Origin*, trans. Patrick Mensah. Stanford: Stanford University Press.

Djebar, Assia (1985). *L'Amour, la fantasia*. Paris: Éditions Jean-Claude Lattès.

— (1987). *Ombre sultane*. Paris: Éditions Jean-Claude Lattès.
— (1993a). *Fantasia, an Algerian Cavalcade*, trans. Dorothy S. Blair. Portsmouth: Heinemann.
— (1993b). *A Sister to Scheherazade*, trans. Dorothy S. Blair. London: Quartet.
— (1995a). *Le blanc de l'Algérie*. Paris: Albin Michel.
— (1995b). *Vaste est la prison*. Paris: Albin Michel.
— (1999). *Ces Voix qui m'assiègent ... en marge de ma francophonie*. Paris: Albin Michel.
— (2001). *So Vast the Prison*, trans. Betsy Wing. New York: Seven Stories Press.
— (2003). *Algerian White: A Narrative*, trans. David Kelley and Marjolijn de Jager. New York: Seven Stories Press.
— (2007). *Nulle part dans la maison de mon père*. Arles: Actes Sud.
Doho, Gilbert (2017). *Le Code de L'Indigénat: ou le fondement des états autocratiques en Afrique Francophone*. Paris: L'Harmattan.
Douai, Aziz and Mohamed Ben Moussa (eds) (2016). *Mediated Identities and New Journalism in the Arab World: Mapping the 'Arab Spring'*. London: Palgrave Macmillan.
Douglas, Allen and Fedwa Malti-Douglas (1994). *Arab Comic Strips: Politics of an Emerging Mass Culture*. Bloomington: Indiana University Press.
Douglass, Kate (2011). 'Life-Writing', in Peter Melville Logan *et al.* (eds), *The Encyclopaedia of the Novel*. Oxford: Wiley-Blackwell.
Drif, Zohra (2017). *Inside the Battle of Algiers: Memoir of a Woman Freedom Fighter*, trans. Andrew Farrand. Charlottesville: Just World Books.
Duncombe, Stephen (2002). *Cultural Resistance: Reader*. London: Verso.
Eakin, Paul John (2020). *Writing Life Writing: Narrative, History, Autobiography*. London: Routledge.
Edwardes, Charlotte 2021. 'The Gen Z Activist Twins of Sheikh Jarrah, Jerusalem', *The Times*, 17 July, https://www.thetimes.co.uk/article/muna-and-mohammed-el-kurd-the-gen-z-activist-twins-of-jerusalem-2-million-followers-and-counting-00cwn6bj5 (accessed 28 August 2021).
El Said, Maha, Lena Meari and Nicola Christine Pratt (eds) (2015). *Rethinking Gender in Revolutions and Resistance: Lessons from the Arab World*. London: Zed Books.
El-Ariss, Tarek (2019). *Leaks, Hacks, and Scandals: Arab Culture in the Digital Age*. Princeton, NJ: Princeton University Press.
El-Saadawi, Nawal (1980). *The Hidden Face of Eve: Women in the Arab World*, trans. Sherif Hetata. London: Zed Books.

— (1986). *Memoirs from the Women's Prison*, trans. Marilyn Booth. London: The Women's Press.
— (1988a). *Memoirs of a Woman Doctor (Mudhakirāt Tabībah*, 1958), trans. Catherine Cobham. London: Saqi Books.
— (1988b). *The Fall of the Imam (Suqūt al-'Imām)*, trans. Sherf Hetata. London: Saqi Books.
Elfarra, Mona. *From Gaza, with Love,* https://fromgaza.blogspot.com/ (accessed 28 August 2021).
Elmarsafy, Ziad (2015). 'Action, Imagination, Institution, Natality, Revolution', *Journal for Cultural Research*, 19:2, pp. 130–8.
Elsadda, Hoda (2010). 'Arab Women Bloggers: The Emergence of Literary Counterpublics', *Middle East Journal of Culture and Communication*, 3, pp. 312–32.
Eltahawi, Mona (2015). *Headscarves and Hymens: Why the Middle East Need a Sexual Revolution*. London: Weidenfeld & Nicolson.
Enderwitz, Susanne (1998). 'Public Role and Private Self', in Robin Ostle *et al.* (eds), *Writing the Self: Autobiographical Writing in Modern Arabic Literature*. London: Saqi Books.
Fanon, Frantz (1963). *The Wretched of the Earth*. London: Penguin Books.
Faqir, Fadia (ed.) (1999). *In the House of Silence: Autobiographical Essays by Arab Women Writers*. Reading: Garnet.
Farouk, Menna A. (2020). 'Egypt Jails Five Women Influencers Over Tiktok Posts', *Reuters*, 27 July, https://www.reuters.com/article/us-egypt-women-socialmedia-trfn/egypt-jails-five-women-influencers-over-tiktok-posts-idUSKCN24S2E4 (accessed 2 September 2020).
Felman, Shoshana and Dori Laub (1992). *Testimony: Crisis of Witnessing in Literature, Psychoanalysis, and History*. New York: Routledge.
Foucault, Michel (1990). *The History of Sexuality*, vol. 1, trans. Robert Hurley. New York: Vintage.
Franklin, Cynthia G. (2009). *Academic Lives: Memoir, Cultural Theory, and the University Today*. Athens, GA: University of Georgia Press.
Freud, Sigmund (1948). 'The "Uncanny"', in *The Standard Edition of the Complete Psychological Works of Sigmund Freud*, vol XVII, trans. James Strachey *et al*. London: The Hogarth Press.
— (1960). *Jokes, and their Relation to the Unconscious*, trans. James Strachey. Abingdon: Routledge & K. Paul.
Frye, Northrop (1965). *Anatomy of Criticism: Four Essays*. New York: Atheneum.

Gauch, Suzanne (2007). *Liberating Shahrazad: Feminism, Postcolonialism, and Islam*. Minneapolis: University of Minnesota Press.

Ghannouchi, Soumaya. *Soumaya Ghannouchi*, http://soumayaghannoushi.com/ (accessed 28 August 2021).

Gharib, Malaka (2019). *I Was Their American Dream*. New York: Clarkson Potter.

Ghonim, Wael (2012). *Revolution 2.0: The Power of the People is Greater than the People in Power*, Kindle edn. New York: HarperCollins Publishers.

Gilbert, Joanne R. (2004). *Performing Marginality: Humour, Gender, and Cultural Critique*. Detroit: Wayne State University Press.

Giles, Michelle (2011). 'Postcolonial Gothic and *The God of Small Things*: The Haunting of India's Past', *Postcolonial Text*, 6:1, pp. 1–15.

Gilmore, Leigh (1994). *Autobiographics: a Feminist Theory of Women's Self-Presentation*. Ithaca: Cornell University Press.

— (1998). 'Autobiographics', in Sidonie Smith and Julia Watson (eds), *Women, Autobiography, Theory: A Reader*. Madison: University of Wisconsin Press.

— (2001). *The Limits of Autobiography: Trauma and Testimony*. Ithaca: Cornell University Press.

Golley, Nawar Al-Hassan (2003). *Reading Arab Women's Autobiographies: Shahrazad Tells her Story*. Austin: University of Texas Press.

— (ed.) (2007). *Arab Women's Lives Retold: Exploring Identity through Writing*. New York: Syracuse University Press.

Gordimer, Nadine (2006). 'Witness: The Inward Testimony', *Al-Ahram Weekly Online*, https://www.masress.com/en/ahramweekly/11668 (accessed 6 September 2021).

Green, Andre (1996). *On Private Madness*. London: Routledge.

Gregory, Derek (2004). *The Colonial Present: Afghanistan, Palestine, Iraq*. Oxford: Blackwell.

Guène, Faïza (2006). *Just Like Tomorrow*, trans. Sarah Adams. Definitions (Young Adult).

Gusdorf, Georges (1980 [1956]). 'Conditions and Limits of Autobiography', in James Olney (ed.), *Autobiography: Essays Theoretical and Critical*. Princeton: Princeton University Press, pp. 28–48.

Habibi, Emile (2001 [1974]). *The Secret Life of Said the Pessoptimist*, trans. Salma Khadra Jayyusi and Trevor Legassick. London: Zed New Fiction.

Haddad, Joumana (2010). *I Killed Scheherazade: Confessions of an Angry Arab Woman*. London: Saqi Books.

Hafez, Sabry (2002). 'Raqsh al-Dhāt la Kitābatiha: Taḥawwulāt al-istratijīyāt al-

Naṣṣyah fī al-Sīra al-Dhātiyyah' (Variegating the Self: Transformation of Textual Strategies in Autobiography), *Alif: Journal of Comparative Poetics*, 22, pp. 7–33.

Hafez, Sherine (2014). 'The Revolution Shall Not Pass Through Women's Bodies: Egypt, Uprising and Gender Politics', *The Journal of North African Studies*, 19:2, pp. 172–85.

Hamdi, Tahrir (2011). 'Bearing Witness in Palestinian Resistance Literature', *Race and Class*, 52, pp. 21–42.

Hankir, Zahra (ed.) (2019). *Our Women on the Ground: Arab Women Reporting from the Arab World*. London: Harvill Secker.

Harcourt, Wendy (2004). 'World Wide Women and the Web', in David Gauntlett and Ross Horsley (eds), *Web Studies: Rewriting Media Studies for the Digital Age*. London: Arnold.

Harlow, Barbara (1986). 'From the Women's Prison: Third World Women's Narratives of Prison', *Feminist Studies*, 12:3, pp. 501–24, www.jstor.org/stable/3177910 (accessed 15 May 2021).

— (1987). *Resistance Literature*. New York: Methuen.

— (1992). *Barred Women, Writing, and Political Detention*. Hanover: University Press of New England.

— (1996). *After Lives: Legacies of Revolutionary Writing*. London: Verso.

Hassan, Salah and David Alvarez (eds) (2013). *Baleful Postcoloniality, Biography*, 36:1.

Helmy, Mohamed M. and Sabine Frerichs (2017). 'Sheherazade Says No: Artful Resistance in Contemporary Egyptian Political Cartoon', in Sarah H. Awad and Brady Wagoner (eds), *Street Art of Resistance*. London: Palgrave Macmillan.

Henderson, Mae Gwendolyn (1993). 'Speaking in Tongues: Dialogics, Dialectics and the Black Women Writer's Literary Tradition', in Patrick Williams and Laura Chrisman (eds), *Colonial Discourse and Post-Colonial Theory: A Reader*. London: Routledge.

Henke, Suzette A. (1998). *Shattered Subjects: Trauma and Testimony in Women's Life-Writing*. New York: St. Martin Press.

Herman, Judith (2015 [1992]). *Trauma and Recovery: The Aftermath of Violence – from Domestic Abuse to Political Terror*. New York: Basic Books.

Hiddleston, Jane (2006). *Assia Djebar: Out of Algeria*. Liverpool: Liverpool University Press.

Hobbes, Thomas (1991). *Leviathan*, ed. Richard Tuck. Cambridge: Cambridge University Press.

Høigilt, Jacob (2019). *Comics in Contemporary Arab Culture: Politics, Language and Resistance*. London: I. B. Tauris.

Hollander, Jocelyn A. and Rachel L. Einwohner (2004). 'Conceptualizing Resistance', *Sociological Forum*, 19:4, pp. 533–54.

Houlihan, Patrick F. (2001). *Wit and Humour in Ancient Egypt*. Ontario: The Rubicon Press.

Howard, Philip and Muzammil M. Hussain (2013). *Democracy's Fourth Wave? Digital Media and the Arab Spring*. Oxford: Oxford University Press.

Hubbell, Amy L. (2010). 'Dual, Divided and Doubled Selves: Three Women Writing Between Algeria and France', in Natalie Edwards and Christopher Hogarth (eds), *This "Self" Which is not One: Women's Life Writing in French*. Newcastle upon Tyne: Cambridge Scholars Publishing.

Huggan, Graham (2001). *The Postcolonial Exotic: Marketing the Margins*. London: Routledge.

— (2013). 'General Introduction', in Graham Huggan (ed.), *The Oxford Handbook of Postcolonial Studies*. Oxford: Oxford University Press.

Hussein, Taha (1929). *al-Ayyām*. Cairo: Dār al-Maʿārif.

Hutcheson, Francis (1750). *Reflections upon Laughter and Remarks upon the Fable of the Bees*. Glasgow: R. Urie for D. Baxter.

Hyndman-Rizk, Nelia (2020). 'New Media/New Feminism(s): The Lebanese Women's Movement Online and Offline', in Rita Stephan and Mounira M. Charrad (eds), *Women Rising in and Beyond the Arab Spring*. New York: New York University Press.

Idle, Nadia and Alex Nunns (eds) (2011). *Tweets from Tahrir: Egypt's Revolution as it Unfolded, in the Words of the People who Made it*. New York: OR Books.

Ilott, Sarah (2015). *New Postcolonial British Genres: Shifting the Boundaries*. London: Palgrave Macmillan.

Irving, Sarah (2012). *Leila Khaled: Icon of Palestinian Liberation*. London: Pluto Press.

Isaacs, Carol (2020). *The Woolf of Baghdad*. Oxford: Myriad Editions.

Jelinek, Estelle (ed.) (1980). *Women's Autobiography: Essays in Criticism*. Bloomington: Indiana University Press.

Jordan, Shirley (2012). 'État Présent: Autofiction in the Feminine', *French Studies*, LXVII:1, pp. 76–84.

Jung, Joo-Young (2016). 'Social Media, Global Communications, and the Arab Spring: Cross-Level and Cross Media Story Flows', in Aziz Douai and Mohamed

Ben Moussa (eds), *Mediated Identities and New Journalism in the Arab World: Mapping the "Arab Spring"*. London: Palgrave Macmillan.

Kahn, Richard and Douglas Kellner (2005). 'Oppositional Politics and the Internet: a Critical/Reconstructive Approach', *Cultural Politics*, 1:1, pp. 75–100.

Kaldas, Pauline and Khaled Mattawa (2020). *Beyond Memory: An Anthology of Contemporary Arab American Creative Nonfiction*. Fayetteville: University of Arkansas Press.

Kamel, Nour and Marcia Lynx Qualey (2021). *The Kitchen, ArabLit Quarterly*, Summer, 4:2.

Kammoun, Raoudha (2010). 'Humour and Arabs', in Carmen Valero-Garcés (ed.), *Dimensions of Humour: Explorations in Linguistics, Literature, Cultural Studies and Translation*. Valencia: Universitat de Valéncia.

Kanafani, Fay Afaf (1999). *Nadia: Captive of Hope: Memoir of an Arab Woman*. Armonk: M. E. Sharpe.

Kanafani, Ghassan (1966). *'Adab Al-Muqāwama fī Filasṭīn al-Muḥtalah 1948–1968 (Resistance Literature in Occupied Palestine 1948–1966*, 2013). Beirut: Manshurāt al-Rimāl.

Karmi, Ghada (2002). *In Search of Fatima: A Palestinian Story*. London: Verso Books.

— (2015). *Return: A Palestinian Memoir*. London: Verso Books.

Kelly, Debra (2005). *Autobiography and Independence: Selfhood and Creativity in North African Postcolonial Writing in French*. Liverpool: Liverpool University Press.

Keraitim, Sahar and Samia Mehrez (2012). 'Mulid al-Tahrir: Semiotics of the Revolution', in Samia Mehrez (ed.), *Translating Egypt's Revolution: The Language of Tahrir*. Cairo: The American University of Cairo Press.

Kerbaj, Mazen (2017). *Beirut Won't Cry: Lebanon's July War: a Visual Diary*. Seattle: Fantagraphics Books.

Kerrou, Mohamed (2012). 'New Actors of the Revolution and the Political Transition in Tunisia', in Clement Henry and Jang Ji-Hyang (eds), *The Arab Spring: Will it Lead to Democratic Transition?* New York: Palgrave Macmillan.

Khaled, Leila (1973). *My People Shall Live: The Autobiography of a Revolutionary*, ed. George Hajjar. London: Hodder and Stoughton.

Khalidi, Anbara Salam (1978). *Jawlah fī al-Dhikrayāt Bayna Lubnān wa Filasṭīn*. Beirut: Dār al-Nahār.

— (2013). *Memoirs of an Early Arab Feminist: The Life and Activism of Anbara Salam Khalidi*, trans. Tarif Khalidi. London: Pluto Press.

Khalidi, Rashid (1997). *Palestinian Identity: The Construction of Modern National Consciousness*. New York: Columbia University Press.

Khalil, Andrea (2014). 'Tunisia's Women: Partners in Revolution', *The Journal of North African Studies*, 19:2, pp. 186–99.

Khamis, Sahar and Katherine Vaughn (2016). 'New Media and Public Will Mobilization in the Tunisian and Egyptian Revolutions of 2011', in Aziz Douai and Mohamed Ben Moussa (eds), *Mediated Identities and New Journalism in the Arab World: Mapping the "Arab Spring"*. London: Palgrave Macmillan, pp. 41–60.

Kharroub, Tamara (2021). 'Arab Women's Activism in a Transnational Media Landscape: Negotiating Gendered Spaces', *Feminist Media Studies*, 21:4, pp. 692–6.

Khatibi, Abdelkébir (1999). *La langue de l'autre*. New York: Éditions Les Mains Secrètes.

Kishtainy, Khalid (1986). *Arab Political Humour*. London: Quartet Books.

— (2009). 'Humour and Resistance in the Arab World: The Greater Middle East', in Maria J. Stephan (ed.), *Civilian Jihad*. London: Palgrave Macmillan, pp. 53–63.

Kristeva, Julia (1992). *Black Sun: Depression and Melancholia*. New York: Columbia University Press.

Laachir, Karima and Saeed Talajooy (eds) (2013). *Resistance in Contemporary Middle Eastern Culture: Literature, Cinema and Music*. New York: Routledge.

Laalami, Laila (2020). 'So To Speak', in Pauline Kaldas and Khaled Mattawa (eds), *Beyond Memory: An Anthology of Contemporary Arab American Creative Nonfiction*. Fayetteville: University of Arkansas Press, pp. 151–6.

Laouyen, Mounir (2002). 'Préface', *L'Esprit Créateur*, 42:4, pp. 3–7.

Lejeune, Philippe (1982). 'The Autobiographical Contract' ('Le pacte autobiographique', 1975), in Tzvetan Todorov (ed.), *French Literary Theory Today: a Reader*. Cambridge: Cambridge University Press, pp. 192–222.

— (2000). *Cher écran . . . journal personnel, ordinateur, Internet*. Paris: Seuil.

— (2014). 'Autobiography and New Communication Tools', trans. Katherine Durnin, in Anna Poletti and Julie Rak (eds), *Identity Technologies: Constructing the Self Online*. Madison: University of Wisconsin Press.

Lewis, Jonathan (2018). *The Algerian War in French/Algerian Writing: Literary Sites of Memory*. Cardiff: University of Wales Press.

Lewis, Kelly (2021). 'Social Media Platforms are Complicit in Censoring Palestinian Voices', *The Conversation*, 24 May, https://theconversation.com/social-media-platforms-are-complicit-in-censoring-palestinian-voices-161094.

Lionnet, Françoise (1988). 'Métissage, Emancipation, and Female Textuality in Two Francophone Writers', in Bella Brodzki and Celeste Scheneck (eds), *Life/Lines: Theorizing Women's Autobiography*. Ithaca: Cornell University Press.

— (1989). *Autobiographical Voices: Race, Gender, Self-Portraiture*. Ithaca: Cornell University Press.

— (1995). *Postcolonial Representation: Women, Literature, Identities*. Ithaca: Cornell University Press.

Llewellyn, Tim (2013). 'Reporting Sabra and Shatila', in Caroline Rooney and Rita Sakr (eds), *The Ethics of Representation in Literature, Art, and Journalism: Transnational Responses to the Siege of Beirut*. London: Routledge.

Lutfi, Huda (2006). 'Mulid Culture in Cairo: The Case of Al-Sayyida 'Aisha', in Maha Abdelrahman *et al.* (eds), *Cultural Dynamics in Contemporary Cairo* (Cairo Papers 27:1–2). Cairo: The American University in Cairo Press, pp. 79–103.

Lutz, Meris (2009). 'Tunisia: Online Activists Rally to Free Fellow Blogger Fatma Riahi', *Los Angeles Times*, 6 November, https://latimesblogs.latimes.com/baby lonbeyond/2009/11/tunisia-blogger-fatma-riahi-arrested-held-incommunicado .html.

Makdisi, Jean Said (1990). *Beirut Fragments: A War Memoir*. New York: Persea Books.

Makey, Alia (1989). *Yawmiyyāt 'Imra'ah fil-Sujūn al-Suʿūdiyyah* (Diaries of a Woman from the Saudi Prisons). Cairo: Dār al-Ṣafā.

Malsin, Jard (2015). 'Egyptian Activist Alaa Abd El Fattah Sentence to Five Years in Jail', *The Guardian*, 23 February, https://www.theguardian.com/world/20 15/feb/23/egyptian-activist-alaa-abd-el-fattah-sentenced-five-years-jail (accessed 2 September 2020).

Malti-Douglas, Fedwa (1991). *Woman's Body, Woman's Word: Gender and Discourse in Arabo-Islamic Writing*. Princeton, NJ: Princeton University Press.

Massad, Joseph (2000). 'The "Post-Colonial" Colony: Time, Space, and Bodies in Palestine/Israel', in Fawzia Afzal-Khan and Kalpana Seshadri-Crooks (eds), *The Pre-Occupation of Postcolonial Studies*. Durham, NC: Duke University Press, pp. 311–46.

Mazloum, Sherine Fouad (2015). 'To Write/to Revolt: Egyptian Women Novelists Writing the Revolution', *Journal for Cultural Research*, 19:2, pp. 207–20.

McLoughlin, Kate, Lara Feigel and Nancy Martin (eds) (2017). *Writing War, Writing Lives*. London: Routledge.

McMillan, M. E. (2016). *From the First World War to the Arab Spring: What's Really Going on in the Middle East*. London: Palgrave Macmillan.

McNeill, Laurie (2014). 'Life-Bytes: Six-Word Memoir and the Exigencies of Auto/Tweetographies', in Anna Poletti and Julie Rak (eds), *Identity Technologies: Constructing the Self Online*. Madison: University of Wisconsin Press.

McNeill, Laurie and John David Zuern (eds) (2015). *Online Lives 2.0, Biography: An Interdisciplinary Quarterly*, 38:2.

— (2015). 'Online Lives: 2.0: Introduction', *Biography: An Interdisciplinary Quarterly*, 38:2, pp. v–xlvi.

Mehta, Brinda J. (2007). *Rituals of Memory: in Contemporary Arab Women's Writing*. Syracuse: Syracuse University Press.

— (2012). '"Un-grievable" Lives? Contesting Illegality in Saud Amiry's "Border Diary" Nothing to Lose but Your Life: An 18-Hour Journey with Murad', *Journal of Arabic Literature*, 43, pp. 458–83.

— (2014). *Dissident Writings of Arab Women: Voices against Violence*. Abingdon: Routledge.

Mernissi, Fatima (ed.) (1988). *Doing Daily Battle: Interviews with Moroccan Women*, trans. Mary Jo Lakeland. London: Women's Press.

— (1994a). *Dreams of Trespass: Tales of a Harem Girlhood*. Cambridge, MA: Perseus Books.

— (1994b). *The Harem Within: Tales of a Moroccan Girlhood*. London: Bantam.

— (2001). *Scheherazade Goes West: Different Cultures, Different Harems*. New York: Washington Square Press.

Mersal, Iman (2011). 'Revolutionary Humour', *Globalizations*, 8:5, pp. 669–74.

Michaelson, Ruth (2017). 'The Dancing, Beer-Drinking Woman who would be Egypt's Next President', *The Guardian*, 3 October, https://www.theguardian.com/global development/2017/oct/03/the-dancing-beer-drinking-woman-who-would-be-egypt-next president-monaprince (accessed 30 January 2018).

Miller, Nancy K. (1988). *Subject to Change: Reading Feminist Writing*. New York: Columbia University Press.

Minh-ha, Trinh T. (1989). *Women, Native, Other: Writing Postcoloniality and Feminism*. Bloomington: Indiana University Press.

Misch, Georg (1973 [1907]). *A History of Autobiography in Antiquity*, vol. 1. Westport, CT: Greenwood Press.

Moore-Gilbert, Bart (2009). *Postcolonial Life-Writing: Culture, Politics, and Self-Representation*. London: Routledge.

— (2011). 'A Concern Peculiar to Western Man? Postcolonial Reconsiderations of Autobiography as a Genre', in Patrick Crowley and Jane Hiddleston (eds),

Postcolonial Poetics: Genre and Form. Liverpool: Liverpool University Press, pp. 91–108.

— (2013). '"Baleful Postcoloniality" and Palestinian Women's Life Writing', *Biography*, 36:1, pp. 51–70.

— (2014). 'Time Bandits: Temporality and the Politics of Form in Palestinian Women's Life-Writing', *Journal of Postcolonial Writing*, 50, pp. 189–201.

Moore, Lindsey (2008). *Arab, Muslim, Woman: Voice and Vision in Postcolonial Literature and Film*. London: Routledge.

— (2018). *Narrating Postcolonial Arab Nations: Egypt, Algeria, Lebanon, Palestine*. London: Routledge.

Mortimer, Mildred (2018). *Women Fight, Women Write: Texts on the Algerian War*. Charlottesville: University of Virginia Press.

Mosteghanemi, Ahlem (1999). 'Writing against Time and History', in Fadia Faqir (ed. and trans.), *In the House of Silence: Autobiographical Essays by Arab Women Writers*. Reading: Garnet.

Mubeen, Haris (2008). 'Humour and Comedy in Arabic Literature (from the Birth of Islam to Ottoman Period)', *Al-Hikmat*, 28, pp. 13–30.

Mühleisen, Susanne (2005). 'What Makes an Accent Funny, and Why?: Black British Englishes and Humour Televised', in Susanne Reichl and Mark Stein (eds), *Cheeky Fictions: Laughter and the Postcolonial*. Amsterdam: Radopi.

Mustazraf, Malika (1999). *Jirāḥ al-Ruḥ wa-l-Jasad* (Wounds of the Spirit and Body). al-Qunaytira: Accent Press.

Nash, Geoffrey (2007). *The Anglo-Arab Encounter: Fiction and Autobiography by Arab Writers in English*. Oxford: Peter Lang.

Nasser, Abdel Tahia (2017). *Literary Autobiography and Arab National Struggles*. Edinburgh: Edinburgh University Press.

Nussbaum, Felicity (2007). 'Towards Conceptualizing Diary', in Trev Lynn Broughton (ed.), *Autobiography*. London: Routledge, pp. 1–10.

Nyman, Jopi (2009). 'Cultural Contact and the Contemporary Culinary Memoir: Home, Memory and Identity in Madhur Jaffrey and Diana Abu-Jaber', *a/b: Auto/Biography Studies*, 24:2, pp. 282–98.

Olney, James (ed.) (1980). *Autobiography: Essays Theoretical and Critical*. Princeton, NJ: Princeton University Press.

Omar Ata, Iasmin (2017). *Mis(h)adra*. New York: Gallery 13.

Orwell, George (1945). 'Funny, but not Vulgar', *George Orwell's Library*, http://orwell.ru/library/articles/funny/english/e_funny (accessed 19 February 2018).

Ostle, Robin, Ed de Moor and Stefan Wild (eds) (1998). *Writing the Self:*

Autobiographical Writing in Modern Arabic Literature. London: Saqi Books.

Papa, Stephanie (2016). 'The Most Important Way to Love and Peace is Justice: A Conversation with Samar Yazbek', trans. Emma Suleiman, *World Literature Today*, November–December, pp. 16–20.

Pappe, Ilan (2006). *The Ethnic Cleansing of Palestine*. Oxford: One World.

Pascal, Roy (1960). *Design and Truth in Autobiography*. London: Routledge.

Pepe, Teresa (2019). *Blogging form Egypt: Digital Literature, 2005-2016*. Edinburgh: Edinburgh University Press.

Philipp, Thomas (1993). 'The Autobiography in Modern Arab Literature and Culture', *Poetics Today*, 14:3, pp. 573–604.

Podnieks, Elizabeth (2001). 'Web Diaries, Cyber Selves, and Global Intimacy: Surfing Secra Terri's FootNotes', *a/b: Auto/Biography Studies*, 17:1, pp. 119–38.

Poletti, Anna and Julie Rak (eds) (2014). *Identity Technologies: Constructing the Self Online*. Madison: University of Wisconsin Press.

Popovic, Srdja (2015) *Blueprint for Revolution: How to Use Rice Pudding, Lego Men, and Other Nonviolent Techniques to Galvanize Communities, Overthrow Dictators, or Simply Change the World*. New York: Spiegel and Grau.

Prince, Mona (2014). *Revolution is My Name: An Egyptian Women's Diaries from Eighteen Days in Tahrir* (*'Ismī Thawrah*, 2012), trans. Samia Mehrez. Cairo: The American University Press of Cairo.

Punter, David (2003). 'Arundhati Roy and the House of History', in Andrew Smith and William Hughes (eds), *Empire and the Gothic: the Politics of Genre*. London: Palgrave Macmillan.

Qualey, M. Lynx (ed.) (2019). 'The Comic Edge: Arabic Humour', *Words Without Borders*, October, https://www.wordswithoutborders.org/issue/october-2019-arab-humor (accessed 23 October 2019).

Reichl, Susanne and Mark Stein (eds) (2005). *Cheeky Fictions: Laughter and the Postcolonial*. Amsterdam: Radopi.

Renfrew, Alastair (2015). *Mikhail Bakhtin*. Abingdon: Routledge.

Reynolds, Dwight Fletcher (2001). *Interpreting the Self: Autobiography in the Arabic Literary Tradition*. Berkeley: University of California Press.

Rice, Alison (2006). *Time Signatures: Contextualizing Contemporary Francophone Autobiographical Writing from the Maghreb*. Lanham: Lexington Books.

— (2012). *Polygraphies: Francophone Women Writing Algeria*. Charlottesville: University of Virginia Press.

Riverbend (2005). *Baghdad Burning: Girl Blog from Iraq*. New York: Feminist Press at the City University of New York.
— *Baghdad Burning*, https://riverbendblog.blogspot.com/ (accessed 28 August 2021).
Rooke, Tetz (1997). *In My Childhood: A Study of Arabic Autobiography*. Stockholm: Stockholm University.
Rooney, Caroline (2011). 'Egyptian Literary Culture and Egyptian Modernity: Introduction', *Journal of Postcolonial Writing*, 47:4, pp. 369–76.
— (2015). 'Sufi Springs: Air on an Oud String', *CounterText*, 1:1, pp. 38–58.
Ross, Fiona C. (2003). *Bearing Witness: Women and the Truth and Reconciliation Commission in South Africa*. London: Pluto Press.
Ryan, Caitlin (2015). 'Everyday Resilience as Resistance: Palestinian Women Practicing *Sumud*', *International Political Sociology*, 9, pp. 299–315.
Said, Edward (1986). *After the Last Sky: Palestinian Lives*. London: Faber and Faber.
— (1991). 'Reflections on Twenty Years of Palestinian History', *Journal of Palestine Studies*, 20:4, pp. 5–22.
— (1999). *Out of Place: A Memoir*. New York: Alfred A. Knopf.
— (2003a). *Humanism and Democratic Criticism*. New York: Columbia University Press.
— (2003b [1978]). *Orientalism*. London: Penguin Books.
Sakr, Naomi (ed.) (2004). *Women and Media in the Middle East: Power Through Self-Expression*. London: I. B. Tauris & Co Ltd.
Salem, Heba and Kantaro Taira (2012). 'Al-Thawra Al-DaHika: The Challenges of Translating Revolutionary Humour', in Samia Mehrez (ed.), *Translating Egypt's Revolution: The Language of Tahrir*. Cairo: The American University in Cairo.
Salih, Arwa (2017). *The Stillborn: Notebooks of a Woman from the Student-Movement Generation in Egypt*, trans. Samah Selim. London: Seagull Books.
Sattouf, Riyadh (2015). *The Arab of the Future: A Graphic Memoir*, trans. Sam Taylor. New York: Metropolitan Books.
Schaffer, Kay and Sidonie Smith (2004). *Human Rights and Narrated Lives: The Ethics of Recognition*. New York: Palgrave Macmillan.
Schami, Rafik (2012). 'Introduction', in Samar Yazbek, *A Woman in the Crossfire: Diaries of the Syrian Revolution*, trans. Max Weiss. London: Haus.
Schmidt, Silke (2012). *(Re-)Framing the Arab/Muslim: Mediating Orientalism in Contemporary Arab American Life Writing*. Bielefeld: Transcript Verlag.

Schwartz, Lowell et al. (2009). *Barriers to the Broader Dissemination of Creative Works in the Arab World*. Santa Monica: RAND, National Defense Research Institute.

Sebbar, Leïla (1982). *Shérazade 17 ans, brune, frisée, les yeux verts* (*Sherazade*, 2014). Paris: Éditions Stock.

— (1985). *Les carnets de Shérazade*. Paris: Éditions Stock.

— (1991). *Le fou de Shérazade*. Paris: Éditions Stock.

Shaarawi, Huda (1981). *Mudhakkirāt Hudā Shaʿrāwī: Rāiʾdat al-Marʾah al-ʿArabiyyah al-Ḥadīthah*. Cairo: Dār al-Hilāl.

— (1986). *Harem Years: The Memoirs of an Egyptian Feminist*, trans. and ed. Margot Badran. New York: Feminist Press at the City University of New York.

Sharafeddine, Fatima (2013). *The Servant*. Toronto: Groundwood Books.

Sheehi, Stephen (2004). *Formations of Modern Arab Identity*. Gainesville: University of Florida Press.

Sheetrit, Ariel M. (2020). *A Poetics of Arabic Autobiography: Between Dissociation and Belonging*. New York: Routledge.

Siegel, Kristi (2001). *Women's Autobiographies, Culture, Feminism*, 2nd edn. New York: Peter Lang.

Slimani, Leila (2020). *Sex and Lies: True Stories of Women's Intimate Lives in the Arab World*. New York: Penguin Books.

Smith, Sidonie (1987). *A Poetics of Women's Autobiography: Marginality and the Fictions of Self-representation*. Bloomington: Indiana University Press.

— (2016). 'Performativity, Autobiographical Practice, Resistance', in Sidonie Smith and Julia Watson, *Life Writing in the Long Run: A Smith & Watson Autobiography Studies Reader*. Michigan: Maize Books.

Smith, Sidonie and Julia Watson (eds) (1992). *De/Colonizing the Subject: The Politics of Gender in Women's Autobiography*. Minneapolis: University of Minnesota Press.

— (eds) (1998). *Women, Autobiography, Theory: A Reader*. Madison: University of Wisconsin Press.

— (2001a). *Reading Autobiography: A Guide for Interpreting Life Narratives*. Minneapolis: University of Minnesota Press.

— (2001b). 'The Rumpled Bed of Autobiography: Extravagant Lives, Extravagant Questions', *Biography*, 24:1, pp. 1–14.

— (2016). *Life Writing in the Long Run: A Smith & Watson Autobiography Studies Reader*. Michigan: Maize Books.

Sommer, Doris (1988). '"Not just a Personal Story" Women's Testimonies and the

Plural Self', in Bella Brodzki and Celeste Scheneck (eds), *Life/Lines: Theorizing Women's Autobiography*. Ithaca: Cornell University Press.

Sontag, Susan (2003). *Regarding the Pain of Others*. New York: Picador.

Sørensen, Majken Jul (2016). *Humour in Political Activism: Creative Nonviolent Resistance*. London: Palgrave Macmillan.

Soueif, Ahdef (2014). *Cairo: my City, our Revolution*. London: Bloomsbury Publishing.

Spivak, Gayatri Chakravorty (1993 [1988]). 'Can the Subaltern Speak?', in Patrick Williams and Laura Chrisman (eds), *Colonial Discourse and Post-Colonial Theory: a Reader*. London: Routledge.

Stanton, Domna C. (ed.) (1984). *The Female Autograph: Theory and Practice of Autobiography from the Tenth to the Twentieth Century*. Chicago: University of Chicago Press.

Stephan, Rita (2020). 'Long before the Arab Spring: Arab Women's Cyberactivism through AWSA United', in Rita Stephan and Mounira M. Charrad (eds), *Women Rising in and Beyond the Arab Spring*. New York: New York University Press.

Summerfield, Penny (2019). *Histories of the Self: Personal Narratives and Historical Practice*. London: Routledge.

Tagore, Proma (2009). *The Shapes of Silence: Writing by Women of Colour and the Politics of Testimony*. Montreal: McGill-Queen's University Press.

Tawil, Raymonda Hawa (1983). *My Home, My Prison*. London: Zed.

Tripp, Charles (2013). *The Power and the People: Paths of Resistance in the Middle East*. Cambridge: Cambridge University Press.

Tsakona, Villy (2020). *Recontextualizing Humor: Rethinking the Analysis and Teaching of Humor*. Berlin: De Gruyter Mouton.

Tuqan, Fadwa (1984). *Riḥlah Jabaliyyah, Riḥlah Ṣaʿbah: Sīrah Dhātiyyah*. Amman: Dār al-Shurūq.

— (1990). *Mountainous Journey: An Autobiography*, trans. Olive Kenny and Naomi Shihab. St Paul, MN: Graywolf Press.

— (1993). *Al-Riḥlah al-Aṣʿab: Sīrah Dhātiyyah*. Amman: Dār al-Shurūq.

Valassopoulos, Anastasia (2007). *Contemporary Arab Women Writers: Cultural Expression in Context*. London: Routledge.

Ward, Abigail (ed.) (2015). *Postcolonial Traumas: Memory, Narrative, Resistance*. London: Palgrave Macmillan.

Waugh, Patricia (1984). *Metafiction: The Theory and Practice of Self-Conscious Fiction*. London: Routledge.

Weber-Fève, Stacey (2010). *Re-Hybridizing Transnational Domesticity and Femininity: Women's Contemporary Filmmaking and Lifewriting in France, Algeria, and Tunisia*. Lanham: Lexington Books.

Weizman, Eyal (2007). *Hollow Land: Israel's Architecture of Occupation*. London: Verso Books.

Whitlock, Gillian (2000). *The Intimate Empire: Reading Women's Autobiography*. London: Cassel.

— (2006). 'Autographics: The Seeing "I" of the Comics', *MFS Modern Fiction Studies*, 52:4, pp. 965–79.

— (2007). *Soft Weapons: Autobiography in Transit*. Chicago: University of Chicago Press.

— (2015). *Postcolonial Life Narratives: Testimonial Transactions*. Oxford: Oxford Series in Postcolonial Literature.

Wolf, Hope (2017). '"Paper is Patient": Tweets from the #AnneFrank of Palestine', in Kate McLoughline *et al.* (eds), *Writing War, Writing Lives*. London: Routledge.

Wrigley-Field, Elizabeth (ed.) (2009). *Iraqi Girl: Diary of a Teenage Girl in Iraq*, dev. John Ross. Chicago: Haymarket Books.

Yazbek, Samar (2008). *Rā'iḥat al-qirfah* (*Cinnamon*, 2015). Beirut: Dār al-Ādāb.

— (2011). *Taqātuʿ Nirān: Min Yawmiyyāt al-Intifāḍah al-Sūriyyah*. Beirut: Dār al-Ādāb.

— (2012). *A Woman in the Crossfire: Diaries of the Syrian Revolution*, trans. Max Weiss. London: Haus.

— (2013a). 'The Syrian Revolution has Changed me as a Writer', *The Guardian*, 3 May, https://www.theguardian.com/books/2013/may/03/samar-yazbek-syrian-revolution-writing.

— (2013b). 'Introduction', in Layla al-Zubaidi and Matthew Cassel (eds), *Writing Revolution: Voices from Tunis to Damascus*. London: I. B. Tauris.

— (2015). *Bawābāt 'Arḍ al-ʿAdam*. Beirut: Dār al-Ādāb.

— (2016). *The Crossing: my Journey to the Shattered Heart of Syria*, trans. Nashwa Gowanlock and Ruth Ahmedzai Kemp. London: Rider.

— (2019). *Tisʿa 'Asharāt 'Imra'ah: Sūrīyyāt Yarwiyna* (19 Women: Tales of Resilience from Syria). Baghdad: Manshūrāt al-Mutawasiṭ.

Yazbek, Samar and Alan Philps (2012). 'The Alawite Woman who would not be Silenced', *The World Today*, 68:5, p. 30.

Young, Robert (2003). *Postcolonialism: A Very Short Introduction*. Oxford: Oxford University Press.

— (2012). 'Postcolonial Remains', *New Literary History*, 43, pp. 19–42.
Zangana, Haifa (1990). *Through the Vast Halls of Memory*, trans. Haifa Zangana and Paul Hammond. Hourglass.
— (1995). *Fī Arwiqat al-Dhākirah*. London: Dār al-Ḥikmah.
— (2007). *City of Windows: An Iraqi Woman's Account of War and Resistance*. New York: Seven Stories Press.
— (2009). *Dreaming of Baghdad*, trans. Haifa Zangana and Paul Hammond. New York: The Feminist Press.
— (ed.) (2017). *Ḥaflah li Thā'ira: Falastīniyāt Yaktubn al-Ḥayāt* (A Party for The Revolutionary: Palestinian Women Writing Life). London: E-Kutub Ltd.
Ziadé, Lamia (2011). *Bye Bye Babylon: Beirut 1975–1979*. Northampton: Interlink Pub. Group.
Zuern, John (ed.) (2003). *Online Lives, Biography: An Interdisciplinary Quarterly*, 26:1.
Zwagerman, Sean (2010). *Wit's End: Women's Humor as Rhetorical and Performative Strategy*. Pittsburgh: University of Pittsburgh Press.

Web Pages (author unknown):

'Algerian Journalist Khaled Drareni Jailed for Two Years on Appeal', *France 24*, 15 September 2020, https://www.france24.com/en/20200915-algerian-journalist-khaled-drareni-jailed-for-two-years-on-appeal (accessed 26 December 2020).
'Israa Ghrayeb: Murder Charges for Palestinian "Honour Killing"', *BBC News*, 12 September 2019, https://www.bbc.com/news/world-middle-east-49682115 (accessed 28 August 2021).
'Manal Al-Sharif: a Driving Force for Change', *United Nations Human Rights Office of the High Commissioner*, 11 January 2013, https://www.ohchr.org/EN/News Events/Pages/ManalAl-Sharifadrivingforceforchange.aspx (accessed 28 August 2021).
'Measuring Digital Development: Facts and Figures', *International Telecommunications Union* 2019, https://www.itu.int/en/ITU-D/Statistics/Documents/facts/FactsFigures2019.pdf (accessed 18 August 2021).
'Samar Yazbek Shares British Pen Literary Award', *Al-Arabiya*, 11 October 2012, on *Youtube*, https://www.youtube.com/watch?v=luuu2ddAr7o (accessed 14 January 2017).
'Syria Gay Girl in Damascus Blog as a Hoax by US Man', *BBC News*, 13 June 2011, https://www.bbc.co.uk/news/world-middle-east-13744980 (accessed 11 August 2019).

Index

Abirached, Zeina, 232
Abou Rached, Ruth, 63n29
Abouzeid, Leila, 48, 49
Abu Jaber, Diana, 233
activism, 21, 25, 31, 32, 43, 72, 82, 114, 227
    cyber, 187, 197, 207, 208–11, 219
    political, 38, 111, 120, 132
Ahmed, Leila, 46, 82
Ahmed, Sara, 89
al-Hassan, Hawra, 55
Al-Maria, Sophia, 233
al-Barghouti, Tamim, 20, 79
al-Essa, Bothayna, 233
al-Ghazali, Zaynab, 42, 53
al-Harthi, Jokha, 233
al-Nahḍa (Arab Renaissance), 14, 40, 56
al-Nakba (catastrophe), 28, 31, 47, 161
Al-Samman, Hanadi, 129, 130, 136
al-Sanea, Rajaa, 233
al-Sharif, Manal, 195, 233
al-shaʿb (the people), 163, 164, 173, 193, 213, 218
al-Zayyat, Latifa, 53, 54, 82
Alem, Raja, 233

Algeria, 20, 22, 24, 31, 52, 84, 85, 89, 90, 93, 94, 96
    Algerian Civil War, 84, 102n
    Algiers, 51
Algerian White (Djebar), 49, 142n17
Alshejini, Lamis, 195
alterity, 88, 92–3, 95, 98, 100
alternative journalism, 200; *see also* citizen journalism
ambivalent laughter, 161, 166
Amin, Ahmad, 16
Amireh, Amal, 224n29
Amiry, Suad, 111, 121, 132, 145
Ammar 404, 210
amnesia (historical), 107, 112, 118
Anderson, Benedict *see* imagined communities
Anishchenkova, Valerie, 3, 16, 17, 92, 218
anonymity, 198–9
anxiety, 119, 153–4, 164–6
    of authorship, 50
Aouragh, Miriyam, 211, 212, 216
Arab
    Arabisation, 93

identity, 18, 46
nationalism, 16, 18, 38, 44, 56
Arab Spring, 20, 22, 35n16, 148, 208
Arabic (language)
   'amiyyah (colloquial of Mashriq), 116, 163, 165
   dārijah (colloquial of Maghreb), 93
   dialectical Arabic, 17
   fuṣḥā (standard Arabic), 93, 56
ArabLit Quarterly, 235n4
Arabo-Islamic culture, 93, 95
archive, 7, 50, 118, 180
artifice (text as), 77, 87
Ashour, Radwa, 31, 46, 64–5, 70, 83, 86, 87, 163
Athqal min Radwā (Heavier than Radwa) (Ashour), 64
audience, 56–8, 62n20, 77, 109–10, 162
authenticity, 11, 58–9, 88, 109
   aura of, 199, 201
   metrics of, 203
autobiographical criticism, 2, 6, 32, 67, 69, 187
autobiographical fiction, 40, 50–3, 84, 96
autobiographical identities, 8, 11
autobiographical pact, 9–10, 110, 141n3; *see also* Lejeune, Philippe
autobiographical project, 71
autobiographical traditions 14–17
autobiography
   Arab(ic), 2, 4, 15, 18–19, 40
   autobiographics (Gilmore), 8, 68–9; *see also* Gilmore, Leigh
   autographics, 232
   autogynography 8, 34n5; *see also* Stanton C. Domna

canonical, 15, 23, 67–8
collective, 52
conventional, 77, 88, 99, 108–10, 151
Francophone, 49, 85, 96–7
performative, 68, 89, 98–9, 218
postcolonial, 11; *see also* life writing
and theory, 5–10, 13
autofiction, 88–9
'awrah (private part of the body), 50, 51

Badran, Margot, 36n21, 40–1, 50, 60n7
Baker, Farah, 201–2
Bakhtin, Mikhail, 174; *see also* carnivalesque
Barakat, Hoda, 106–7
Barreca, Regina, 154–7
Basrawi, Fadia, 233
battlefield, 106, 130
Ben Mhenni, Lina, 186–7, 220
Benstock, Shari, 7, 67
Bergson, Henri, 167
Bernard, Anna, 152
Berque, Jacques, 16
Beverley, John, 108; *see also* testimony
Bey, Maïssa, 65, 70–1, 96
Bhabha, Homi, 181n3
biography, 61n9
blogger, 187, 205–8, 211–13
blogs and blogging, 189–94, 216, 220
body, 50, 54, 68, 96, 124, 214, 220, 175
Booth, Marilyn, 45, 233
border crossing, 46, 47, 82, 121, 127, 129, 132, 136, 138, 139
borderline (concept), 122–3, 127; *see also* Green, André
bricolage (of genre), 80–1, 229
Brisley, Lucy, 125

Brodzki, Bella (and Celeste Schenck), 66–7
Bromley, Roger, 118
Bugeja, Norbert, 12, 102n16
Butler, Judith, 115, 151, 157, 214

carnival (festival), 162, 167–9, 171, 178
carnivalesque, 167–9, 171–8; *see also* Bakhtin, Mikhail
Caruth, Cathy, 124–5
censorship, 32, 50, 51, 53, 62n21, 187, 191, 193, 195, 201, 205, 210, 212, 216, 219, 220, 228
Ces Voix qui m'assiègent (Djebar), 52, 61n19, 94
circulation, 50, 58, 87, 105, 118, 180, 188–9, 191, 198, 201, 227
citizen journalism, 200; *see also* alternative journalism
colonialism, 1, 11, 13, 19, 22, 39, 46, 72, 89, 228
comedy, 145, 146–9, 150, 153–4, 158, 175
communication platforms, 192
Cooke, Miriam, 36n21, 40, 50, 119, 165
counter-discourse, 121, 174
crossfire, 112–14, 119
The Crossing (Yazbek), 121–32
Cubilié, Anne, 127, 201
curfew, 137, 145, 151–3, 155, 160

Dabaie, Marguerite, 232
de Man, Paul, 58, 75, 81
decolonisation, 10
 de/colonising the subject, 8, 9, 12
Deir Yassin (Palestine), 74, 80, 101n6
Derrida, Jacques, 103n22

dialogism, 69, 98
diary, 15, 86, 115, 145, 149, 151–2, 230
 digital, 192, 198, 201
dictatorship, 166, 179, 181, 211, 213, 215
digital culture, 186, 187
Djebar, Assia, 49, 51–2, 78, 79, 94–6, 99
Drif, Zohra, 63n26
Duncombe, Stephen, 26

Egypt
 Egyptian revolution, 41, 71, 72, 162–3, 165, 167, 168–9, 170, 176, 178
 Egyptian women, 41–3
El-Ariss, Tarek, 198–9
El-Saadawi, Nawal, 16–17, 48, 53–4, 128
Elfarra, Mona, 198
Elsadda, Hoda, 221n2
emancipation, 20, 21, 41, 43, 46–7, 56, 82
ethics, 118, 88
 of marketing literature, 119
 of recognition, 59
 of representation, 124, 134
ethnicity, 8, 90, 108, 146, 157
exile, 55, 56, 79, 121
experiment(al), 52, 57, 70–2, 76, 77, 88–9, 144, 157, 234

faḍḥ (exposure), 198–9
Fanon, Frantz, 27; *see also under* resistance literature
Fantasia, an Algerian Cavalcade (*L'Amour, la fantasia*) (Djebar), 51–2

INDEX | 263

Faqir, Fadia, 23, 231
'Faut-il aller chercher des rêves ailleurs que dans la nuit?' (Bey), 70, 84, 86
feminism, 43, 46
   Arab, 2, 36n21, 42
   and autobiographical theory, 5–10
   Cyber, 194
   intersectional, 112
   Islamic, 60n7
   Islamic feminist writing, 42
festive laughter, 168
Foucault, Michel, 27
fragmentation
   of genre 52, 55, 76, 81
   of subjectivity; identity, 67, 72, 84, 89, 98, 101n4
Francophone
   author, 49, 90, 92, 95, 96, 103n22
   writing, 39, 85, 97
Frantz, Rosenthal, 34n12
Freud, Sigmund, 147, 153

gender, 2, 5–9, 13, 24, 28–9, 42, 47, 54, 67, 69–70, 84
   and femininity, 131, 136
   and masculinity, 136, 160
   and postcolonial humour, 145–9
   and race, 62n20
genre, 3–18, 22–5, 38–46, 55, 58, 65–7, 72–3, 77, 84, 88, 108, 190, 201
Ghannouchi, Soumaya, 198
gharīb (stranger), 98
Gharib, Malaka, 233
Ghonim, Wael, 206, 221n3
Gilmore, Leigh, 8, 48, 68–9, 127; *see also under* autobiography
Golley, Nawar Al-Hassan, 23–4, 44, 75

Gordimer, Nadine, 117
gothic, 74–5
Green, André, 122–3; *see also* borderline (concept)
Gregory, Derek, 20, 137
Gusdorf, Georges, 6, 12, 15, 66, 190

Haddad, Joumana, 128
Hamdi, Tahrir, 110, 228
Hankir, Zahra, 231
harem, 41, 46–7
Harlow, Barbara, 2, 26, 30, 36n22, 55, 57, 79, 188, 234; *see also* resistance literature
Henderson, Mae Gwendolyn, 62n20, 69, 98
Henke, Suzette A., 141n9
Herman, Judith, 125, 142n14, 172
Hiddleston, Jane, 52
historiography, 51
Hobbes, Thomas, 181n4
Høigilt, Jacob, 235n2
home, 46, 50, 86, 115, 139–40
   as women-specific space 24, 106, 135, 159, 178
Howard, Philip (and Muzammil M. Hussain), 211
Huggan, Graham, 20, 59, 191
   the postcolonial exotic, 59
humour
   ambivalent laughter, 161, 166
   Arab, 147–8, 164
   feminist, 146, 147, 157
   humorous resilience, 159
   incongruity theory, 182n5
   political, 162, 164–6, 179, 180, 182n8
   postcolonial, 145–9, 168, 182n7

humour (*cont.*)
  superiority theory, 146
  women's, 146, 154, 157, 179
Hussein, Taha, 14, 39, 82

identity
  Arab, 16, 18, 46
  in autobiography, 66, 68, 218
  and the collective; communal; national, 17, 21, 38, 113, 132, 138, 139, 152, 156, 213
  cultural, 3
  digital, 191, 194, 199
  and discourse, 40
  and the female, 52
  and gender, 7, 131
  and the individual, 40
  and postcolonial subjects, 11, 19, 22, 75, 85
ijtihad (reasoning; quest), 77–8, 80
imagined communities, 212, 143n26
Internet, 180, 188, 191–4, 196, 198, 202–5, 215
intersection
  of feminism and postcolonial frameworks, 5, 24, 38, 40, 43, 53, 112
  of humour and diary writing, 149
  of metatext and autobiography, 231
  of power discourses, 29, 30, 79, 110, 157, 179
  of voices, 25, 68, 69
intertextuality, 6, 80, 165
Iraq, 19, 41, 54–6
Iraqi Girl: Diary of a Teenage Girl in Iraq, 222n10
Isaacs, Carol, 233

Jelinek, Estelle, 7, 67
The Journey (Al-Riḥlah: Ayyām Ṭālibah Miṣriyyah fī Amrīkā) (Ashour), 46, 47
journey (*riḥlah*), 46–7, 82, 132, 137–8

Kaldas, Pauline (and Khaled Mattawa), 232
Kanafani, Fay Afaf, 46
Kanafani, Ghassan, 2, 26, 79, 188
Karmi, Ghada, 149
Kelly, Debra, 12–13, 97, 94–5
Keraitim, Sahar (and Samia Mehrez), 170
Kerbaj, Mazen, 232
Khaled, Leila, 45
Khalidi, Anbara Salam, 43–4
Khalil, Andrea, 219
Khatibi, Abdelkébir, 103n22
Kishtainy, Khalid, 148
Kristeva, Julia, 142n13

Laachir, Karima (and Saeed Talajooy), 2, 192
Laalami, Laila, 225
labour
  domestic, 130
  of migrants, 134, 137–9
  of research, 78, 80
  of writing, 86–7
language issues, 93–4, 197–8, 204
laughing revolution, 163, 179
Lejeune, Philippe, 9, 190–1; *see also* autobiographical pact
Lewis, Jonathan, 105n27
life writing
  Arab, 17–22

Arab women's, 22–5
digital, 189–94
postcolonial, 10–14, 17–22, 32, 150, 152
liminality, 52, 73, 88
Lionnet, Françoise, 8, 69, 75, 152; *see also métissage*

Maghreb(i), 18, 49, 57, 85, 90, 93, 95–6
Makdisi, Jean Said, 101n8
Makey, Alia, 53
malleability
  of gender roles, 131–2
  of genre, 6
marketing
  exoticism, 59
  of literature, 58, 63n30, 119, 208, 218
Mashriq, 18
McLoughlin, Kate (and Lara Feigel and Nancy Martin), 144
Mehta, Brinda, 28, 140
memoir, 15, 231
  Arabic, 39, 40–4, 47
  culinary, 233
  see also prison accounts
Mernissi, Fatima, 47
metatext(ual), 70, 73, 76–7, 84, 87, 230–1; *see also* Waugh, Patricia
métissage, 81
metrics of authenticity, 203
migrant workers, 132, 137, 138
mirror (trope), 66–7
Misch, Georg, 6, 66
modality (of autobiographical writing)
  multiplicity of voices, 69
  performative view, 68
  positionality, 68

Moore-Gilbert, Bart, 10–11, 12–13, 19, 150
Moore, Lindsey, 50
Mosteghanemi, Ahlem, 99
Mubarak (Hosni), 162, 165, 167, 170, 172–4, 181
Mudawanāt (blogs), 202
mūlid (also *moulid* or *mawlid*), 169–70
multiplicity
  of forms and voices, 52, 53, 67, 69, 69, 70, 72, 73, 81, 83–4, 229
  of identity, 90, 94, 98, 100
muqāwamah (resistance), 36n24, 161
Muslim, 41, 42, 51, 53, 79, 91, 113
Mustazraf, Malika, 49

Nasser, Abdel Tahia, 3, 17, 38, 82, 163
national narrative, 3, 10, 54, 127, 152, 180, 193
national struggles
  ḥirāk (popular movement; uprising), 1, 20, 21, 180, 205, 234
  revolution 2.0, 221n3
  twentieth-century, 39, 42, 44
  uprising, 19, 20, 31, 111, 112, 118, 120
  see also resistance
native informant, 118, 151
Nobel Peace Prize, 186, 187, 206
non-fictionality, 10, 49, 203
Nothing to Lose But your Life (Amiry), 132–40
Nulle part dans la maison de mon père (Djebar), 61n18

Olney, James, 100n1
Omar Ata, Iasmin, 232

The Open Door (al-Zayyat), 82
orientalism, 1, 19

Palestine, 45, 47, 73, 74, 79, 138, 139
participatory space, 197
Pascal, Roy, 6
Philipp, Thomas, 15
Photography, 214
Prince, Mona, 145, 178
prison accounts, 40, 42, 49, 54–5
Punter, David, 74

qarīn (double), 73, 75

resistance
  and culture, 26–8, 41, 55, 65, 79, 226
  resistance 2.0, 188
  see also national struggles;
    muqāwamah
resistance literature, 21, 26, 28–9, 33, 46, 57, 60, 120, 188, 228, 230, 232
  literature of combat, 36n23; *see also*
    Fanon, Frantz
  see also Harlow, Barbara
return (tope of), 74
Return to Childhood (*al-Rujūʿ ila-l-Ṭufūlah*) (Abouzeid), 50–1
Revolution is My Name (*'Ismī Thawrah*) (Prince), 162–81
Reynolds, Dwight F., 16, 38, 39
Rice, Alison, 85, 90
Riverbend, 199–201
Rooke, Tetz, 60n2
Rooney, Caroline, 180, 185n29

Said, Edward, 10, 34n9, 155
Sakr, Naomi, 196

Salih, Arwa, 48
Al-Ṣarkhah (The Scream) (Ashour), 71, 72
Sattouf, Riyadh, 232
Schami, Rafik, 117
Scheherazade, 128–32, 136
The Search (al-Zayyat), 53, 82
Sebbar, Leïla, 128, 143n18
self
  fragmentation, 70, 75, 81, 92
  deprecation, 147, 157–8
  fictionalisation, 75, 76
  representation, 75, 76, 83, 108, 111, 120, 127, 189, 194, 196, 202, 204
selfhood, 3, 9, 11, 16, 19, 66, 67, 84, 97, 189
Shaarawi, Huda, 41–4
Sharon and my Mother-in-Law (Amiry), 149–62
sīrāh dhātyyah (autobiography), 14
sitr (concealment), 51, 95, 198, 199
Slimani, Leila, 232
Smith, Sidonie (and Julia Watson), 8–9, 99, 189, 199
Sontag, Susan, 214, 141n8
Soueif, Ahdef, 163
spectrality, 74
Specters (*Aṭyāf*) (Ashour), 71–83
Spivak, Gayatri, 151, 183n16
Stanton C. Domna, 7
subjectivity *see* selfhood
Syrian revolution, 112, 118, 120, 129

tadwīn (blogging), 202
Tahrir Square (also *Mīdān al-Taḥrīr*), 163, 170–2, 178

Tawil, Raymonda Hawa, 53
testimony
   shahādah, 140n2
   testimonio, 108–9, 121, 127; see also Beverley, John
   trans-border testimonies, 121–40
   see also witness, bearing
tragicomedy, 161, 179
trauma
   theory, 124–5
   and (un)naming, 125
   and unspeakability, 124, 125–6
Tripp, Charles, 27
A Tunisian Girl (Ben Mhenni), 206–21
Tunisian revolution, 166, 207–13, 220
Tuqan, Fadwa, 17

L'une et l'autre (Bey), 83–100
unveiling, 41, 50, 95, 199

Waugh, Patricia, 76; see also metatext
Web 2.0, 188
Whitlock, Gillian, 58, 189, 196, 204
witness, bearing, 1, 31, 54, 107, 110, 116–18, 200; see also testimony
A Woman in the Crossfire (Yazbek), 111–20
writing process, 54, 77, 99

Yazbek, Samar, 111–32

Zangana, Haifa, 54–5, 79, 232
Ziadé, Lamia, 232
Ziadeh, May, 45

EU representative:
Easy Access System Europe
Mustamäe tee 50, 10621 Tallinn, Estonia
Gpsr.requests@easproject.com

www.ingramcontent.com/pod-product-compliance
Lightning Source LLC
Chambersburg PA
CBHW050212240426
43671CB00013B/2309